TAROT
FOR
LIGHT
SEERS

TAROT
FOR
LIGHT
SEERS

Also by Chris-Anne

<u>Card Decks</u>
The Light Seer's Tarot
The Muse Tarot
The Sacred Creators Oracle
The Tarot of Curious Creatures
The Light Seer's Pocket Tarot

All of the above are available at your local bookstore,
or may be ordered by visiting:

Hay House USA: www.hayhouse.com®

Hay House Australia: www.hayhouse.com.au

Hay House UK: www.hayhouse.co.uk

Hay House India: www.hayhouse.co.in

CHRIS-ANNE

TAROT FOR LIGHT SEERS

A Journey Through the Symbols, Messages, & Secrets of the Cards

HAY HOUSE LLC
Carlsbad, California • New York City
London • Sydney • New Delhi

Published in the United States by: Hay House LLC: www.hayhouse.com®
Published in Australia by: Hay House Australia Publishing Pty Ltd: www.hayhouse.com.au
Published in the United Kingdom by: Hay House UK Ltd: www.hayhouse.co.uk
Published in India by: Hay House Publishers (India) Pvt Ltd: www.hayhouse.co.in

Interior design and illustrations: Chris-Anne and Valentina Abusabbah
Original illustrations by Pamela Colman Smith with guidance from Arthur Edward Waite,
first published by William Rider & Son, London, in 1909
Author photo: Jessica Crandlemire

Cataloging-in-Publication Data is on file at Library of Congress
Hardcover ISBN: 978-1-4019-7872-3
E-book ISBN: 978-1-4019-7873-0
Audiobook ISBN: 978-1-4019-7874-7

10 9 8 7 6 5 4 3 2 1
1st edition, October 2024
Printed in China

FOR my incredible parents,
mike and ♡
CORRINE

thank you for giving me
Permission to be myself,
OVER and OVER AGAIN.

I love you.

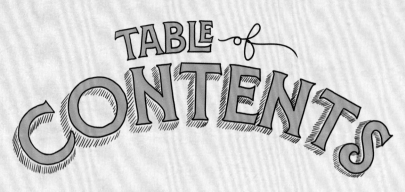

TABLE of CONTENTS

the MAJOR arcana

the MINOR ARCANA

Dearest

LIGHT SEER

Dearest Light Seer,

    I've been imagining publishing this extended guidebook for *The Light Seer's Tarot* for a long time. So much has changed since 2017 when I began sketching the first drafts of the cards. The world has changed, the tarot industry has changed, and I have changed. But what has not changed is the need for *Light Seers,* for people like us who actively seek out hope and healing and who, in doing so, often inadvertently become beacons of light for those around them. This is especially true during times of great challenge, and right now, Light Seers are needed more than ever. *I'm so glad you're here.*

    Whether you are new to tarot or a long-time seeker, you may wonder how to live more fully as a Light Seer. You may have many questions about lightwork and shadow work, and you may be curious how they can help us to better understand ourselves and those around us. How can they, for example, help to make the world a better place? Or how can our cards make us more aware of light and shadow so that we can initiate meaningful change in our lives? I believe that working with our internal light can heal our hearts, our minds, and our bodies, and that cards can offer direct access to these profound changes. I want you to know that if you already have a different set of definitions for light and shadow (or for some of the healing concepts I will share) that I wholeheartedly invite you to hold your beliefs close to your heart. I will always encourage you to give preference to your own intuitive thoughts over mine (and over anyone else's!), as I believe that translating the light of our own souls means we must learn to listen *within* first.

On the Art of Perception, Intuition and SEEING

There is a subtle frequency that vibrates within all of us. When we choose to listen, it provides very quiet cues about the true nature of things. Sometimes, these cues manifest as senses or as fleeting feelings. Sometimes, they show up as metaphors or as images in the mind's eye, or perhaps they are less subtle and they arrive as physical sensations or as more insistent thoughts. How these cues show up will be different for each one of us, as every mind has a different set of signs and signals that it uses to interpret the Universe around it. The language of the intuition is highly personalized, and *it wants to be understood*. Even if you're not consciously aware of it, you already have a personal dialect of signs and symbols that you can call on when you are reading your cards. Humans are excellent at translating metaphors and symbols into concrete ideas, and your unconscious mind is a master at this. It has taken your past experiences and blended them with everything you've studied and learned, and it has created your very own encyclopedia of meaning. Your dialect is like an ever-expanding library of signs, and it is the interface that allows you to monitor the world's subtle frequencies and *to make sense of them*.

I am going to assume that, as card reader or as someone who is tarot-curious, you have already been in touch with the quieter side of your intuition. *How do you personally interpret the world? Do you know what your cues are? Perhaps you've written a list?* You may get goosebumps when you hear something that is true or emotionally moving . . . or perhaps your eyes water instead. Maybe certain symbols, numbers, or colors mean something specific to you . . . or your heart may feel warmer and more expansive when you are headed in the right direction. Even though every tarot card has a prescribed set of meanings and traditional interpretations, you can (and should!) also use your personal intuitive vernacular to add nuance and depth to their meanings. The more serious you get about understanding your personal cues and what they mean, the more succinct, consistent, and clear they will become during your readings.

If you are hoping to expand your personal intuitive vocabulary, you *do* have the capacity to turn up the volume on your inner nudges, if you want. Ask Spirit to speak a little louder! You get to decide how loud your intuition is and how you receive your information. You can ask for more specificity and detail. The real trick is to become devoted to really exploring and getting to know your inner landscape, and to notice when and how it changes. Sometimes our intuitive thoughts are so subtle that we barely notice them, but they are there. Ignore them, and they may slowly shift out of tune. Practice listening to them, and they will begin to resound louder and more precisely. Getting to know your cards will offer countless opportunities to listen and practice the art of interpretation. And if you are hoping to expand your growing list of symbols and their significance, the art of tarot offers a rich tapestry of metaphor and meaning. I have included a chart of the most common tarot symbolism in the back of this book, just for this.

During a card reading (or even when you are simply listening for insights from the Universe), it may help to keep a notebook handy to track any thoughts or images that arise. If you have an inner nudge or a visual representation come to mind and you're not sure what it means, write it down along with a reminder of the question you asked. Take note of the situation that you were in when you did the reading. Eventually, you will look back on this list, and you will see that certain symbols will repeat themselves for specific situations, and you will understand what your intuition was trying to say. *We can use the 20/20 vision of hindsight to help us develop our foresight!* You can quickly expand your conversation with your intuition this way, and this method works for all intuitive arts, including tarot. When your library of specific symbols becomes clearer and more conscious, your ability to hear the subtle whispers from the Universe will ramp up quickly. The very first step of mastering our intuition is to remain aware of the quiet cues and the subtle murmurs of our inner voice, and it is also, quite conveniently, the very first step toward being a super detector of *light and shadow* too.

On Light AND LIGHTWORK

It's easy to understand that light and shadow are two sides of the same coin. One gives meaning to the other, and to truly understand one, the other must also be understood. Light both creates shadow and illuminates it. It dispels it yet also defines it. Night and day. Yin and Yang. Good and evil. The duality that lives in light and shadow has been an integral part of spiritual teachings and philosophies for as long as humans have been recording deep thoughts. *For real.*

Light is what guides us toward our highest self. It's expansive and connected. It's inspiring and abundant, and it shines rays of truth, generosity, and gratitude. It sheds illumination on our inner brilliance, and it helps us to nurture the positive aspects of our identity. Light*work*, or the effort it takes to notice and share this light, is the process of fostering love and compassion in our hearts, and then beaming these elevating energies into the world. A result of sharing genuine and authentic light with others is that it *almost always* initiates a spark of desire inside of *their* hearts to do the same. (Light is magic and contagious that way.) I have had so many paths of self-discovery illuminated by other seekers who showed me their bright love. And these gleaming paths of honest love tend to remind others that uncovering their own incredible radiance is an exciting and tangible possibility. Which, in turn, is a gift that they will eventually give to others as they begin to shine a little brighter. To me, this means that as lightworkers we strive to become catalysts for positive change in the world, and that doing this work means practising our ability to bring bright love into all our actions, intentionally. *No matter what career or social situation we find ourselves in.* I will be the first to admit that I do this *very* imperfectly, as it's a pretty monumental task, and so much easier said than done. Sometimes life is incredibly hard. And sometimes people can really suck. And yet showing up *in love* and *as love* is something that I attempt to learn more about, always.

Over the years I have noticed that this heart-wide-open-love-beaming skill does get easier with practice, and that it comes bundled with a wonderful secondary effect: the world responds to you with more openness and opportunity. With more curiosity. The serendipity and the synchronicity flow more steadily. And things seem to fall into place. Life gets easier and more joyous, and you may even begin to see magic *everywhere*. The more we focus on love, the more our ability to see light residing in every corner grows. Because wherever you look for it—in interactions, relationships, and circumstances—*there is always light to be found*. That said, if you want to bring the love, you first need to notice where the love is *missing*, right? Thus, as a result of wanting to share light, we also become super-sensors and excellent shadow detectors, because, as you already know, shadows are the places where the light is *not*. Our cards can help us to see this contrast more easily. They can point us in the direction of love and show us the potential light that lives inside of our stories. And they can crack open old paradigms and hardened mindsets, showing us the places where our own light needs to be let in.

On Shadow AND Shadow Work

While light shows up as our love, our aspirations, our virtues, and the parts of us that we willingly share with the world, shadow holds our fears, our pain, and the parts of our mind that we may even hide from ourself. It is the container for our shame, our guilt, and our sadness and often makes an appearance in our ugliest reactions and defense mechanisms. Shadow can run deeper than light, and often escapes the watchful stare of the mind's eye, and when aspects of our personality or memories become too painful to face, we tend to tuck them away. Whether intentionally or subconsciously, we shuffle them into the dark corners of our psyche and into the unconscious realm of the *shadow*. This is akin to stowing away forgotten items in a neglected attic, obscured by cobwebs and dust due to our reluctance to confront them. In the darkness they remain hidden to us, and consequently, unresolved. And even though we can't *see* them, they still affect the way we unconsciously (and often unexpectedly!) react to situations in our lives. Have you ever had a terribly strong reaction to something (like feeling instantaneous anger) without understanding why you've had such an extreme response? Or maybe there's a personality trait that really rubs you the wrong way, yet it doesn't seem to bother others in the same way? Those are likely coming from the unconscious information stored within the shadow.

Shadow *work* is rooted in the psychological teachings of Carl Jung, who explained the shadow as the unconscious part of our personality that our conscious mind does not identify as *self*. We may feel pain and assume its origin comes from something external (as in, it's someone else's fault) instead of seeing that it actually comes from within, and that it's rooted in a past memory. In these cases we can project our pain onto others, shifting the focus to the outside world. In shadow work, we often find that our anger toward something or someone will mirror a frustration we harbor toward ourselves, or that we are unduly upset by a character flaw that is something we also possess *and dislike*. It's as if a film of dust from that forgotten attic obscures our ability to see that our instinctual responses are coming from somewhere within us, and that they are rooted in prior painful experiences that are *deeply* hidden. It's not for the faint of heart, this shadow work stuff, and yet ignoring that stack of dusty boxes at back of your psyche means that you will miss the opportunity to soothe, reassure, comfort, and forgive those unseen parts of self that need it most. *Gentle and compassionate shadow work can be a game changer.* This realm of shadow is not just a hiding place for our fears and flaws. It's also a really beautiful reservoir of potential healing, wisdom, and creativity. By daring to explore our innermost emotions, especially the ones that feel imperfect, frightened, and that are seeking refuge in the dark, we can open our hearts to profound healing and transformation.

And as it happens, tarot is one of the very best tools for illuminating those parts of self that we struggle to see. The cards allow us to gently pry open that attic and peek inside *if we want to*. Their fresh perspectives sweep into our conscious awareness and help us to recognize, understand, and love the parts of ourselves that we haven't been accepting. They clear away the dust. *It's a wonderful thing to be able to call out that inner saboteur and figure out why they've been meddling in our decision-making!* By integrating these inner fragments consciously . . . lovingly . . . we can heal rifts with our hearts, forgive ourselves and others, and find tremendous harmony in our lives.

There are many different methods to work with shadow and tarot cards, but I want to offer some simple advice to get started. When the cards offer you a challenging piece of advice or a perspective that is hard to accept, notice the feelings that arise. Much like listening for your personal intuitive cues, you can also listen for the reactions and the feelings that emerge from the shadow. Again, you will have to spend some time focusing on your inner landscape, and over time it will become easier to distinguish where your thoughts are coming from. While everyone's experience is different, hints arising from the *intuition* usually feel subtle, floaty, expansive, or exciting. They usually provide a direct, instantaneous, and definitive answer with no logical explanation or reasoning behind it. And while they are usually to the point and precise, they may feel like they make no sense, especially when we are reading cards *for others*. The clarity or calmness that accompanies intuitive messages is often in stark contrast to the messages that arise from the shadow. The shadow tends to be more emotionally charged and judgemental. Perhaps there will be an instant judgement of a card's message, or a sense of fear. You may feel like you are closing off or pulling back, or your mind may chatter wildly, offering a barrage of reasons or explanations why the message you see in the card cannot be true. It may sound like you are trying to convince yourself with the subtle sounds of excuses, reasons, and worries. Messages that float in from the intuition usually feel a little gentler or more neutral, whereas thoughts arising from the shadow can feel more volatile or protective. And intuitive thoughts are usually accompanied by a clear sense of *knowing*. A directive. Where shadow thoughts can often quickly cascade into scenarios of things that could go wrong, pushing us to move *away from something we don't want* instead of *toward something we do*. None of these are carved in stone, of course, but I offer these suggestions as starting places—and as a way to get curious about the inner workings of your mind and heart. If you notice things feel more like they are emerging from the shadow, *ask yourself why, with no judgement.* Maybe there is information there that will help you to heal your beautiful heart. Maybe the information *was supposed* to come from the realm of shadow because it actually holds the key to your future and was striving to be heard. Exploring past the cobwebs requires both the shadow *and* the light in our hearts, because light and shadow go hand in hand. You really can't be an effective lightworker without working with shadow. And you can't do profound shadow work without knowing how to move toward the light. As the 10 of Swords would say, watching the sun peek over the horizon is the highest task of a bruised heart, and in my opinion, this is some of the greatest work we can do in this lifetime.

Dancing with Duality: Creating the Light Seer's Tarot

When I started working on *The Light Seer's Tarot*, I knew I wanted to create a deck that would be equal parts light and shadow. Of course I dreamed the deck would reach others, but in the beginning, this was the deck I really craved to use in my personal practice. I felt called to read with a healing deck—one that was aligned with contemporary spirituality and 21st-century life, that included relatable, free-spirited characters who took *responsibility* for their own sunshine and light. I imagined a deck of intuitive guides casting light onto the truth and unveiling our shadow aspects as they shared their wisdom. My goal was to create an optimistic and happy deck that would lift me up, without sacrificing tarot's incredible ability to illuminate deeper meanings that hid beneath the surface. It had to be insistent enough to prod me to take responsibility for my thoughts and actions, while also inspiring me to do the deeper healing work when I was ready.

This goal was steeped in duality, as is the wonderful tradition of tarot itself:

Light and Shadow.
The delightful and the difficult.
The mundane and the magical.

Did I have the skill to create a deck that held this balance? Could I create images that would offer all of these things? It was a design challenge that I was thrilled to take on. The first card to show up was the 4 of Wands. I was sitting at a busy coffee shop, and she showed up as the first real sketch I had done in years. I have a distinct memory of having sore cheeks as I doodled the first version of the card. She had a personality I hadn't seen in a tarot deck before, and she felt . . . alive . . . with her boho sunshine and a colorful yurt. She made me smile uncontrollably, and as I drew, I witnessed two kindred souls dance themselves into form on the page in front of me. After drawing that first card, I was hooked.

During the process I began living and breathing tarot in a way I hadn't before. I started noticing the archetypes *everywhere*, witnessing the different ways that tarot's quintessential lessons showed up in the world around me. Sitting in cafes and parks, I became enamored with the details of other people's interactions and ways of being in the world. Sometimes I caught fragments of their stories or snippets of conversations, and I turned them into characters. They were sketched as small stills in notebooks, and on every paper, napkin, and back of bill that were within reach.

Some cards were an absolute joy to create.
I felt their light. Their wisdom. Their strength.
Other cards were very painful.
Shadowy. And drenched in difficulty, like their meanings.

I felt like I was walking the entirety of the Fool's Journey——albeit out of order. There were moments when I took all my own enthusiasm, creativity, and excitement and poured it into the suit of Wands. I took my worries, my mental chatter, and my insecurities, and I poured them into the Swords. When I felt love and compassion, a Cups card would show up. Every time I worried about money, I allowed my mind to wonder what my 5 of Pentacles card would look like. I watched for experiences that would embody each card in its most potent light.

The Tower card was born in the middle of the night, when the cry of an animal, whose nest was clearly being raided, roused me from my sleep. When one of my best friends lost her teenage son to suicide, I poured both my love for her and my despair for her loss into the 3 of Swords. And when I lived with the intention of seeing the cards in real life, they all showed up for me to capture, one by one, in the most human yet magical of ways.

During my 18 months with the archetypes, I truly obsessed over every line, color, symbol, and expression. It wasn't until the fifth card was created that I truly began to understand what the deck wanted me to do with it. When I looked at the completed Queen of Pentacles, I took a deep breath, mesmerized by the grace and wisdom of this regal guide. I slowly took in her palpable compassion and love, and I nodded. I *got* it. I whispered to her, "I want to know how you love the world as much as you do. How can you love so deeply?"

She winked back and she spoke her mantra: *"Let it be healing."* And I am pretty sure it was she who guided me the rest of the way, because as I designed the rest of the cards one by one, I repeated this simple statement over and over:

$$\Bigg(\ \bigg(\ \bigg(\quad \begin{array}{c} \textit{"Let it be healing."} \\ \textit{"Let it be healing."} \\ \textit{"Let it be healing."} \end{array} \quad \bigg)\ \bigg)\ \Bigg)$$

Sometimes, other words floated into my mind . . .
"Please allow people to see their shadow in new ways."
"Please illuminate our weaknesses, gently."
"Help us to integrate our shadow-selves while always leaving space for the light."
"Please allow us to see shadow without becoming so enamored with it that we get lost in our reasons, excuses, or our victimhood."

"Let it be healing." I whispered the mantra into the wee hours of the night, producing and imagining the rest of the cards, meeting each new guide as they arrived.

Each one with a unique set of lessons. With its own story. Thinking back on the experience, it's actually hard for me to figure out if I drew this deck to life or if it moved my hands to be drawn. As an intuitive artist, I often birth my creations this way. They come with their own personality, and vision or yearning for what they will become. And during the process, whenever I lost my way—curiously moving around in the dark with my pen, pencil, or stylus—I breathed into the Queen's mantra, and my hand would be nudged in the right direction. *"Let it be healing."*

As a deck mom, it has been an absolute joy to see how far and wide the vibrations of this magical collaboration between me and Spirit have reached. I want to take a moment to thank you for taking a chance on this little deck of mine. And for giving it a loving home. For making it yours and adding your own magic to its story. *The Light Seer's Tarot*, I believe, has taken on a sort of mind and energy all its own. I am sure that its collective magic has grown over time, becoming an incredible matrix of love and healing. When I tune in to the energy of *Light Seer's* now, it is something of a marvel to me. It's stronger. More succinct. Wiser. And more healing. It's something that is definitely no longer "mine," but rather "ours."

When I check in on its energy today, I am overwhelmed with the amount of healing work that it has been a part of. My tears begin to flow when I imagine all the candlelit tarot journaling sessions, the laughter between friends, and all the secret dreams that the deck has been privy to. I am so honored that it has had the chance to accompany so many beautiful souls as we build brighter futures, shift and transform realities, and make the world a better place to be. I am so grateful that you have, in your own way, welcomed this deck into your sacred space and made new memories with it in the process. Thank you!

Incredible miracles happen when we blend cards, intention, and love! As you explore the sunshine-and-shadow-laden path of the Light Seer, I hope you hear it whisper that shadow is a profound tool, and that light is an awesome endgame. Wishing you light and blessings on the path!

Sending giant love and epic magic to you,

xo **Chris-Anne**

Pssst. If you want to go deeper with your cards, I have created the LightSeersTarot.com website, where you will be able to find more materials to support your tarot journey. To connect with others who use the deck, use the hashtag **#LightSeersTarot** to find one another online.

TAROT AS A TOOL for HEALING

The goal of *The Light Seer's Tarot* has always been that it would be used as a healing tool, and healing has been big on my radar over the last few years. My personal experiences with burnout and going back to school to study acupuncture have all required me to hold healing as the primary focus in my day-to-day. And when I look out into the collective, I see that same need for healing mirrored back to me—we are all in need of a little TLC these days. When I sat down to re-imagine the original guide, I knew it had to include a few key changes that reflected the way the world has woven itself into something new, beginning with the 22 cards of the Major Arcana. The Majors hold potent energetic medicines that are highly effective for healing, and I believe that we can draw down these energies from the ethers and ask them to help guide us on our journeys toward wellness. Each Major has its own spread in this guide, so if you already know a specific archetype that you want to work with, simply go to that section of the book and try the spread that is meant for that particular card.

Healing art.

Did you notice that most of the cards in this deck include points of light and rays of energy? These layers represent my fiercely anchored beliefs about the positive effects of energy medicine, and the way our bodies have an innate capacity to heal. If you pay extra attention to the rays of light, dots, and lines when you lay out your cards side by side, you will see how the energy flows through the deck. Those dots of light often line up perfectly, and they can add a nuanced layer of meaning to your readings. If you ask, they will tell you a story of transformative light that flows between the messages of the cards, and they can guide you in the direction of your own curative insights. Designed to be a visible translation of healing energy, I hope that they will serve as subtle visual cues for where and how to seek out wellness. Sometimes the cues will point to conditions of our minds or our hearts, and other times they will point to spiritual wellness or the physical body. Whenever I read with these cards, the wisps of energy running through the deck play an integral role in the way the artwork speaks to me.

Okay, but can cards heal?

I used to imagine that we could read cards and then use the interpretation to change our thoughts or emotions. This would, of course, call forth some magical restorative vibes to help us heal. And while I know that this type of spontaneous phenomenon is *very* possible, my vision around the mechanisms of healing has expanded tremendously in the last few years. For most of us, it's not quite that easy, and we need a little more help to truly call in those cosmic miracles. After working one-on-one with patients in the clinic and working with energy via massage, touch, and acupuncture needles, the way I sense and see energy has shifted, and the profound nature of those little dots and rays of energy on the cards has become, for me, even more meaningful.

When we get hurt, there are subtle energies that can stop flowing through our body. Instead of moving fluidly, they can stagnate and become stuck . . . often in our meridians, tissues, fascia, or viscera. (Remember those painful memories that we relegate to the abandoned attic of our mind? They can cause some real friction in our energy systems, and this often shows up in parts of the body that we don't even associate with the original trauma or pain!) Energy blockages will slow down our body's energy system and cause strange hiccups and blips in both the body and the mind. This can mean that changing our thoughts to call in the big miracles can be a little trickier done than said— because those *sticky-tricky* energies that caused the energy block in the first place have changed the way the energy moves, creating a new pathway that can become a learned loop. If we end up repeating these loops over and over, our pathologically misfiring energy can actually lock our thoughts into place. Sometimes, "changing our thoughts" can feel impossible, because what we actually require to make it happen is not simply the desire to do so. Sometimes, we need to change the way we *perceive,* and we need a jolt of *new paradigm* or a jostle of *fresh perspective* to get things flowing freely again.

In this way, tarot can be the perfect catalyst for loosening and releasing stuck energy. It can help gently nudge your thoughts and emotions back on track, or even forge a new route for your energy system by bringing you into a vibration that allows your energy to course through your systems more fluidly. It can help you to create the necessary conditions for healing. Thoughts can, after all, change heart rates and hormones . . . blood pressures and immune systems. They can change your muscle tension, your sleep patterns, your respiratory rate, and your brain chemistry. In some cases, to heal the mind and the emotions, we need to heal something physical—and in other situations it's the other way around. Sometimes it's the mental-emotional flow that needs a pattern interrupt in order to heal the physical body. *Because it's all connected.*

Am I suggesting that tarot messages replace conventional medicine? *Of course not.* But they can help unstick the stuck, as they are balms for the soul and can help us to change the patterns that occur as a result of the way that we think. They can swoop in and temporarily short-circuit a negative looping thought pattern, or they can pause emotional pain for long enough for us to see a new way forward. These 78 pieces of cardstock and ink can jumpstart new ways of *feeling and being* . . . and become veritable catalysts for some incredible healing.

Tarot Basics for the New Cardslinger

If this is your first experience with the tarot, welcome! What an absolute honor it is to share this beautiful practice with you. Know that there is no right or wrong way to read with the cards. Some people use cards to better understand who they are and what they want, others look to the cards to highlight shadow aspects of self, while others use the cards in a predictive manner. How you use the cards is totally up to you.

There is no need to memorize every card meaning before you begin to work with the cards. I created the artwork on each card to deliver a clear message to you, and each character is a sacred guide to your own intuition. Your first impression of the card is the best meaning! Do your best to pay attention to your own ideas and thoughts when you pull a card, even before you find the meaning in the guidebook. This guidebook is meant as a reference and a resource, and it should bolster your own unique conversation with the cards. If I had one piece of advice for the new reader, it would be to trust in your ability to do this. You totally can.

The fastest way to really get to know your cards:

I highly suggest a technique called pathworking to learn more about the personal messages that the cards have for you. Pathworking is having an imagined conversation with the card's character during your own creative visualization/meditation time. To get started, you simply ask a question and pull a card. When you're ready, hold the card in front of you and really look at the landscape or the character of the card. Notice the details as best you can, without worrying about remembering everything perfectly. Trust that you'll remember the details that you need to remember. Next, close your eyes and imagine that you are going into the card. (You may want to turn on some quiet music and make sure you've got some alone time to do this.) When you find yourself inside of the cardscape, look around and see if there is anyone to talk to or learn from. Ask your question to the people you run into and see what happens. And yes, this is totally imaginary, and yes, it feels like child's play. You'll probably feel like you're making it all up, and that's great . . . because you are. But if you simply go with the flow and trust the images you receive, you'll start getting answers from your subconscious mind, and you'll be amazed at the type of wisdom you can receive from your own inner guidance system with this simple technique. Give it a try! You'd be amazed at the information you receive from your own inner guidance system.

New to pathworking?
I've made you an audio meditation to walk you through this fav practice of mine. (It's free!) Go to **www.chris-anne.com/TarotforLightSeers** or take a photo of this strange little code with your phone to access your audio experience!

I made a MEDITATION FOR you ♡ ⟶

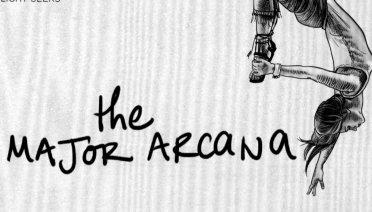

the MAJOR ARCANA

Most tarot decks are based on the same basic structure: 22 Major Arcana cards and 56 Minor Arcana cards. The structure of *The Light Seer's Tarot* deck featured in this guidebook (as well as the names of the cards and their most basic meanings) is based on the *Rider-Waite-Smith Tarot*. Published in the early 1900s, the RWS deck itself was a product of hundreds of years of card-reading traditions that came before it, and its metaphysical and esoteric symbolism has informed and inspired most modern decks.

The 22 Majors (of all tarot decks) are the big guns of the tarot. They often convey the "major" energies, or the overarching archetypal energies that surround major life events, transitions, or lessons. The journey of the Major Arcana begins with the Fool card, who falls off the cliff to begin a cycle, and ends with the World card when the cycle is complete. If you pull a lot of Majors in one reading, there may be significant change going on!

the MINOR ARCANA

The Minors are often seen as energies surrounding day-to-day experiences and decisions. Traditionally, the Minor Arcana is broken into four suits that align with the four elements. Fire is expressed via the suit of Wands, and it deals with inspiration, creativity, and passions. Water is felt through the suit of Cups, which mainly deals with emotions, relationships, and how we feel. Air is communicated through the suit of Swords, and the Swords help express the mind, our ideas, and how we communicate and think. And earth is manifested through the suit of Pentacles, which form messages of physical security, wealth, and health. The Aces of each suit usher in the elemental energy of their suit, and as the numbers on the cards increase, the energy and the lessons heighten.

Each suit has a set of "Court" cards: Page, Knight, Queen, and King. These Court cards can often be the trickiest cards to master in the tarot. They are messengers that can be seen as people, energies, or situations. If a reading is heavy on Court cards, it can mean that there are a lot of people or opinions affecting the situation. Each card has a personality, and my favorite way to read Court cards is imagining the character speaking up in the middle of the reading.

Tarot can seem overwhelming when we first get started. Daily card pulls is a good way to jump in, if that feels right for your practice! There are no set rules, decided-upon meanings, or governing bodies when it comes to tarot. It is really a relationship between you, your intuition, and the cards, so as with any great relationship, you'll build trust over time.

a note on
↑ UPRIGHT CARDS AND REVERSALS ↓

UPRIGHT

REVERSED

Some readers use upright cards only, and many a case has been made that there is no need to read with reversals, as the full energy of the human condition is contained within the 78 cards. I believe this to be true. Others prefer to read with reversals, giving us 156 messages to work with. A reversal is when you pick a card and the image is upside down. I have chosen to include the meanings for upright, Light Seer, and reversal messages, Shadow Seer, as keywords in the guidebook, but of course I leave it up to you how you interpret the cards.

There are three main ways that people tend to read reversed cards:

① Reversals can convey the more negative or shadowy traits of a card's energy. With a card like the Magician, his power to manifest when the card is facing upward may turn into his power to manipulate when the card is flipped upside down.

② Sometimes, reversals are seen as the opposite of the upright, original meaning. (This is why some of the Shadow Seer keywords seem to be more positive than the Light Seer keywords.)

③ Most of the time, I choose to read reversals as blocked or stagnant energy around the card, because blockages can highlight important opportunities for healing. There will be a few times in the deck when the reversed Shadow Seer message seems slightly more "positive" than its Light Seer counterpart, and this is because there are cards that are slightly easier to navigate when their energy is blocked.

A lot of reversals showing up in the same spread can indicate an overall stagnation or negative mindset, or even that the querent is temporarily blocked from their goal. For individual cards in a spread, the surrounding cards always help me to decide which messages are meant to be highlighted. The surrounding cards are usually a fabulous indicator of how the card's energy is meant to be interpreted. If you aren't sure about reversals, I would suggest beginning with upright cards. Read all the card's keywords as a starting point, and I suspect you will know very quickly which ones need to be focused on. Trust your gut. You've got this.

Connecting with your cards

Start by choosing your light and shadow cards.

Before you get started, take a moment to connect with the cards. By simply flipping through this book (or the deck, if you have it handy) with the intention to see each card and feel its unique energy, you will be getting yourself acquainted with the many archetypes, stories, and themes. As you spend time noticing the different characters and scenarios, take note of your visceral reactions to the cards. The image that brings you the most joy will be your light card, whereas the card you feel the most aversion to will be your shadow card. Your shadow card may bear an image that you really don't like, and that's totally okay. This is something that you should do intuitively, without lingering on which meanings you prefer. As you explore the cards, ask yourself:

Which one feels the most inspiring?
Which one feels like it really "gets" you?
Which one feels like a giant yes in your system?
(These help you define your **light** card.)

Which one do you feel the least attracted to?
Which one just turns you off?
Which one makes you the most uncomfortable?
(These help you define your **shadow** card.)

Go ahead and pick your two cards now.

Your light and shadow cards will be your trusted allies and guides as you work with the tarot system, and they will become your messengers along the path. Often, the card you choose as your light card will feel the most like where you are headed, and it will represent who you want to be. Consider it to be a special nod from the cards when it shows up in a reading, because it's going to be your big, badass YES card—the card that lets you know you are on the right track.

Conversely, your shadow card will be the one that stirs up the most feelings of discomfort. Quite often this is because this card has an important lesson to teach you. Spend some time with your shadow card now if you'd like. Maybe find its meaning in the guidebook and pull out your journal. What lesson does the card have for you right now? What is it about the card that rubs you the wrong way? Maybe it's the character in the card, or the situation they seem to be in? Perhaps they remind you of a time in your life or a person from your past?

Most important, try to discern how this card could have a positive influence on your life if you were easily able to accept the wisdom found on the card. We can often learn a great deal about the challenges that we are facing inside of our darkest shadows.

As you work with your tarot deck, your shadow card will serve as a gentle reminder that some aspect of your situation is being blocked by a shadow that you've created, and that there is a massive opportunity to turn things around by working with a more positive mindset.

Readings and Spreads

There are so many ways to set up a reading, and as you work with the cards, you will find your own favorite ways to shuffle, draw, and interpret them. Usually, you will come to the cards with something you want to learn about: a project, a relationship, or an idea. Decide in advance the type of spread you are going to use to gather information from your cards. Will you choose one card? Or more? How will you lay the cards on the table? *(Pssst. There are some ideas for spreads on the following pages!)*

① Clearly meditate on the situation or question

② Shuffle the cards any way you'd like

③ Holding your question in the front of your mind, choose your card(s)

④ Read your card

After you have flipped the card over, take some time to sit with its meaning. I suggest spending some time looking at the imagery before jumping into the guidebook. Answers that come from your intuition will always offer the most insight. Here are a few questions that will help you tune in to your own interpretations:

• What does the card make you think of?
• How does the card make you feel?
• Does it remind you of a specific situation?
• Does the character seem to have qualities that remind you of anyone?
• How could the character, scenario, or lesson on the card help you to better understand your current situation?
• If they had advice for you, what would it be?

When you've taken note of your own intuitive interpretations, go to the guidebook to see if there's anything more you can learn from the card.

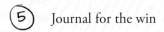 Journal for the win

To go deeper with your reading, journal about your experiences with the card! When you do a reading, something on the cards will call for your attention. It may be as simple as the time of day or the type of landscape that the artwork portrays. It may be an emotion, an item, or a pair of shoes on the card that remind you of so-and-so. These little nudges from the cards allow you to connect your own inner knowing with the message that the card conveys about your situation. And it is in this connection—in your own interpretation of the message—that the magic lies.

LIGHT SEER'S Spreads

I want to introduce you to a light and shadow technique that will have you placing cards in their upright and reversed (Light Seer and Shadow Seer) positions on purpose. I know intentionally turning your cards is a bit unorthodox, but I find the most healing messages can come through when we force the reversals and uprights in a reading! Arrows in a spread indicate that the cards are meant to be placed in a specific orientation. If there are no arrows, place them as they were pulled. *Of course, you can always choose to place the cards however you'd like. There are no rules.*

LIGHT ~and~ SHADOW SPREAD

A spread for light and healing

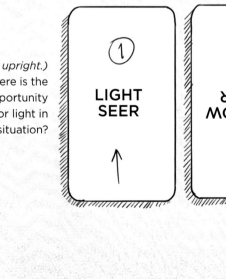

(Place upright.)
Where is the greatest opportunity for light in this situation?

① LIGHT SEER ↑

↓ SHADOW SEER ②

(Place reversed.)
Where is the greatest opportunity to heal shadow in this situation?

Light of the Day Draw

① LIGHT

A simple spread for choosing a card of the day

(Draw a card and place it upright or reversed as pulled.) What message of light do you have for me today?

Soul Joy Spread

A spread for finding and sharing purpose-fueled soul joy

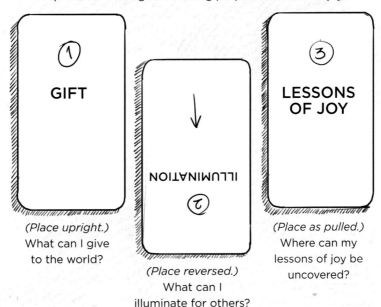

① GIFT

↓

② ILLUMINATION

③ LESSONS OF JOY

(Place upright.) What can I give to the world?

(Place reversed.) What can I illuminate for others?

(Place as pulled.) Where can my lessons of joy be uncovered?

LIGHTWORKER ACTIVATION SPREAD

A spread for changemakers

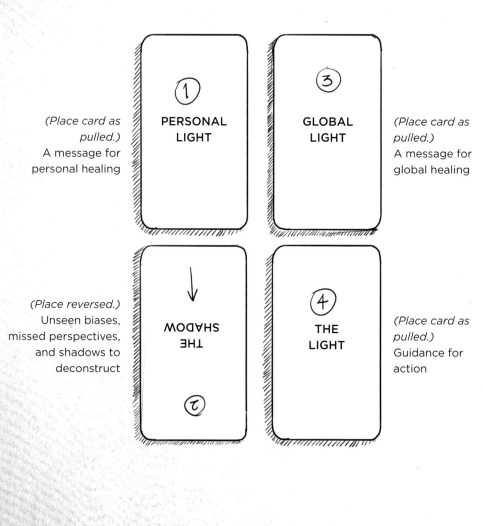

(Place card as pulled.)
A message for personal healing

① PERSONAL LIGHT

③ GLOBAL LIGHT

(Place card as pulled.)
A message for global healing

(Place reversed.)
Unseen biases, missed perspectives, and shadows to deconstruct

② THE SHADOW

④ THE LIGHT

(Place card as pulled.)
Guidance for action

(Place upright.)
How can I best bring this aspect of my shadow into the light? How can I acknowledge, accept, and integrate this part of my shadow into my conscious life?

③
ILLUMINATION

↑

①
WHAT IS CURRENTLY HIDDEN?

(Place card as pulled.)
What aspect of my shadow self is presently beneath the surface, unseen or unrecognized?

②
SHADOW LESSONS

(Place card as pulled.)
What lesson does my shadow have for me? Understanding this can be transformative!

Shadow
ILLUMINATION
SPREAD

Before you start this spread, I encourage you to center yourself. Take a deep breath, perhaps light a candle, and set the intention to approach your shadow with curiosity and compassion. Spend time with each card, allowing their messages to speak to you. Journaling your thoughts can be incredibly revealing and healing during this exploration.

TIP

the ANCESTRAL healing spread

(Place the Devil here.)
This powerful archetype
will help interpret card 3.

(Place the Star here.)
This powerful archetype
will help interpret card 4.

CALL ON THE ENERGY and WISDOM of the ARCHETYPE to CLARIFY your ANSWER

③

ANCESTRAL
CONVERSATION

④

ANCESTORS
SPEAK

*(The Devil will help you
interpret this card.)*
What stories are you holding
on to? What do they want
you to liberate?

*(The Star will help you
interpret this card.)*
How can you let go and embody
hope? What wisdom from your
beautiful ancestors do you hear?

♡
the
Calling IN
love
spread

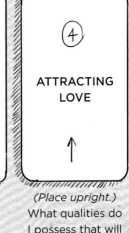

①	②	④
RECOGNIZING LOVE	**SEEKING LOVE**	**ATTRACTING LOVE**
↑	↑	↑

(Place upright.)
What qualities will my future partner have?

(Place upright.)
Where can I seek them? Who will they remind me of?

(Place upright.)
What qualities do I possess that will attract my partner?

↓

BLOCKING LOVE

③

(Place reversed.)
What shadow aspect of mine is blocking this union?

the Anxious LOOPS — SPREAD —

THE ROOT

EMBRACE IT

TRANSMUTE IT

HEAL IT

I am.
Why am I feeling fear and anxiety?

I am safe.
A loving message to my heart and mind

I am love.
Compassionate action steps of transformation and change

I am here.
Illuminate the path towards healing

healing
THE BODY AND mind

A spread for working with our capacity to heal

What past experiences
are affecting my health?

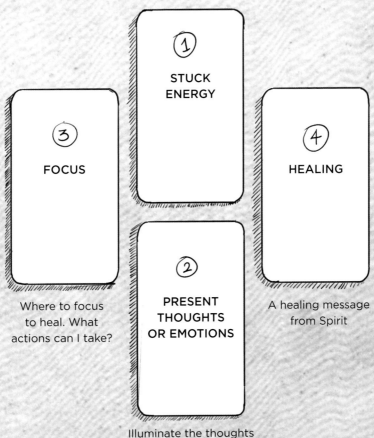

①
**STUCK
ENERGY**

③
FOCUS

④
HEALING

②
**PRESENT
THOUGHTS
OR EMOTIONS**

Where to focus
to heal. What
actions can I take?

A healing message
from Spirit

Illuminate the thoughts
or emotions that can
affect my health

EPIC MISSION
— AND —
Badass Dreams

A spread for calling in big sacred dreams and for taking action towards goals

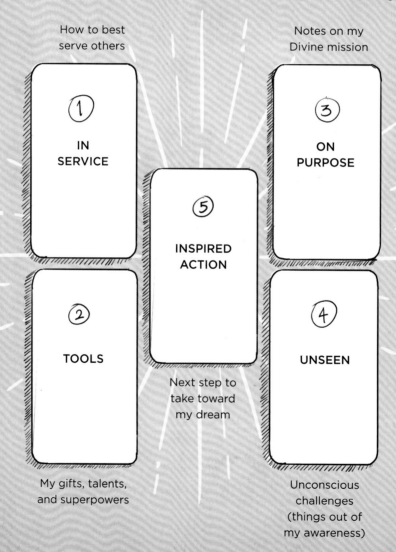

How to best
serve others

Notes on my
Divine mission

① IN SERVICE

③ ON PURPOSE

⑤ INSPIRED ACTION

Next step to
take toward
my dream

② TOOLS

④ UNSEEN

My gifts, talents,
and superpowers

Unconscious
challenges
(things out of
my awareness)

the MAJOR Arcana

The Major Arcana are the epic, major energies of the deck that relate to important milestones of the Fool's Journey (or the Hero's Journey.) These 22 cards encapsulate the breadth of our human experiences, captured in 22 moments between *the Fool*'s first leap of faith and the final rising and completion of the journey in *the World*.

{FIRST STEPS of A NEW JOURNEY}

Tiny red dots in hair: seeds of POMEGRANATES (from the Priestess)

Staff: protection on the journey

YELLOW DRESS:
- optimism
- happiness
- new ideas
- mental activity
- building confidence.

the Fool

Amethyst CRYSTAL: healing, protection, crystals often serve as gateways to the higher realms. Naivete.

TRUST? feet are slightly stuck

VIBRATING strings of light drawing her to her new FUTURE

all is POSSIBLE

Falling into the seed of life → SACRED GEOMETRY for first step of creation, consciousness, electromagnetic spectrum of light, {Blueprint of the universe}

INITIATION

0. the Fool

LIGHT SEER: new beginnings, potential, adventures, enthusiasm, awakening, innocence, optimism, fresh opportunities, a transitional period of awakening, light-heartedness, and being spontaneous

SHADOW SEER: naivete, assuming you already have the answer, rash or impulsive choices, lacking experience, analysis-paralysis, foolishness

A FOOL STORY

On the edge of an epic journey, the Fool peers into the abyss below and senses the seed of life calling out to her. She sees the opportunity and stardust swirling, and she knows that her dream begins with this single step. She's not sure what she will learn or exactly where she's headed, but she has clarity about one thing: she will need to jump in order to begin. With her crystal amplifier to guide her, and her wand to protect her, she feels her toes slide past the threshold of her current reality. She sends one last intention prayer up to the Universe and lets go, feeling the rush of the unknown rise up to meet her. She falls into the void, where her beautiful future awaits.

THE FOOL'S MESSAGE

Every dream achieved begins with the seemingly "foolish" notion that there is something bigger out there. Something greater. Something epic to explore and to become. This childlike optimism comes from deep within your knowing, and it reminds you that you *can* achieve the magical things that you've been dreaming about. Your journey of the soul begins with a single step, and the time has come to enthusiastically turn toward the future and take a Divine leap of faith. You may not feel ready. You may not *be* ready. Yet there is magic in the air, and the Universe is waiting to support you with infinite love and guidance. Surrendering to the call of the Fool means putting deep trust and unwavering faith in the unknown. It means remembering that everything is happening *as it should*. With your curiosity in tow, it's time to swan dive into the seed of potential that awaits. This is how you will claim the reward that the abyss is offering.

Sometimes, in shadow, the Fool marks moments in life when you long for something fresh and new. If your life has become too conventional, find your sense of freedom by shaking things up a little! Remember that during the genesis of something different, extreme recklessness and impulsivity can create unnecessary obstacles on your path. Have you been ignoring good advice? Trust your instincts and tune in to both intuition *and* experience. Take any precautions you need to take, and prepare for a stable landing. It's time to optimistically fall toward an exciting future!

I awaken my soul PATH AND I am Ready for adventure

QUESTIONS FOR THE SEER
- If you knew the Universe would catch you mid-flight, where would you leap?
- Name one thing you could learn today that would help prepare you for tomorrow?
- Imagine two wise guides named Playfulness and Enthusiasm.
  What counsel do they have for you?
- How much do you trust yourself to try new things and succeed?

"Trust fall. *Foolishly? Maybe.* But this is how dreams are launched."

THE FOOL'S
TRUST FALL SPREAD

A spread for starting new journeys

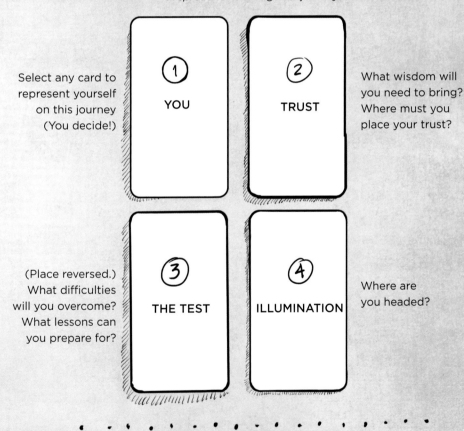

Select any card to represent yourself on this journey (You decide!)

① **YOU**

② **TRUST**

What wisdom will you need to bring? Where must you place your trust?

(Place reversed.) What difficulties will you overcome? What lessons can you prepare for?

③ **THE TEST**

④ **ILLUMINATION**

Where are you headed?

HEALING WITH THE FOOL

fear, trust issues, analysis-paralysis, respiratory disorders, asthma, foot problems, vertigo, being accident prone, ADHD, healing the inner child

Archangel
METATRON'S CUBE TATTOO
contains all the sacred geometric
shapes and frequencies
that exist in
the universe.
CUBE REPRESENTS
harmony and SKILL
in creation, the
highest frequencies.
AND IT
REMINDS us to pay
attention to our
thoughts. ALL IS
RECORDED IN THE
AKASHICS.

∞ INFINITY
(Lemniscate)
for INFINITE POWER.
· ALL IS ONE
· cycles of creation
· INFINITE POSSIBILITY

the
Magician

GRASS:
the
energy to create
something new arises
from the present.
grass seeds fading as
the magician creates
a new reality from
his hands.

As above,
so BELOW.

♡ HERMETIC WISDOM,
YOUR HEART and
intention is
REFLECTED in THE
COSMOS.

SPINNING CAULDRON:
Spiral galaxy
with a WHITE HOLE
center.
where matter
is transformed
AND
CREATED
anew.

4 elements:
△ FIRE
△ AIR
▽ WATER
▽ EARTH

1. the Magician

LIGHT SEER: skill, natural talents, power, manifesting your desires, creativity, possessing the resources you need, transformation

SHADOW SEER: unused potential, latent talents, questionable intentions, manipulation, selfishness, unfocused or blocked creative energy, a need to bolster your self-confidence

A MAGICIAN STORY

Deeply entranced by his state of co-creation, the Magician harnesses the power of the elements with the skill of a masterful alchemist. In doing so, he unites the world above with the world below. He shapes his reality by aligning the Cosmos and the earth into the present moment. He doesn't believe he is creating his reality through thought alone . . . rather he is aligning his life with one of the many possibilities that already exist in the swirling ocean of potential. He brings his *imagined world* to reality by moving ideas from the ethereal plane to the physical plane, and he gives them shape, life, and form. He is a powerful manifester who speaks the ancient languages of the elements, healing, training, and magic. With the infinity sign stitched into his hood, and Metatron's sigil tattooed on his arm, he is reminded of his innate ability to connect to the perpetual cycle of Source energy that flows between the Cosmos and the earth. He speaks steadily, *"As above, so below,"* and his creation bubbles up from his Universe cauldron. The Universe whispers back, *"As within, so without."* He is grateful for his emerging creation before it arrives . . . and he *believes*. Oh, how he believes. *And so it is.*

THE MAGICIAN'S MESSAGE

A potent message of your ability to create your life and manifest your dreams, this card asks you to connect to your creator spark. You have all the tools you could ever need, so beautiful creator, *go create!* Do you feel the magic in your veins? You can activate it by focusing your energy, willpower, desire, and actions. Even if it seems latent right now, know that it is there, waiting to be called upon. The Universe will indeed support your goals and bring them to fruition when you consciously step into your personal power. Every breath in and every breath out are opportunities for you to carve new realities and perspectives, and you can use them to succeed by making space for your rock-solid belief! *Trust yourself!*

Your connection to your desire is crucial right now, as being clear on your goals will reshape the material world around you. If you are feeling less than inspired, it's time to find your muse. Find the catalyst. Find your *why.* In shadow, dispel any unchecked or misaligned intentions you may have. Power can transform yet can also *corrupt absolutely,* so why not be a good mage and use your mindset to create something for the greater good? With everything you need sitting in front of you like a giant cosmic vortex to be called upon, what is it that you will bring to life?

I manifest the LiFe
I Desire THROUGH
energy AND INTENTION

QUESTIONS FOR THE SEER
- What tools do you have at your disposal that you aren't fully utilizing?
- How does magic appear in your life? What does it look like? Feel like? Sound like?
- Are you sharing your skills and talents with others, and using your magic for the good of the Universe? Or are you short-changing your potential and using it only for personal gain?

"For your faith is the key to your connection.
And your connection is the key to your power."

the COSMIC CAULDRON of Dreams

A Spread for Manifesting Dreams

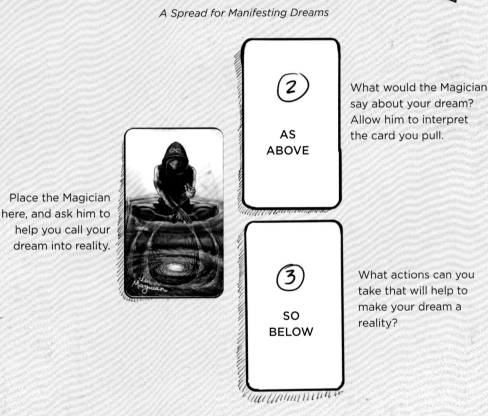

2

AS
ABOVE

What would the Magician say about your dream? Allow him to interpret the card you pull.

Place the Magician here, and ask him to help you call your dream into reality.

3

SO
BELOW

What actions can you take that will help to make your dream a reality?

HEALING WITH THE MAGICIAN

central nervous system issues, boosting energy, brain fog, neurological or cognitive functions, improving body and mind's abilities to heal, speech disorders, carpal tunnel, migraines, vision problems, memory disorders, self-confidence

Runes:

ᛗ MANNAZ:
Humankind.
Self-
Actualization

ᛚ LAGUZ:
Water, flow,
INTUITION, DREAMS

the veil: subconscious

chakras connecting
to SOURCE

ᛈ PERTHRO:
Hidden knowledge

ᚹ WUNJO: joy

2. the High Priestess

👁 THIRD EYE OPEN
AND her EYES are
BOTH OPEN and closed
at the same time.
She can see the un-
see-able and, LIKE
INTUITION, ONCE you
notice something,
(LIKE her open eyes)
you can't UN-NOTICE
IT

starlight hair:
(she is the Cosmos)

Crescent moon:
Divine feminine,
the unconscious
MIND.

SCROLL
EARRINGS:
WISDOM, DIVINE LAW,
esoteric
knowledge

Pomegranates:
Fertility, abundance,
Goddess
Persephone

CROSS of ✚
the FOUR directions:
OMNIPRESENCE,
Sometimes seen as a
SOLAR CROSS
(balances the
MOON)

BLUE COLOR:
SPIRITUAL/
MYSTICAL

2. the High Priestess

LIGHT SEER: dreams, powerful visions, psychic insights, serendipity, meditation, introspection, intuition, arcane or hidden knowledge, a spiritual experience

SHADOW SEER: keeping secrets, gossip or mistruths, hidden agendas, fear of intuitive abilities, not paying attention to your inner voice

A HIGH PRIESTESS STORY

The High Priestess sits at the threshold of the Akashic Records, with one foot softly rooted in this conscious reality and the other one dipping deeply into the unconscious realm. Between light and dark, she stills her mind and connects to the field of information above her. Eyes fluttering, she senses the tingling sensation of the glyphs, and as the symbols trickle down, she accesses the mysteries beyond the veil. Oh, sweet elucidations of wisdom and insight! Even though her eyes are closed, she invites you to look deeper and see the unseen vision that they hold. With ancient wisdom and a deep connection to the ethers, she understands your path with profound clarity. Her keys: intuition and mystical illumination. She is the keeper of the arcane secrets of the universe. She trusts in her Yin energy—waiting instead of pushing, receiving, and rooting instead of reaching—for she knows that patience allows emerging magic to germinate in the void. In stillness, she invites you to find your innate seer and to step into your own translation of the mysteries.

THE HIGH PRIESTESS' MESSAGE

Sacred insights and profound wisdom are flowing to you now, and to access them, you must tune in to your intuition and submerge your thoughts into her subconscious realm. In order to translate her mystical undertones, you must be willing to pull meaning from beyond the edges of conventional perception. Search for the light and the shadow in the quiet corners of your mind. The Divine whispers emanating from your soul at this time hold an important message for you, and the bridge between the enigmatic realm of the Priestess and your conscious understanding of the signs will be found through quiet introspection. *Trust your ability to understand her subtle nudges.* The language of the unconscious mind reveals itself through metaphor, prophetic dreams, or as ancient memories that resurface to be processed. *In stillness.* Pay attention to synchronicities, any nagging feelings of being off track, as well as hunches that move you in a new direction. The Priestess wants you to know that you already have access to the answers you seek, and by insisting on the truth, you will find them. Are you having trouble translating your intuition? In shadow, this card suggests that you may be actively blocking messages from your Higher Self. Instincts that point you toward new experiences hold the seeds for your future, and ignoring her whispers now will only delay the arrival of this truth, for the knowledge she holds transcends our willingness to listen. Seek to see more, bright seer, and your inner sight will show you the way.

I already have the answers I seek, and by following the TRUTH I will find them.

QUESTIONS FOR THE SEER

• How do you connect with your intuitive heart? Do you feel it, see it, hear it, and know it?

• Do you receive messages of both shadow and sunshine from beyond the veil, and do you treat them with equal importance?

• When you quiet your mind, and you listen for one word that the High Priestess is sending to you today, what is it? And why does it make sense for you right now?

INTUITION
upgrade
s p r e a d

*Ask the High Priestess to offer suggestions
for your daily intuitive practice*

①

② EYES SHUT

③ EYES OPEN

Place the
High Priestess
here.

What is
blocking
my intuition?

Where should
I look?
What can I do
to see?

> "You see more than you know.
> You know more than you think.
> You think more than you need.
> Slow down, and listen, for your inner sight
> is a vast landscape of truth."

HEALING WITH THE HIGH PRIESTESS

forgotten memories, thyroid / hormonal imbalances, lymphatic system, hypothalamus,
pineal gland, blocked intuition, serotonin, melatonin and sleep disorders, kidney stones

Mother Gaia:
Sacred feminine,
fertility,
Holding us all
with her Love

Branches & Leaves:
Nature,
B e a u t y,
creatrix of Life

Full moon
scepter:
Nourishing
Power

{ Daughter
of Heaven
and Earth

School of
Fish:
abundance,
a situation
teeming with
Life,
Spiritual
Gifts

Pregnant with
the World:
Growth,
Expansion,
Creation energy.

3 the
Empress

Moss:
being grounded

Expectation of
Prosperity

"You are love. You are ruler. You are nurturer. You are creativity
and the miracle of life entwined. You are *all of* these things, and you
are safe to breathe life into the world that you desire to create."

3. the Empress

LIGHT SEER: the Divine feminine, prolific creativity and creation, fertility, unity, empathy, motherhood, the Goddess, sensuality, nurturing, abundance, unconditional love, lushness, a new relationship or business

SHADOW SEER: infertility, emotional overwhelm, shutting down, the need for self-care, disharmony, negligence, being materialistic, being overprotective of your creations, being overly dependent on others

AN EMPRESS STORY

The Gaian Empress looks out over the earth, *her favorite creation*, and she sends out a low nurturing hum from deep within her core. A vibration of love. Of grounding energy. Of positive answers and outcomes. Her echo reverberates through the fish that swim around her and into the ground beneath her, and she watches it all teem to life with infinite creator potential. With an exhale of love, she leans on her moon scepter and sends gravitational harmony to the oceans and earth. She reminds us that the earth is abundantly fertile, and that it can evolve and co-create whatever it can imagine for itself: Mossy forests. Oceans. Health. Romance. Epic love stories. Creative insight. Soul-nurturing stories. And every miracle of life one could imagine.

THE EMPRESS' MESSAGE

The Empress reminds you that you have the potent fertile energy of the Divine Goddess within you. You also have a generative imagination that you can use to envision and create your life with ever more love, connection, healing, and more abundance. Feel free to take her literally—with her full belly and dynamic warmth on display, she offers a nod to your positive outcome and to your ability to birth the reality you desire. In romance, she often signals a yes, and she affirms that you are on the right track in your endeavors. She suggests a time of profound healing and blessings and wants to remind us that her bountiful abundance is always available to us all. Simply look around you, and you'll find her regenerative beauty everywhere! It's time to take some luxurious self-care time to nourish your body with compassion. (Deep breath in, my love.) Remember that no excuses are bigger than the magic of life itself. No blockages are too big for her Gaian miracles. If you are feeling a lack of inspiration or not able to see the infinite possibilities that are popping from every cell and swimming around in your energy body, it's the perfect time to bring your dreams from the ethereal realms and ground them. Share them. Start them. *Birth them.* Trust in this expansive and flourishing energy to wash through your physical temple and bloom! Embody her radiating creativity, and then continue to move calmly and gracefully in the direction of that which whispers yes. This card often predicts the creation of the magnificent, so keep growing, beautiful seer, and work with the nature of your situation instead of against it.

I am ready to give birth to my abundantly rich future.

QUESTIONS FOR THE SEER
- What areas of your life need more mothering and are asking to be held and nurtured?
- What would unconditional self-compassion allow you to birth?
- Sensuality and creativity are gifts from the Gaian Empress. How do they support you?
- What outcomes have you been nurturing? What have you been growing in the light *and* in the dark? (You get to decide what seeds you plant in your creative cave and which ones you birth. You get to decide which ones to water and tend. You decide how long you wait before the harvest and how you share the harvest with those around you.)
- Finish this sentence: I am ready to give birth to _____.

an empress spread for PROLIFIC CREATIVITY

(Ask the Empress to offer suggestions for your daily intuitive or creative practice and to help interpret the other cards from the Muse's perspective.)

② THE BLOCK

③ THE UNCREATED

④ THE MUSE

Place the Empress card here.

What is holding back my creativity/intuition?

What will I create next? Where should I start?

A message from the Muse

HEALING WITH THE EMPRESS

creative blocks, fertility and reproductive system issues (endometriosis, cysts, fibroids, etc.), estrogen issues, breast disorders, weight issues, mother wounds, ties with community, postpartum depression, attachment disorders, dependency issues

LIGHT: DIVINE ILLUMINATION AND guidance

Ram's head:
Connection to Aries
pioneering SPIRIT
and leadership,
stubbornness and
DETERMINATION

HANDKERCHIEF IN
POCKET: ability
to support others
emotionally and to
show EMPATHY as
he leads

Chess piece: strategy
AND success, the
material WORLD,
a PROTECTOR and
PROVIDER, being
ANALYTICAL.

Ankh: Ancient
Egyptian
symbol of Life AND
eternal Life,
PROTECTION.

Mars throne:
STATUS, POWER.
AUTHORITY,
ASSERTION. ANGER,
WARRIOR ENERGY

4. the Emperor

Chess board
Floor: PLANNING, WISDOM, VISION

RED AND GOLD:
PASSION, WEALTH,
POWER, AUTHORITY

4. the Emperor

LIGHT SEER: the Divine masculine, authority, power, a natural leader, entrepreneurship, structure, strategic and analytical thinking, taking action, calculated risk, looking after others, promotion, success

SHADOW SEER: unchecked power, being overly pragmatic and rigid, corruption, a desire for control, selfishness, defensiveness, being stubborn, ruling with an iron fist

AN EMPEROR STORY

The Emperor is a creative, innovative leader, and he knows it. He sits on his Mars throne, contemplating his next move and watching over his domain with the control, assuredness, and the consistent guidance of a skilled leader. He tempers his fiery Aries energy with discipline and strategy, structure, and consistent action, for he knows that this is how he will find his success. His ram's skull hanging on the wall is a constant reminder that he must use his power wisely and that selfish motives will lead to his demise. A wise leader looks after his people, shares his energy in service to them, and understands that his strength is a direct reflection of his relationship with others. He understands that the unity of the whole is his greatest asset. Well, that, and his collection of imported chess boards. He learns to listen to other's needs as he moves toward his goals. If he is overly pragmatic and forgets to marry his logical mind with his compassion and his heart, he risks being too strict and structured. His disciplined success radiates when he leads with service in his heart and follows with the strategy in his head.

THE EMPEROR'S MESSAGE

The Emperor's message is one of ambitions met and success found. Often seen as the card of the Divine masculine, the leader, or the businessman, it asks you to build a better world by moving forward methodically—using both your determined heart and your compassionate intelligence. While becoming your own Emperor means infinite possibility for your success, it also means that you must truly lead your own evolution. Mastering this leadership power in your life means addressing any personal issues you harbor around authority, control, and willpower. You may need to work your magic within the structured confines of "establishment," but remember that the organizing principles of societies and sciences are fluid over time. Remain flexible and keenly aware of your energetic boundaries and motives, especially where others are concerned. Find opportunities to be of service to others as you build your empire, and choose strategic logic over daydreams and emotional desires. Pay close attention to the needs of those you are leading along the way. Integrity, deep trust, and respect are the energies of the Emperor. Step into this energy of success and rise, sweet Light Seer! Embody confident, compassionate leadership and exercise sovereignty over your own reality. The world is yours for the making.

I lead the circumstances in my world with confidence, harmony, and generosity. ♈

QUESTIONS FOR THE SEER
- Do you feel stable and reliable? What is your relationship with responsibility like?
- What strategies or plans have you been meaning to implement? Whatcha' got in mind? Write them down and formalize them!
- What are you building, and what will it look like when you are done?

"Leading others means being of service to others.
Protect your energy as you move toward success."

~ the ~
CHECKMATE STRATEGY SPREAD

A spread for finding your personal power and success

What power do you
have access to that
you aren't currently
aware of / using?

**YOUR
POWER**

Place the Emperor
here. (His wisdom will
help you to interpret
the next two cards.)

Checkmate! What
is the strategic
next step to take?

**EMPEROR
SPEAKS**

**POWER
MOVES**

A message about
embodying success
and leadership energy

HEALING WITH THE EMPEROR
head and face issues, prostate issues, bone disorders, brain/cognitive disorders,
challenges with authority figures, father wounds, healing feelings about male figures,
rifts with the Divine masculine

"As a seeker, you hold the power to vibrate with a little more light
as you ascend upwards . . . Up towards the One Cosmic Love that shines
down and illuminates the path for us of all."

SPIRITUAL SYMBOLS
FLOATING AROUND
HIS HEAD: ONENESS,
NON-DENOMINATIONAL
ALL PATHS WELCOME,
SPIRITUAL TEACHINGS,
WISDOM, PATHS

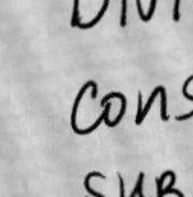

PAPAL
CROSS:

HOLY TRINITIES,
A LINK to the
DIVINE, also
CONSCIOUS,
SUBCONSCIOUS,
and SUPERCONSCIOUS

MANDALA GATEWAY:
ascension,
the DIVINE

STAIRS:
BRIDGE BETWEEN
the DIVINE
AND the MUNDANE,
the path to
enlightenment

MINDFULNESS,
MEDITATION,
PRESENCE and
JOY ARE
PORTALS of
CONNECTION

5 the
Hierophant

5. the
Hierophant

LIGHT SEER: powerful lessons, a spiritual leader or guide, a time to have faith, awakening, enlightenment,, in service of Spirit, finding your own path, an awakened soul, new paradigms, transformation and transcendence

SHADOW SEER: old systems or structures that are no longer relevant, dogma, rebelling against societal norms, a need to let go of old ways of thinking, abuse of power, stagnation, ego-based leadership, a need to connect with Spirit

A HIEROPHANT STORY

The Hierophant is the keeper of the sacred, and he sits at the steps of a spiritual pilgrimage. Every stair is a lesson that is unique to the individual who walks the path.

He has always known that his primary path in life was to show others the doorway, and he sits smiling at the base of a step-by-step spiritual journey, welcoming guests with open arms. *Hieros* is a Greek word meaning "sacred," and *phant* has its roots in the Greek "to show." As he warmly greets those who arrive, he reminds them of their own Divine makeup. "You are made of God-stuff," he calls out, "fashioned with the same forces of creation that inspired the stars." As an awakened master, he is the personification of the gateway between Divine Source and the people he serves.

He holds in his mind's eye the energies of all religions, and he recognizes that— organized or not—there is deep wisdom at the heart of all spiritual teachings. "It's the people who fail us," he winks. He lives a life of humility and service, but always in a way that demonstrates self-love. His T-shirt displays the prongs of the original Hierophant's trinity scepter, because he openly holds admiration for the old Gods and for the many wondrous faces of the Divine that speckle our expanding Universe.

THE HIEROPHANT'S MESSAGE

As you search for your Divine truth, you create frameworks of understanding that help you to expand your consciousness and that ground your faith into your reality. Your own spiritual beliefs should support you at this time, and if they don't, you are being asked to activate a deepening of your faith in order to find the guidance that you seek. When the Hierophant shows up in a reading, he is asking you to grow and to hold more light within your being than you ever have in the past. If you've been stuck in an old tradition, system, or structured way of acting or being, it is time to let that fall away in order to make space for a better version of you. The Hierophant serves as a gateway between Divine Source and the seeker, so be open to new paradigms, perspectives, mentors, or teachers coming into your life at this time. He may show up in a variety of lessons or circumstances. Look to the repeating patterns around you, and strive to understand your own internal compass. Know that while there is wisdom in the teachings of the mystics, the voice of your own heart is the one voice that matters the most. It's time to find the wisdom of the heavens, within.

I am my own Guru. The guidance I need is Rooted in my faith, my belief, and my unique essence.

QUESTIONS FOR THE SEER

• Are you listening to the wisdom of your heart, or placing other people's messages above your own?

• Is there an old way of doing things that you are holding on to? What would happen if you let go of an outmoded way of life?

• What beliefs or belief system is getting in the way of your dreams?

the HIEROPHANT'S
steps to spirit spread

Carefully select a card to represent your faith by looking through the cards face up and choosing intuitively. (You get to decide!)

① **FAITH**

② **RENEW**

How can I strengthen my connection to the Divine? How can I renew my spiritual or religious faith?

What actions or daily practices would help me at this time?

③ **DEVOTION**

④ **YOU, THE GURU**

My incredible spiritual capacity, a message from Spirit

HEALING WITH THE HIEROPHANT

skeletal system, shoulder or arm problems, ancestral or generational trauma, TMJ, rigid joints, hearing disorders, throat disorders, obsessive or compulsive thinking, lost religious or spiritual faith, pessimism, trauma caused by systems or patriarchy

SPIRALS: the HYPNOTIZING nature of love

MERKABA: a PORTAL. INTERDIMENSIONAL travel. SPIRITUAL GROWTH, Connection. FROM ancient EGYPTIAN MER = LIGHT, KA = SPIRIT, BAH = BODY

HOLDING HAIR: She is Choosing to fall in love

Tattoos of SPIRITUAL SYMBOLS: LESSONS LEARNED IN the Hierophant CARD, and Brought into her Relationships.

6. the Lovers

CUPID'S ARROW: LOVE, PARTNERSHIP

"Mastering self-love is the key to balancing the duality of any relationship. As with all willing partnerships, the choice to step into vulnerability must be made consciously."

6. the Lovers

LIGHT SEER: a choice, dualities, harmony, a lover or romantic relationship, friendship, unity, choosing to allow yourself to fall in love, healthy boundaries, soulmates

SHADOW SEER: a break in communication, disharmony, the need to find self-love, giving away power in a relationship, the loss of self, too many expectations of others, manipulation, an imbalanced partnership, codependency

A LOVERS' STORY

The world slows as two souls gaze attentively at each other. Like Yin and Yang, these entwined figures embody the concept of duality. Two hearts. Two energetic systems. She carries with her the initiations and the tattoo markings that remind her of lessons learned in card 5 (the Hierophant.) Who she is today is a result of everything she has done and experienced—her wounds, her desires, and her beliefs—will all carry forward into this forthcoming relationship. The orbiting spirals of emotion and attraction lull the couple into euphoria, and yet she knows there always comes a choice: to *really* allow herself to fall into this partnership and merge with this new energetic offer . . . *to become a part of a totally new creation*, or to block off her heart and not fully experience what this love has to offer.

Her hair flows toward him, and attraction threatens to whisk her away. Will she lose her bearings? Will this new opportunity blossom? She remembers that clenching on to any one thing in fear will not actually keep it with her in the long run. Cupid marks her arm with a new sigil, and she bravely takes one step closer to this man—his graying hair a sign of a long life of challenges and joys lived before this moment—promising to remain true to her heart no matter what happens, and to love herself so completely that she can support this pairing with her own light, her love, and her magic.

THE LOVERS' MESSAGE

Magnetism like magic is coming into your life. You are sitting on the cusp of a new connection, union, or partnership: the type of profound connection when two souls are intertwined, and their entanglement forever marks their individual paths. You may be deepening into the truest of loves, a kinship of kindreds, or the heaviest of romances. This relationship has the power to change your trajectory and fill your heart with all the passion and spark of two souls in momentum. Often this card signifies that an important choice needs to be made. Which experience do you really desire? Will you embrace the hypnotic energy that unwinds between people who are deepening their connection? Will you merge your energy and shift into this relationship or not? Falling deeply into trust will be necessary in order to create a lasting bond, and growth around vulnerability, honesty, desire, and intimacy is being called into the light to be healed. While partnerships are beautiful gifts on the path, you must also seek to give fully without weakening your resolve to remain whole. Remember that self-love is the key to balancing the duality of any relationship..

MY HEART IS OPEN TO DEEPLY MEANINGFUL RELATIONSHIPS AND I EXPAND INTO THIS UNION with LOVING TRUST.

QUESTIONS FOR THE SEER
- Are you able to bring yourself *fully* to a partnership at this time?
- What shadow might you be projecting onto others in your relationships?
- Are you open to collaborating with others? Or to having a romantic relationship with another soul? If yes, how are you calling them in? If no, why not?
- What steps have you been taking to inform the Universe that you are here and that you are ready?

THE LOVERS'
MERKABA
spread

*Ask the Merkaba (a portal connecting the light body
to the higher realms) what it wants to tell you about love*

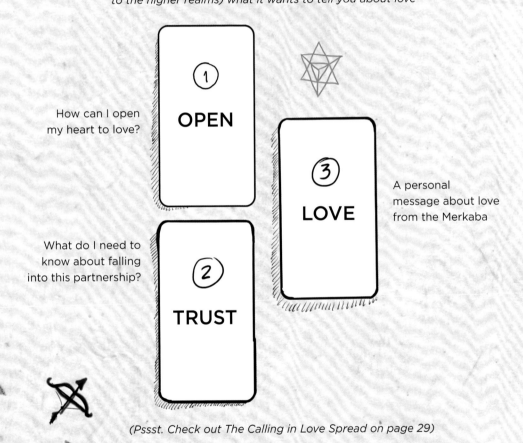

How can I open
my heart to love?

① **OPEN**

③ **LOVE**

A personal
message about love
from the Merkaba

What do I need to
know about falling
into this partnership?

② **TRUST**

(Pssst. Check out The Calling in Love Spread on page 29)

HEALING WITH THE LOVERS
cardiovascular issues, insomnia, hot flashes, nightmares, left and right brain unity,
skin rashes, STDs, libido issues, balancing systems in the body, broken hearts, indecision

HARNESSING THE MAGIC
IN BOTH LIGHT AND SHADOW

CHARIOT
LIGHTS:
BRINGING
your magic
with you

STAR CANOPY OF
the UNIVERSE:
DIVINE HELP AND
GUIDANCE

WATER: USING
INTUITION

TWO HORSES:
DUALITY, YIN-YANG

● RED: PASSIONS
● PURPLE: CROWN
CHAKRA, INTUITION

YELLOW: SOLAR
PLEXUS CHAKRA,
EGO, WILLPOWER,
DETERMINATION

7. the Chariot

Velocity
SPEED,
Gathering
Momentum

GETTING all of the UNIVERSE'S
ENERGY flowing in one direction

"It's now. Today's determined actions will amplify your
sense of purpose and resolve tomorrow."

LIGHT SEER: victory, speed and action, determination, harnessing and uniting opposing energies, success, travel, confidence, willpower, being in control

SHADOW SEER: haste, a lack of energetic focus, a need for self-discipline, aimlessly charging ahead, self-doubt, lack of control

A CHARIOT STORY

The charioteer is perched steadily atop his carriage, galloping toward his destination. Energetic reins of light and shadow flow down from the Cosmos and direct his movement, and while these celestial forces seem like they are headed toward opposite paths, he coaxes them forward toward one destination. They rush ahead quickly, working with one another as he remains laser-focused, determined, and on the move. He controls his trajectory through sheer willpower—and rushes to the best version of his future by taking inspired action. He knows his time is precious and that he must act in order to ride the momentum of this energy. To stay is to stagnate, and he wants to evolve, knowing that lessons will unfold as he speeds on to these new experiences. Looking up at the starry sky, he knows he is never alone, and that Spirit is with him, always. The spinning shadow and light energy twists into a path before him, showing him the way forward. Galloping ahead, he feels his power rise. And from the back of his throat, the words "**I am**" begin to emerge, and he smiles . . . feeling fully alive and ready to take on the world.

THE CHARIOT'S MESSAGE

The Universe constantly gifts us with the opportunity to become more. Push ahead with determination, beautiful seer, because you will get there. Your evolution is imminent right now, and this is a magical moment for taking inspired action. You can do this, so charge ahead and find extreme optimism! The Chariot reminds you that while you are on the way to your goal, you need to make decisions about your best path forward. If you feel pulled in two different directions, work on coaxing both of these energies toward the same target. There's a way to get them both on the same page! Seek to align your task with your purpose, leaving room for any spiritual desires that you may have. This will add momentum as you fly upward toward your goal. Get ready, because completion and achievement are yours to be had! In shadow, charging ahead without paying attention to your path can sometimes be harmful to those in your wake, so take care not to trample on others on your way up the mountain. Choose the thing you really want . . . and if you aren't sure what that thing is, then you may need to buckle down and find your north. (It's self-discipline time!) The Chariot teaches us that *inaction* is the same as *deciding to stay where you are*, and that your evolution includes lessons that *require* your movement. Choose to ride the peaks and valleys with focus, confidence, and control. Set your goals. Make your plans. And spark your dreams!

I CHOOSE WHO I am BECOMING AND I RUN TOWARDS IT WITH CONVICTION AND CONSISTENT MOTION

QUESTIONS FOR THE SEER

- Where are you headed? Without clarity on your innermost desires, it's impossible to send your chariot in the right direction. Check in with your solar plexus to find answers if you are unsure.
- Does your chariot feel a little stuck in the mud? In what areas of your life have you been stagnant for too long? What would give you the boost you need to start moving?
- How are you planning for the journey ahead? Chart your route. Make a list.

OPPOSING eNeRGIeS
UNiTE SPREAD

A spread for when you have two opposing choices, voices, or desires.
Before you pull your cards, get clear on your two desires.

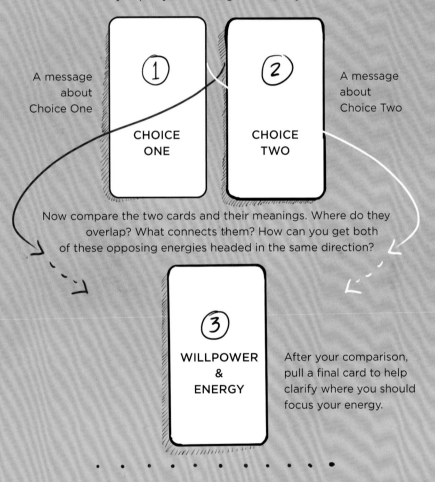

A message
about
Choice One

①

②

A message
about
Choice Two

**CHOICE
ONE**

**CHOICE
TWO**

Now compare the two cards and their meanings. Where do they
overlap? What connects them? How can you get both
of these opposing energies headed in the same direction?

③

**WILLPOWER
&
ENERGY**

After your comparison,
pull a final card to help
clarify where you should
focus your energy.

HEALING WITH THE CHARIOT
chest and stomach issues, strength/mobility issues, physical rehabilitation, fitness or
weight-loss goals, quick-moving ailments, negative mindset, help sticking to meditation
or daily routines, adrenal fatigue, ulcers, foot or leg problems, lack of control, travel
sickness, feeling directionless, lack of willpower and self-discipline

LEO
CONSTELLATION

Balance Between
human AND ANIMAL,
Her position
shows her
confidence and
willingness to
be vulnerable.

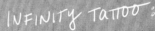

INFINITY TATTOO:
Eternal Strength
and ENDURANCE,
balance of
RESTRAINT
and POWER.

LAMB:
INNOCENCE,
Purity, INNER
Peace AND
Calmness, control,
SPIRITUAL Faith,
Gentleness and
Compassion.

HEART:
compassion,
empathy,
love,
INNER-
STRENGTH.

Strength

○ GREEN: HEART CHAKRA
○ YELLOW: SOLAR PLEXUS CHAKRA (WILLPOWER)
● WHITE : PURITY

8. Strength

LIGHT SEER: fierce serenity, courage, calmness, quiet strength, inner strength, influence, purity, innocence, spiritual matters, compassion, graceful leadership, gifted healer, spiritual matters, sometimes lust or animal instinct

SHADOW SEER: blocked by fear, self-doubt, stuck in a flight-or-fight response, a dysregulated nervous system, a need to exercise self-control, being guided by the lizard part of your brain, self-destructive impulses

A STRENGTH STORY

Strength's nature is so calm and gentle that even the baby lamb feels safe in her presence. She stands quietly . . . serene and relaxed . . . and allows this energy to guide her every move. Beneath her soft and youthful exterior lies the strength and the courage of a lion. In times of peril, she always has access to the steady wisdom that resides within, for she has merged with the Spirit of her animal guide, and he leads her to an inner refuge of deep peace. The kingly beast has taken up residence within her heart where she has been slowly learning how to embody his courage and wisdom. Her quiet, humble bravery and her honest motivations have impressed him, so he gifts her an understanding of fierce power . . . and she promises to embody it, fully. Whenever she is faced with danger or uncertainty, his empowering sovereignty will allow her to exude grace and confidence, and to bravely stand against the monsters of the world. Roaring warmly though her kind smile, he fills their heart with a consistent, peaceful gratitude. And together, with their shared compassion, they exert gentle influence and control over their domain.

STRENGTH'S MESSAGE

Be brave, sweet seer. Embody your light and shine courageously in the face of danger or uncertainty. Step into patience and fierce serenity as you exert your graceful influence for the greater good. There is great fortitude in your calm heart, and a gentle demeanor will not be mistaken for weakness when you share your gift of relentless love with the world. Allow confidence and composure to guide you toward your desires without the use of excessive force or aggression. Mindful awareness will be much more useful than rigid control right now. In shadow, sometimes the beast we need to tame is not one that exists in the outside world. You can handle anything that lands on your path, so don't try to forcefully domineer your way into a specific outcome. When paired with a willingness to adapt and learn, your consistent, peaceful energy can be incredibly persuasive. This card reminds you to stand strong in your beliefs and desires, and to remain steady as you bring compassion to your current situation. You are powerful, and your purity of heart will be a beacon of strength and inspiration to those around you.

I deliberately shine my compassion and STRENGTH, and I use THEM for GOOD.

QUESTIONS FOR THE SEER
- How do you find courage in the face of shadow? Do you remember to call on your guides to lend their support?
- Sometimes the beast we need to dominate is within us. What part of your personality needs some gentle guidance?
- When faced with a challenge, how do you react? Or respond? Does fear play a role?
- Are you being taken advantage of (or walked on) because of your soft nature?
- Fearless serenity is grounded power. When do you feel powerful in life?

> "In the meadow of Strength and Innocence, the fierce serenity of the lion and the lamb will teach us the profound essence of peace."

INNER STRENGTH outer CALM SPREAD

③ MY OUTER COURAGE

① MY INNER GUIDE

∞

② MY INNER PEACE

How the outside world views my influence, my power and boldness. How can I foster bravery?

A message from my guide about where I can find my inner fortitude

How can I cultivate and maintain inner peace when the outer world feels chaotic?

HEALING WITH STRENGTH
personal power, vital life force, sexual addiction, heart and heart chakra, cardiovascular disorders, immune system, muscular endurance and strength, rage and anger issues, inner critic, inner self-talk, blood disorders, dental problems

LIGHTS AND STARS:
the PRESENCE of the DIVINE, DOWNLOADS, Connection with SOMETHING greater than self.

9. the hermit

MEDITATING:
Time away, inner focus. Solace, inner magic AND LIGHT.

Knowing WHO you are and what you're made of.

LAMP LIGHT:
Guidance and ENLIGHTENMENT, Seeking truth, Hope, comfort or PROTECTION.

(she left her lantern at the base of the mountain because she no longer needs it. Her light comes from the INSIDE.)

DOTS: the TRAIL of LIGHT she left behind, RIPPLES of change or BREADCRUMBS from the UNIVERSE.

"The guest of honor is your own soul."

9. the
hermit

LIGHT SEER: inner reflection, meditation, contemplation, soul searching, inner wisdom, spiritual mentor, experience, finding your guide within, taking time away from the chaos of a busy life, time out, "hermitting"

SHADOW SEER: withdrawing from society, isolation, loneliness, ignoring your inner voice, forever seeking without healing, losing your sense of purpose, feeling like a misfit

A HERMIT STORY

She walks the path, using her lantern to light her way through the dark corners of the night. She has learned all she can from her current situation, so she drops her candle, her devices, her connections to other people's opinions and voices—she even leaves her trusted tarot cards behind—for she knows that it is time to set the traditional tools aside and walk the rest of the path alone. It's the only way that she will be able to hear the beating pulse of her own spirit . . . her only true guidance. Her heart leads her to the top of her inner mountain to spend some time in quiet contemplation. She looks out at the horizon and understands that her own internal compass may shift after she passes through this process of integrating her shadow and light. Here, at the precipice of her knowing, she sits in introspection. She forges her faith. She listens. She uplevels her belief. She feels. She journeys. She learns. *Oh! An enlightenment. An awakening. An illumination!* When she is ready, she knows she must say good-bye to her hermit experience and return to her life below. If she doesn't, she risks becoming too isolated and withdrawn. She knows she wants to experience the richness and fullness of life, *with others.* With gratitude, she leaves her steady candle burning brightly at the foot of the path, where it will illuminate the way for others. She no longer needs it to see where she is headed, as she has become her own brightest light and can safely illuminate her way home.

THE HERMIT'S MESSAGE

It's time to pause—and to make space in your busy life for sacred aloneness and self-care. If you are feeling disconnected from your spiritual north, this time of solitary withdrawal will help you to connect with your own compass and recalibrate. Take a hiatus from your daily life and commit to creating a space for quiet contemplation. The luminous energy of the Hermit will gift you with inner wisdom about your soul purpose, spiritual awakening, and your best way forward. In his lamplight, you will find your way back to your guiding principles. It is truly the right time to go within to uncover the intensity of your light and your love. Sometimes, we run the risk of being so introspective that we lose our connections to others, or worse—we can dive so deeply into our stories of struggle that we inadvertently begin to believe that our wounds will be a part of our forever identity. In the deepest trenches of self-discovery, we must remember that our continual search for our own healing and inner truth does not mean that we are not already whole and healed. Emerge from your inner retreat with beautiful insights from Spirit and allow yourself to navigate the path with your brightly illuminated heart. Trust your ability to move ahead in the dark with only your own strong light to guide you.

Inner-Sage. Inner-Mentor. Inner-Guide.
Show me my brightest LIGHT so that
I may see with all of my HEART.

QUESTIONS FOR THE SEER
• How comfortable are you doing things by yourself and spending time alone?
• Do you give yourself permission to pause when you need to?
• What would your inner sage say about your healing journey?
  Are you over-identifying with your struggle or your challenges?

the HERMIT'S INNER LAMP

A spread for finding your way

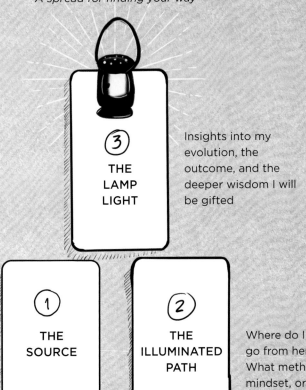

③

**THE
LAMP
LIGHT**

Insights into my
evolution, the
outcome, and the
deeper wisdom I will
be gifted

①

**THE
SOURCE**

What needs
to be healed?
Where does
my healing
journey begin?

②

**THE
ILLUMINATED
PATH**

Where do I
go from here?
What methods,
mindset, or
approach
could help me?

HEALING WITH THE HERMIT

mental confusion, self-compassion, attention disorders, back issues or difficulty standing,
night blindness, fear of the dark, chronic pain, burnout, vitamin deficiencies, colds or flus,
light sensitivity, eye strain, emotional wounds, social anxiety, loneliness

YOGA TREE POSITION ON TOP OF WHEEL:
Balancing Life's Ups and Downs

LUCKY DICE: Fate, Luck

ELEMENT SYMBOLS:
▽ EARTH   △ AIR
▽ WATER   △ FIRE

SPINNING
WHEEL DISKS:
SPIRALLING UP
through Lessons
and KARMIC CYCLES,
DIFFERENT TIMELINES
and POSSIBILITIES

ROULETTE
wheel:
← FATE, chances,
the UNKNOWN
POTENTIAL

the WHEEL

Chaos Symbol:
- UNPREDICTABLE NATURE of Life
- CREATIVE POTENTIAL WITHIN chaos
- EMBRACING change AND UNCERTAINTY
- INTERCONNECTEDNESS / the BUTTERFLY effect
- BALANCE BETWEEN ORDER AND CHAOS

10. the wheel

LIGHT SEER: changes, fate, destiny, a lucky break, cycling up through karmic lessons, the chaos of creation, a turning point, serendipity

SHADOW SEER: misfortune, karma, a need to relinquish control, the ups and downs of life, the inevitability of change, an unexpected setback

A WHEEL STORY

She spins her wheel with all the wonders of curiosity and creation in her eyes. She whispers her quintessential invocations as she spins: *"Here we go. All or nothing: Randomness. Synchronicity. Fractal and repeating. Patterned and karmic. Luck. Fate. Freedom."* She lets the wheel go and stands over her spinning disks, gleefully watching the eight arrows of chaos slip in and out of probabilities. They simultaneously point to the eight stages of the year, and to the roulette of possibilities for the seeker's answer. All the while, perched on one foot, she knows that she has harnessed all the light and all the shadow to create this destiny. If she leans too far in either direction she may fall out of balance and land at the bottom. She's fallen before and she will do it again, each time learning and growing from the experience. *But not this time.* She isn't really sure if it's her luck or Divine intervention that keeps her at the top of the wheel today. She does know, however, that every time the wheel spins, she feels as though she is cycling upward through the very same lessons. And those lessons vibrate a little differently each time, getting easier to navigate or getting more intense depending on her ability to maneuver her mindset. She has learned that her perspective is an extraordinary asset, and she prepares to throw the lucky dice she carries around her neck. She shakes them in her hand, kisses her knuckles, leans toward her badass belief, and winks at faith. With a giggle, she casts her lot and hopes with all her wishful thinking that her magical mindset will keep her balanced at the top once more, and she readies her footing as it begins to spin again.

THE WHEEL'S MESSAGE

Get ready, sweet soul, for the wheel is about to gift you a moment of Divine fortune and charmed outcomes! Synchronicity is afoot, so look for opportunities to propel your life ahead. Be prepared for fortuitous meetings or a lucky fork in the path that will change everything for the better. If you're open to spotting opportunity, it's yours for the taking, as beautiful turning points are all around you right now! Just follow the breadcrumbs of serendipity and fate toward your happy ending. Remember that the wheel is always spinning, and things are never the same as they were before. Learn to enjoy this constant regenerative energy, knowing that with every spin we have another chance to cycle upward toward our own expansion and enlightenment. Trying to control the outcome of the Wheel of Fortune would prove to be impossible, so don't! Destiny oscillates in ups and downs, and this dynamic and ever-changing force is yours to harness and work with. (You do have a say in the matter!) Grab your lucky dice and see the spinning of the wheel for what it really is: all the beauty of a lifetime of experiences, waiting to spin forth and be lived.

I allow The Transformative eNergies of FaTe To exPaND my exPerience.

QUESTIONS FOR THE SEER

- Are you trying to control the outcome of events in your life to the point of stifling your ability to see serendipity?
- Do you believe that your destiny is written, or do you believe that you create your own future? Would one of these perspectives help you more than the other at this time?
- Wheel of Truth: What part of your current situation have you created through choices that you may now regret? Can you release and transmute your feelings around your past, so that you can free up the present and spin the wheel in your favor?

"Embrace the flow of life's continuous cycles."

SPINNING *your* OWN **LUCK** with THE WHEEL

A spread for calling in the magic of luck and synchronicity

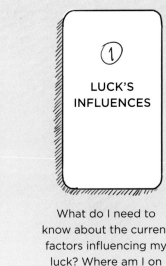

①

**LUCK'S
INFLUENCES**

②

**SERENDIPITY'S
SPIN**

③

**LUCK. FATE.
FREEDOM.**

What do I need to
know about the current
factors influencing my
luck? Where am I on
the wheel?

How can I invite more
serendipity, luck, and
magic into my life?

Advice for where
I am headed next.
What actions or
perspectives will
positively influence
my opportunities?

HEALING WITH THE WHEEL
digestive issues and organs, cycling mood disorders, sleep cycles and circadian
rhythm, diseases that have flare-up cycles (lupus, multiple sclerosis, rheumatoid arthritis,
eczema, etc.), epilepsy, blood-sugar imbalances, pessimism

SWORD:
CUTS through
DECEIT and
UNCERTAINTY,
TRUTH,
     CLARITY

11. Justice

SCALES of JUSTICE:
BALANCE and FAIRNESS,
Weighing Actions,
Integrity and
     CONSEQUENCES

← THEY ARE MADE
WITH mini CAULDRONS
(OR PLANTERS)
BECAUSE our actions
and INTENTIONS have
consequences on the
Magic we can WIELD
(AND the GROWTH
     we can
     EXPERIENCE.)

BLACK and
WHITE DOTS:
DUALITY,
LIGHT and
   SHADOW

REFLECTION:
Self-Reflection and
Examination, HONESTY,
Shadow WORK, MOTIVATIONS,
a Reminder that our
Karma, MINDSET, and our
choices are MIRRORED back
to us through LIFE.

"True equilibrium between actions and consequences
is only found through honest self-reflection."

11. Justice

LIGHT SEER: natural law, balance, karma, truth, wisdom, legal matters, fairness, cause and effect, integrity, objectivity, perspective, accountability

SHADOW SEER: consequences, retribution, karma, injustice and inequity, dishonesty, imbalance, a need to take responsibility for your past actions, past experiences, facing regret, difficulty in legal matters

A JUSTICE STORY

Justice holds her sword out skillfully, and she tunes in to the question asked of her. She feels the changing winds pick up and pass through her hands, and she waits for the feeling of balance to arrive as she whispers her values: *morality, intention, truth, integrity.* While her sword can be used for slicing through the darkness in order seek truth, she prefers to use it more gently, picking up on the thoughts and intentions of the seeker. In this way she can balance and weigh their outcomes objectively. Justice believes that actions provoke reactions, in things being either right or wrong, and understands truth as well as deception. She believes in the universal moral code that she upholds, and easily sees the errors in other people's thinking. In shadow, she witnesses the way our emotional state can easily cloud our judgement. The connection to ego. *The lies.* She watches how quickly we tend to see things from our very limited perspectives, often condemning others before having all the facts. She knows that fear will usually cause us to act in ways we are not proud of, and that the only elevating path lies rooted in deeper truths. She understands, yet holds us accountable regardless, and with a steady hand she asks us to look at our responsibilities, our choices, and our excuses, *with love.*

JUSTICE'S MESSAGE

Your past actions have brought you to right here, right now. Justice asks you to learn from your experiences: the good, the bad, and the fugly, and take it all and grow from it. This energy is not about perfection, but about fairness and honesty. It highlights clarity of motivation and intention, and it asks you to be realistic about the cause-and-effect of your actions. If there is something you need to rectify, rectify it! Seek radical integrity at this time, for it will help you to understand where you could have done a better job, while also seeing where another person was doing their best with the tools that they had. Justice speaks to accountability and resolution, and she reminds us that *honesty always brings us back to balance.* Your best opportunities for growth and success will integrate both optimistic positivity and curiosity about your own actions. If you've learned from a past mistake, *be proud of your progress.* This is how we grow! If the truth feels foggy and unclear, or if life's choices have you feeling disoriented, the Justice card asks you to seek equilibrium through truth and fairness. In your current situation, be impartial as you reframe your reality and work to remove any negative emotional charge from the equation. This will allow you to act out of integrity and realign with your core values so that you can restore harmony. If you're stuck in a dispute or a legal matter, Justice upright often speaks to the outcomes leaning in your favor. Don't allow fear to turn you into someone you're not, and seek a variety of perspectives before judging another person's actions to be "good" or "bad." Remember that the true path of "goodness" is not always black or white, but it is—always—one of love.

MY GOOD KARMA is DELightfULLY LOVING AND can BE THE MOST MOTIVATING of TEACHERS.

QUESTIONS FOR THE SEER
• Where in your life are you out of balance?
• If you've made a mistake, how can you learn from it and do a better job next time?
• Justice and injustice are tightly bound concepts. What injustices can you right with thoughtful action and inspired service?
• If you have been harmed by an injustice, can you move toward forgiveness in order to heal? What does it mean to truly make amends?
• Are fairness and rightness the same thing?

JUSTICE & BALANCE

A spread for cultivating clear judgement and aligned action

③ BALANCED ACTION

① BALANCED HEART

② BALANCED MIND

What actions are for my highest good and the highest good for all?

In what areas of my life can I cultivate better emotional balance? Where can I foster more harmony and light?

In what areas of my life can I work on cultivating clearer judgement?

• • • • • • • • • • • • • • • •

HEALING WITH JUSTICE
balance issues, vertigo, ear disorders (Ménière's, etc.), metabolic disorders, cardiovascular disorders, liver, hypertension, lower back pain, kidney issues, stress because of legal/equity issues, diabetes

Ⓘ Pause button in the Cosmos

"ⅠⅠ" angel numbers: DIVINE Timing

aerial SUSPENSION: a Time of SURRENDER

BRIGHT HALO: Spiritual awakening

the ¹²Hanged Man

Runes of KNOWLEDGE and WISDOM in the WATER:

- ᚦ THURISAZ - Protection / Defense
- ᛈ PERTHRO - LUCK, DESTINY, Chance
- ᛞ DAGAZ - BREAKTHROUGH, a new DAY
- ᛗ mannaz - Mankind, Shared EXPERIENCES
- ᛟ OTHALA - ancestors, WEALTH
- ᚺ HAGALAZ - Change, SURRENDER
- ↑ TIWAZ - JUSTICE, Power
- ᚷ GEBO - Partnerships, a GIFT
- ᚱ RAIDO - JOURNEYS, the PRESENT moment

"By fully surrendering and accepting what is, the epiphany of the present brings inner peace."

12. the Hanged Man

LIGHT SEER: surrendering to the will of the Cosmos, an intentional pause, reflection, letting go, embracing the new, realigning with your heart and purpose, new wisdom found, spiritual teachings, sacrifice, enlightenment, acceptance

SHADOW SEER: stagnation, self-sabotage, holding on to something that isn't meant for you, stubbornness, a tendency to be a martyr

A HANGED MAN STORY

Strapping into an aerial yoga sling to prepare, the Hanged Man prepares herself for total surrender and for the pause she knows is required of her. The Hanged Man archetype is often attributed to the Norse God Odin as he swings on the Tree of Yggdrasill. In the Odin myth, he hung for nine days and nights, surrendering to death in order to glean wisdom from the runes. By letting go—in sacrificing himself *for himself and his own wisdom*—he was gifted access to the deep mysteries of life that were carved into the language and symbols of the runes. Our Hanged Man has come to a place in her journey where a similar surrender is necessary, and like Odin, she is intentional in her actions. She checks the straps, and pushes beyond her current boundaries and releases it all. And from this flipped vantage point, she reaches toward the magic that awaits and toward her own runic insights. By fully surrendering and accepting what is, the epiphany of the present brings inner peace.

THE HANGED MAN'S MESSAGE

Flow with it. You are being asked to let go of something that is no longer necessary in your life, *so let it go, beautiful seer.* The Hanged Man is offering you the chance to look at something from a completely different perspective—one that brings with it incredible new opportunities for your life. While the Hanged Man often signifies a standstill, it also offers the ideal intermission to re-evaluate that thing (that idea, viewpoint, relationship, or career issue) that's got you hanging in limbo and feeling stationary. When you flip your thinking, new insights and vantages will shift into place that will swing you higher than you are imagining right now. Divine wisdom spills forth in moments of deep flow, so give yourself permission to lean in to this pause whether it's intentional *or not*. Resistance to change may have you stuck in a place that isn't for you, and you may need to take a few steps back to course correct as you make space for a better future. Don't fret if it feels like you are sacrificing one thing in order to gain another. This alternative way of seeing will allow you to break free from old programming and tap into a whole new framework from which to see the world. Spiritual insights will spill forth to support your shift, so open your heart to the bigger plan. While pausing in introspection, be careful to not fall into old patterns of thinking. Swing clear of learned helplessness or desires to step into the role of the martyr at this time. It's okay to do this deep dive *just for you*. Know that your path—and your dream—may look unfamiliar to you after you relinquish the need to direct the outcomes. Surrender to the will of the Cosmos and realign your life with its sacred patterns. The Universe already knows which life-altering lesson is the key to your happiness, and your Higher Self has so much wisdom for you when you intentionally pause to listen.

I lean in to my WORLD of LIMITLESS miracles, SURRENDERING to the DIVINE WILL of the COSMOS.

QUESTIONS FOR THE SEER
• What is it that you are grasping too tightly for? Is it a thing? An idea? Or a belief?
• Do you surrender to the "reality" that there's nothing else you can do right now?
• If you let go of your feelings about your situation, what would you learn?
• Is there something in your life that that is stopping your flow? Perhaps the only way to grow is to continue on without it?

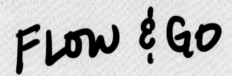

A spread for surrendering to the present moment

Where would I benefit from letting go? Where I am over-controlling or clinging too tightly?

In what areas of my life should I welcome alternative viewpoints?

HEALING WITH THE HANGED MAN
organs of nutrition, back and spine disorders, depression, pain, circulatory issues, lymphatic stagnation, muscle atrophy or weakness, varicose veins, leg cramps, suspended states, control issues, martyrdom, anxiety and stress, fearing change or loss

SCYTHE:
End of a HARVEST CYCLE,
Time to PLANT
AGAIN. (FROM a
DISTANCE, a BURIAL
and a PLANTING
LOOK the Same.)

Reaper:
TRANSITIONS,
endings

STAR in
MIDDLE:
New Beginnings,
THE UNIVERSE,
the DIVINE,
a REBIRTH

13.
Death ∞ Rebirth

REPEATING
FOREST:
New Landscapes, GROWTH,
Cycles of Transformation

"After decay, the ground is abundantly fertile."

13.
Death ∞ Rebirth

LIGHT SEER: cycles of transformation, rebirth and renewal, transition, change, new beliefs, newfound awareness, endings, a symbolic death, an initiation process

SHADOW SEER: clinging to the past, fear of change, sentimental attachments, forces of destruction, mortality, end of hope, mourning loss

A DEATH / REBIRTH STORY

The reaper steps into view and stares at the seeker. He knows his appearance usually causes panic, and he wants us to know that he isn't usually meant to be taken literally. He's here to share his healing wisdom and to illuminate the potential he holds to transmute and transform your life. Taking one step closer, he pushes back his hood to reveal his inner landscape—a blossoming forest, teeming with life. Its trees mimic the land you already know, yet it has the brightest of opportunities shining down from its center. Familiar territory, but vibrating at a higher dimension. He reminds us that before this new world can take root, something old must cease to be. This is the natural ebb and withering of things that are no longer being nourished, and the dying of one form so that it can shift into another. Peacefully, he watches his old reality fall away to make space for this new birth. Gently, he opens his cloak to you during this metamorphosis, knowing that it will mark a major change in your life, and that you will emerge transformed.

DEATH / REBIRTH'S MESSAGE

You are on the cusp of a massive transformation, and it's time to mourn the end of one phase while celebrating the birth of another. Energy cannot be created or destroyed. Its *potential* changes. And transforms. The Death/Rebirth card in your reading suggests that you are on the cusp of a massive transformation, and that it's time to mourn the end of one phase while celebrating the birth of another. The energy of transmutation and rebirth signals a beautiful transition that will allow you to expand your consciousness and move closer to your own Divine essence. A cycle in your life is coming to an inevitable end, and you may be experiencing the end of a relationship, a belief, a career path, or an outdated plan for the future. (Deep breath in if this scares you, sweet shadows and light! This change is needed!) Know that clinging to the past will only block the flow of positive energy at this time. If you are longing for days gone by, know that this card is gently urging you to release what is already losing energy, and to focus on the things that are actively gaining momentum. Welcome the possibility of something new, and allow this major phase to come to a graceful end. Having gained the lessons and wisdom you needed to move on to the next chapter, you can now look toward the magic of this newfound horizon, because underneath its morbid exterior, the death card heralds exciting times filled with the brightness of so much potential! *New light awaits.*

I Let go of the PasT AND I aDD energy to New Beginnings.

QUESTIONS FOR THE SEER

- Is there an attachment that is holding you back or keeping you from experiencing this birth of your true nature?
- What comes next, after you release the past?
- What magic are you ushering in and birthing? What new experiences and opportunities are you excited about?
- If you could be reborn, what life would you choose to birth yourself into? And (this one is a biggie) would your current values, confidence, determination, faith, lifestyle, and attitudes be able to sustain you inside of that ideal life? What would need to change?

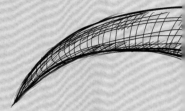

THE FOREST of REBIRTH

A spread for letting go and stepping into transformation

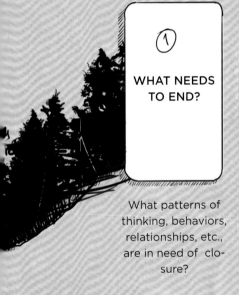

① WHAT NEEDS TO END?

② THE CHANGE

③ THE FOREST OF REBIRTH

What patterns of thinking, behaviors, relationships, etc., are in need of clo-sure?

What attitudes or actions will make this process smoother? In what ways am I changing?

What new potential lies on the horizon of rebirth? What beautiful new beginnings will emerge?

• • • • • • • • • • • • • • • • • •

HEALING WITH DEATH/ REBIRTH
intestines, colon, trauma, recovering from a serious illness, miscarriage, grief, menopause / andropause, cognitive dissonance

14
Temperance

Sun and moon:
BALANCE

SUN: ILLUMINATION
and ENLIGHTENMENT

the
Angel
HERMAPHRODITUS,
Child of Venus
and MERCURY/
HERMES and
APHRODITE:

COLORS FROM
Kaballistic magical
Teachings

○ GOLD: CENTER of TREE
OF LIFE, BALANCE,
Beauty, HARMONY,
SPIRITUAL awakening

● PURPLE: UNION of WISDOM and
UNDERSTANDING

NON-DUALITY,
balance of
OPPOSITE
ENERGIES

⊙ Sun

TATTOOS: △ HARMONY of ELEMENTS,
alchemical philosopher's stone
⊗ Vesica Piscis: UNION and DUALITY,
INTERCONNECTEDNESS

Temperance
14.

LIGHT SEER: alchemy, blending energies, harmony, moderation, masculine and feminine balance, duality and amalgamation, the fluidity of time, meditation, the perpetual motion of life, neutrality, restraint, patience, purpose, resilience, mindfulness, spiritual growth

SHADOW SEER: clashing interests, oil and water, extremes, disharmony, a need to practice moderation in some aspect of your life, severity, polarity, impatience

A TEMPERANCE STORY

The angel of Temperance is a master alchemist. Processing the energies of life, she weaves them into potent experiences and lessons, which she will then turn into spiritual gold. She sits, quietly. After the teachings of the Hanged Man's powerful pause and Death's transformational rebirth, she finds herself in a place of perfect balance. And all of the elements are waiting to be spun into something new. You will see the alchemist's symbol for gold tattooed on her arm, a mark of her transcendental and seraphic magic. She is able to effortlessly wield opposites: the Yin and Yang, the Divine masculine and feminine, past and present, the heavens and the earth . . . the material and the spiritual. This is her purpose and what gives her such an incredible strength of Spirit. She seeks balance and equilibrium. And when blending different parts of self, she always weaves something uniquely truthful.

The ease with which she holds the energy of the sun and the moon in each hand seems deceptively easy. The sheer strength it takes to harness, hold, and fuse these opposites is tremendous. She accomplishes the impossible with grace, fluidity, and certainty. She reminds you that in the realm of the Divine, *everything is possible* . . . and that *that future* which you can imagine for yourself is also something that can be alchemized and created. By the Gods. Or by the way they work through you. Sometimes, you can even balance different options and straddle two different paths at the same time, because with the magic of meaning and purpose, you can fuse the elements of life any which way you desire.

TEMPERANCE'S MESSAGE

Temperance ushers in harmony, alchemy, and non-duality. It's time to bring yourself to a beautiful equilibrium by seeking moderation and balance. Sometimes, this means that you must blend more than one idea together or seek more than one solution to find the perfect answer for your unique situation. Sometimes, you are being asked to look at your life's overall balance and flow. Tune in to your purpose and ask *what you really want to experience with your one precious life.* Are you balancing the right ingredients to create your desired experience? Or are things a little out of whack? Make a note of where you are choosing to focus most of your energy right now. Maybe you've been overdoing it in your social life? Or not socializing at all. Too much work vs. too much rest? Being wholly materialistic vs. wholly spiritual? Life often swings between polarities, and Temperance guides us to avoid the extremes. This energy can also show up in relationships when we are focusing on a partnership that is depleting more energy than it is replenishing. And it is present when we become obsessed with scrolling, binging drinks or food, or overspending. We live in a world of extreme passions and heated hustle, so slowing down the desire for excess in any one area of your life may be harder than you think. Clearing your energy of extremes and over-indulgence will foster a dynamic, nourishing flow that is aligned with your perfect alchemical purpose. Trust yourself to find this flow . . . if something feels off, it probably is off—so seek your equilibrium and allow Temperance to gently nudge you back on track. Stay away from "all or nothing" choices and prepare to walk the middle path of moderation and non-extremism. With all your beauty and all your flaws, this is a chance to call forth and blend your most genuine dreams and desires into something uniquely yours. You are entering a phase of alchemical gold, and choosing to transmute and alchemize the different stories and visions for your life will offer mental clarity and peace. As you set new timelines in motion, which parts of your life do you want to bring with you? Chart your course mindfully and honestly, and in this way, you will achieve your most sincere amalgamation of authentic Self.

I walk the MIDDLE PATH and I NOURISH WHOLENESS

QUESTIONS FOR THE SEER:
- Are you overdoing it in one area of your life?
- Sacred flow. What does that day look like for you? Or that week?
- Can you bring two different solutions together at this time?
- Money talk. Are you overspending or underspending?

"Peace is housed in the heart that transmutes and alchemizes imbalances."

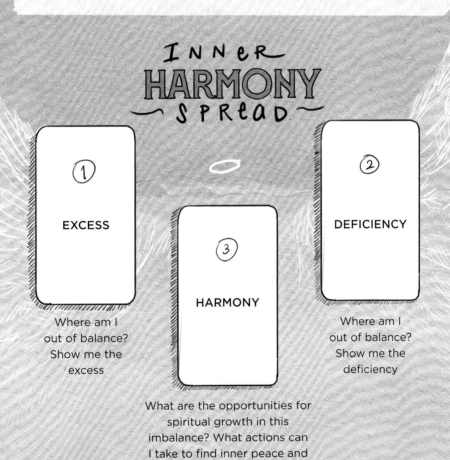

INNER
HARMONY
~ SPREAD ~

① EXCESS

Where am I
out of balance?
Show me the
excess

② DEFICIENCY

Where am I
out of balance?
Show me the
deficiency

③ HARMONY

What are the opportunities for
spiritual growth in this
imbalance? What actions can
I take to find inner peace and
establish balance?

HEALING WITH TEMPERANCE
borderline or bi-polar disorders, hormone imbalances, over-indulgence,
gut microbiome imbalances, hips and thighs

GOLD HORNS OR
GOLD FLECKS IN HAIR :
DISTRACTIONS, the false beauty
of ILLUSIONS... OR the LIGHT and
MAGIC that Lies hidden in the SHADOW.

CHAINS TATTOO :
VICES, addictions,
feeling STUCK

GOAT TATTOO :
CAPRICORN,
Baphomet

UNICURSAL HEXAGRAM :
magical symbol for
BANISHING AND INVOKING —
for calling on CHANGE

15. the Devil

an invitation
to LOOK at
shadow or to
INDULGE in
pleasure.

STRINGS:
The trap
of addiction

"What disguise does your anchor wear, sweet light?"

¹⁵·the Devil

LIGHT SEER: vices, addiction, a need for liberation, healthy vs. unhealthy sexuality, materialism, the healing found in darkness, being trapped in your own stories, manipulation, lying to yourself, temptation, delving into your shadow self

SHADOW SEER: release, freedom from addiction, on the cusp of a breakthrough, liberation, not wanting to see your own role in a negative circumstance, realizing that you are giving away your power, feeling helpless, breaking the chains

A DEVIL STORY

The Devil reaches out his hand, gently wooing you, welcoming you into his circle. His intensity is as much physical as it is spiritual. On one hand, he offers a release from the mundane—a time to break free from the rules and the chains that you placed upon yourself. He offers you the chance to dance in ecstasy and liberation, and he will accompany you to the darkest corners of your heart in order to see the places where the light needs to be let in. In this way, he offers great healing, and a chance to witness and release your own shadows. *Freedom.* He lures you in with promises of pleasure, material abundance, and all the earthly feels. On the other hand, he hides the fact that while he will bring you to the darkness, you will be left to your own devices to find your way home. He doesn't remind you that this path can lead to addiction and imprison you, because he knows that you already knew that before he arrived. He cannot make choices for you, and he does not force his energy upon anyone. He invites. That is all. He is both the *invoking and the banishing*, the vice and the liberation, and the feeling trapped and the feeling free. Smoothly, he extends his hand, waiting for you to accompany him. Some who have joined him have become too dependent on him, and thus feel manipulated under that hand. Alone. Chained. Desperate. Yet, like all teachers in the tarot, he is not good or evil. *He just is.* He represents a dark illumination. A choice. Your falling and your willingness to heal.

THE DEVIL'S MESSAGE

Oh temptation, sweet temptation. The Devil represents everything in life that we are addicted to. The things that can entrap us, enslave us, or overtake our lives. These addictions can be of the garden variety—alcohol, drugs, sex—or they can be a little more difficult to detect. Being addicted to how others make you feel, to co-dependent relationships or technology, or even being addicted to your own stories and excuses are examples of how his vices can be a little more nebulous. This is a nudge to delve into your own shadows. *Illuminate the things that hold too much sway over your attention.* And break free from those things that are vying for your time, your energy, and your love . . . if they also leave you feeling empty. Remember that addictions don't necessarily look scary and demonic . . . until they do. Seek liberation from the bindings that are keeping you trapped and untether yourself. In darkness, look to fragmented aspects of the self as a source of light. Self-forgiveness and self-compassion will be your greatest guides.

In the DARKNESS I am FREE To HEAL everything.

QUESTIONS FOR THE SEER
- What aspect of you is seeking liberation from self-imposed chains?
- What is holding too much attention right now?
- What healing message of self-acceptance and forgiveness does the shadow hold?
- Freedom calls. Do you need to dance a little more?

Shadow Stories

A spread to uncover the shadows in the stories we tell ourselves

① SHADOW STORIES

What aspects of your story are you addicted to or may be contributing to harmful or unhealthy patterns in your life?

② SAFETY IN SHADOWS

How are your shadow stories serving you? How do they empower you to remain in unhealthy patterns?

(i.e., I am depressed, so I don't need to get out of bed to do that thing I don't want to do, or I have a fear of visibility so therefore I don't need to grow my business any further.)

③ BREAKING CHAINS

You've got this. What steps can you take to clear out and illuminate these illusions? What steps can you take that will lead you to self-awareness, liberation and ultimately, freedom?

· · · · · · · · · · · ·

HEALING WITH THE DEVIL

materialism, compulsive behavior and addictions (shopping, sex, drugs, alcohol, people, technology, etc.), addiction-related ailments (liver, lungs, etc.), eating disorders, stress-related disorders, sleep apnea, the genital system

Lightning STRIKE:
UNexpected
Circumstances,
Sudden
Disruptions

16. the Tower

BUTTERFLIES:
Transformation
and CHANGE

EMBERS:
FINDING awe
and BEAUTY IN
THE moment.

HAZELNUTS:
IN Celtic
mYTHOLOGY
associated
with WISDOM,
KNOWLEDGE AND INSPIRATION...
DISINTEGRATING as
CHAOS Sets IN.

Squirrel SYMBOLISM:
Preparation,
Resourcefulness,
FLEXIBILITY
Renewal,
ALERTNESS

"While the jolt of the Tower is visceral and often frightening, know that you are safe. And that the magic of starting anew bubbles from this rupture."

16. the Tower

LIGHT SEER: unexpected change, chaos, the rug pulled from beneath your feet, beliefs challenged, new awareness and perspectives, a shift in the matrix, changing timelines, destruction, foundations crumbling, being unsure of who you are, change

SHADOW SEER: life becoming stale, refusing to change, fear of the unknown, avoiding a disaster, denial

A TOWER STORY

This squirrel has been hoarding nuts for the whole season. He's been making his nest, organizing his assets, and lining his bunker with extra supplies. **Everything. In. Perfect. Order.** Until suddenly, it's not. Out of the blue a storm erupts, bringing electric change to his plans. One flash and his home has been hoisted out from underneath him. His super safe, secure provisions of precious hazelnuts begin to dissipate in front of his eyes, and even his belief about the nature of his own reality is being tested. He's paralyzed . . . at first by fear, and by the sky, which seems to be falling. He watches, stunned and speechless. And even though it's chaotic, abstract, and surreal, he can't help but notice the floating embers, like fireflies in the sky. Amidst chaos, he *still* sees the beauty in the landscape. He blinks, eyes stinging in the heat, and the tiny flames seem to move and transform like butterflies. *Are they flames or butterflies?* Through the smoke, he can't really tell. All he knows is that nothing will be the same after the sparks go out.

THE TOWER'S MESSAGE

Whoa. Buckle up. Massive shifting is *what's up* right now! Simply put: expect the unexpected. Even if you've been squirreling away and meticulously planning for the future, the Universe is about shake things up. Sometimes we resist change to the point that the Universe forces a shift in a destructive and chaotic way. (Because change is necessary.) Other times, these dramatic transitions cause *not-so-subtle shifts* in our belief systems, and they fundamentally change the way we see our reality. When life is dishing out crumbling structures and fluctuating paradigms, there is nothing to do but to *be in the moment.* The true lesson of the tower is just to be with it all. Find the beauty in it. Find the humanity. While totally new territory can be intimidating, there is also a strange beauty in this deconstruction—as all the elements for a better life will be found among the rubble. Trust that you will be held by the Universe, and you'll become stronger and more resilient as a result, as life only throws us the curveballs that we can handle. Tower energy in your life marks a period when you get to re-evaluate, redirect, re-establish, and realign. These moments are powerful opportunities to rebuild something foundational from the ashes. Use this moment to rebuild something extraordinary. Something moving. Shifting. Expanding. It's magic in the disguise of unpredictability. Know that the brightest of lights will pierce through the pandemonium of change that you are experiencing, and that you will find your own brightly lit truth in the darkness of the Tower. It's time to step into a stunning display of your blazing potential.

In chaos, I move towards the brightest light.

QUESTIONS FOR THE SEER

• How flexible are you in times of fast change? How could staying in the present help you to stay grounded as you build your future?

• In the debris of a tower, our brightest lessons are found. What can you take away from this?

• What have you learned about yourself? When things break apart unexpectedly, how does your incredible resilience help you to persevere?

LIGHT IN the UNEXPECTED

A spread to help navigate the unexpected

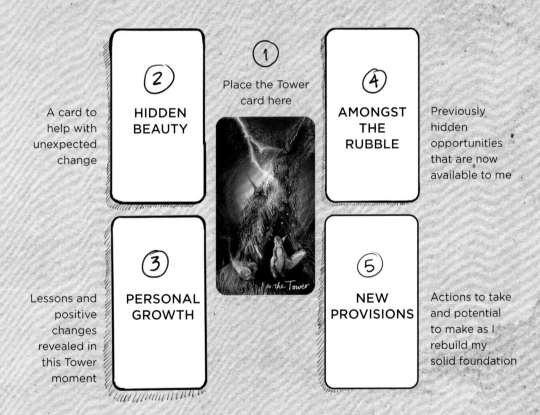

① Place the Tower card here

② **HIDDEN BEAUTY**

A card to help with unexpected change

③ **PERSONAL GROWTH**

Lessons and positive changes revealed in this Tower moment

④ **AMONGST THE RUBBLE**

Previously hidden opportunities that are now available to me

⑤ **NEW PROVISIONS**

Actions to take and potential to make as I rebuild my solid foundation

HEALING WITH THE TOWER

psychological or emotional breakdowns, unexpected diagnosis, infection, elimination of toxic substances from the body, immune system reactions, surgical interventions, recovery after illness, a healing crisis, a catalyst for changing lifestyle/choices, muscular system

WISHES SPIRALING UP

STAR:
HOPE, GUIDANCE
IN THE DARK,
INSPIRATION

STRING:
HOLDING on to
hope, Connection
to UNIVERSE
and FAITH

8 - POINTS :
DIRECTIONS,
COSMIC ORDER,
STAR of
ISHTAR

WATER POOL:
SUBCONSCIOUS
MIND, INTUITION,
healing...
Reflecting COSMOS / DIVINITY
(Oneness, as above So BELOW.)

Manpala:
Manifesting,
Magic AND
Joy

"Draw energy from your brightest inner light,
because you know exactly what you came here to do."

17. the Star

LIGHT SEER: expectations fulfilled, wishes granted, opportunities, healing after traumatic events, knowing you are on the right path, soul-purpose, inspiration, renewed hope

SHADOW SEER: loss of faith, diminished hope, disappointment, missed opportunities, being overly-sensitive, despair

A STAR STORY

After living through the chaos of the Tower, the Star emerges from the ashes with her own warm feelings of renewed hope. She can't pinpoint exactly why she's feeling this way, yet she is. With a deep breath in, she steps out of the galaxy pool and sits at the edge of the earth. *Warmth. Beaming. Light.* There is so much to do from here. So many things to see, and so many places to go! She looks up, and instantly remembers where she came from . . . and feels grateful to have this beautiful opportunity to live, renewed. What a gift from the Gods! A spiritual being in a flesh-and-bones experience, she reaches her heart up to the stars, and connects with their guiding glow. Subtly, at first, ancient memories begin to stir within her soul. A remembering. A re-awakening. A connection long forgotten. And now she knows what she is. And what she came here to do. Her timeline glows the most beautiful of hues as inspiration pours down from the stars. Pure. Honest. Divine. Hopeful and expectant, she tugs on her light and watches as her miracle starts to flow.

THE STAR'S MESSAGE

Allow yourself to sink into the dream-like inspiration of the Star. She sends a message of Divine timing and renewed expectations, and she guides you to reach for that string of serendipity and faith. She promises you that your expectations will be met if you find your conviction, your hope, and your excitement. Your future is increasingly bright! Find unwavering optimism and determination, because you are truly being blessed by the Universe at this time. Your core purpose—along with your light—is beginning to shimmer at the surface of your reality, and your path is being intrinsically tied to your biggest missions and brightest opportunities for expansion. You are stepping onto a path of fulfillment and happiness with starlight to guide you!

Allow your innate essence to shine through any residual darkness right now. Uncover any limiting beliefs or self-doubt that you are holding on to, finding the courage to voice any unexpressed emotions. The past no longer has the weight to hold you down, so release every bit of outgrown energy that is anchoring you to old memories. As you let go, you will focus on the future and find your biggest source of inspiration and love there. Release and ascend. The stars are aligning in your favor, and it's time to embody your trust in them again.

I expect miracles.

QUESTIONS FOR THE SEER
- If you knew that your success would be guaranteed, what would you do with your life?
- What's the biggest, most badass future you can envision for yourself?
  Where would you be in 3 years? 5 years? 10 years?
- What does inspiration feel like in your body? Invite it in, then describe it.
- If you had to choose one word to describe your soul's purpose, what would it be?

the STARLIT DREAMS SPREAD

A spread for finding hope and optimism

| | ② HOPE | ③ OPTIMISM | ④ BRIGHT FUTURE |

Place the Star
card here

How can I find
or cultivate
more hope?

A message
about optimism

What action can
I take to grab
ahold of my
brightest
Starlight?

Tune in to the Star's Feelings of Hope Before pulling your cards

HEALING WITH THE STAR

psychological or emotional breakdowns, disassociation, bladder issues,
fluids and filtration problems, water retention, reproductive health, depression,
fatigue, loss of faith, creative blocks, feeling unmotivated

MOON: the SUBCONSCIOUS, DREAMS, INTUITION,
ILLuminating the dark night, SHADOWS,
fears, GUIDANCE and hope in the DARK.

NIGHT: fears,
that which we
cannot see, the
unknown,
worries, anxieties

Dog and WOLF:
Duality, Illusions.

Tamed vs. WILD,
CIVILIZED vs.
INSTINCTUAL,
intellectual vs.
emotional

WATER: INTUITION, the
subconscious REALMS,
emotion, the cyclical
nature of our
emotions, the INFLUENCE
of nature,
our connection
to the unconscious/
shadow aspects
of self.

18.
the Moon

HAND REACHING
FOR LIGHT:

Letting go, trusting
our ability to thrive,
trusting and
following intuitive
information

DAPPLED OCEAN FLOOR:

LIGHT and SHADOW, SPARKS
of SPIRIT, the Depths of our
minds, the PSYCHE and THE
SECRETS HELD WITHIN, the
UNIVERSES we create WITHIN
our THOUGHTS and our MINDS

"Trust your intuition and float."

18.
the Moon

LIGHT SEER: illusions, hidden truths, the unknown, trusting your intuition, facing your fears, the watery nature of the unconscious mind, mystery, symbolism and metaphor, perception, uncertainty, dreams

SHADOW SEER: fears that block you, difficulty separating reality and illusion, linear thinking, inability to process a spiritual or mystical experience, mental confusion, misinterpretation, anxiety, fear

A MOON STORY

A wolf and a dog howl up at the moon. One aloof, wild, and cunning, the other friendly, eager to please, and affectionate. One is a potential danger and the other her companion, but from this distance and in this light, she finds it hard to discern which is which. When they both turn to her and begin to advance, she struggles to tell them apart in the dark. The shadows and light play tricks in the reflecting water, making it impossible to see the details of the path she is walking. Were they both running at her? Or away from her? She panics, imagining the worst, and she trips into the water, flailing desperately. Her mind races—her layered dress is suddenly so heavy, and somehow her head is underwater. She struggles, wrapping herself up in the many layers, trying to discern up from down. Air. Motion. Gasp. *She needs air.* And just when her fear is about to overtake her, a stream of light grazes her hand. *The Moon.* She pauses. Surrenders. And she finds her bearings. The moonlight streams down through the water, and she notices how it dances on the bubbles around her, and the way that they float upward, guiding her to safety. She realizes that the moment she stopped struggling was the moment she began to float to the surface. Drifting in the liminal, she surrenders, and when she finally breaks through the surface, she breathes in all the magic of the moment. With renewed trust, she thanks the moon for its light and its guidance, and she reaches for the shore, where a wagging tail meets her with affection.

THE MOON'S MESSAGE

When faced with uncertainty and illusion, it can feel like we are drowning. Trust that you will be okay, even if you can't seem to distinguish up from down right now. When you stop struggling to see that which you simply cannot see, you will experience a deep release that will allow you to float to the surface of your truth. The Moon card asks you to go within, and to calmly listen to the whispers of your own intuition. There is Divinity here. And magic. She asks you to find comfort in the darkness and in the unknown. For until the sun comes up, certain things may remain obscured behind shadows of the moonlight. Indeed, many creative seeds and new beginnings will not sprout until they are germinated by the gentle beams from the moon. When you choose to fall into the Moon's still waters, your inner wisdom will embrace you, and then push you toward the light. Trust any nudges that lead you toward clarity, as the moon's gentle caress offers you the key to your subconscious mind. As you submerge your thoughts in her shadowy messages, pause to seek. *And seek to feel. And feel to float. And float to thrive.* Follow your breath all the way up to the surface. She will reinvigorate your imagination and resurrect your spark as long as you reach beyond your own fears in order to find her. Sometimes, this card illustrates that you cannot possibly know everything about your situation at this time. And sometimes, her shadow creates thick illusion, even for the most discerning eye. Dive into the Moon's healing embrace, breathe into and past any insecurities that you notice you are holding on to, and let her dimly lit magic guide you home.

I am safe, and I Reach new Levels of unconscious Knowing as I Surrender to the will of the Universe.

QUESTIONS FOR THE SEER

- How does fear create illusion and distrust in your life?
- How do you respond when you can't interpret things with 100% certainty? Does it affect your emotions? Your choices? Your perspective?
- Even though the path may be dimly lit, are you willing to move ahead?

A spread for releasing fear, trusting instinct, and seeing truth

Pack mentality: What conditioning (learned behaviors, societal or cultural norms) are playing a role in my life at this time? Do they hold me back or do they protect me?

① **THE DOG**

② **THE WOLF**

Wild knowing: What can I do to unleash my wilder nature? How can I listen to my instincts, find my freedom, and express my beautiful, untamed, and unique energy?

What hidden fears, anxieties, or repressed emotions are playing a role in my situation? How can I let them go?

③ **THE SHADOW**

④ **THE UNTAMED**

How can I embody and integrate both *learned* and *instinctual* wisdom? How can I move ahead, releasing my fears and stepping into my untamed authenticity?

HEALING WITH THE MOON

fears and phobias, menstrual cycle issues, psychosomatic illnesses, mental health–related physical symptoms, stress-related issues like eczema, etc., sleep disturbances, anxiety, neurological events, nerve pain, mystery symptoms, subconscious stress, mood disorders, PTSD, legs and feet

SUN: *light, clarity, vitality,*
the conscious mind.

MANDALA: the UNIVERSE,
wholeness, cycles,
self-Realization,
Journey of
    enlightenment.
    SHINING the
    light of TRUTH,
    Dispelling shadows
    AND *fear.*

19. the Sun

RAY of SUNLIGHT:
Regenerative
power of NATURE,
Healing.
Working with
the elements

DANCING:
Celebrating Life,
Joy, Positivity,
Energy, Happiness,
Peace, Wonder

SoweLu (SOWILO):
the SUN Rune,
guidance, Success,
    accomplishments,
        VICTORY

19. the Sun

LIGHT SEER: joy, inspirational success, abundance and fulfillment, exuberant creativity, positivity, love, manifesting dreams, inner beauty, a "yes" card, self-actualization, a ton of happiness

SHADOW SEER: delays, negative mindset, self-doubt or lack of confidence, thoughts that are blocking positive outcomes, a need to tune out a negative mindset and to find inspiration

A SUN STORY

Only in these moments, under the warm sun, does she feel totally alive. Her heart chakra vibrates. Her solar plexus radiates, and she feels nurtured by the sunlight and by the energy of life itself. She steps into her power and her confidence, and she calls out to the small photons . . . the particles of light and heat that burst forth from the sun . . . and she imagines them showering down, all around her. They create the most spectacular patterns, cascading both frequency and tone, and they fill up her energy body with a vibrant and potent life force. Each elemental particle comes bundled with tiny bits of cosmic information. Patterns of knowing. States of being. *The capacity to love.* And an overabundance of magic. She begins to dance, hearing the messages held within these ancient rays of joy. She can't see them, but she can feel them flooding her system. She feels connected to this positive frequency, and she celebrates under the spinning heavens, opening up to life itself.

THE SUN'S MESSAGE

The sun radiates life down to everything he touches. Shining brightly, he creates a path of illumination, love, and harmonic abundance. This is a card of joyful celebration and a vibrant sign of sunny success! Call on your warrior energy and move to the vibrating rhythm of the sun's vitality and essence. Expect to find bliss and be ready to take inspired action based on radical positivity and generosity. Allow others to bask in the warm glow of your beaming heart and your inspired mind. People will feel drawn to you when the Sun card arrives (um, hello charisma!). Live it up! Dance, sing, move or express yourself, unabashedly. If you have been going through tough times, the Sun reminds you that the dawn is coming soon. In shadow, it asks you about your mindset and wonders if you've lost your enthusiasm. Or perhaps you're having trouble accessing your optimism because it feels a little too utopian? *Nothing is impossible for this glowing energy*, so pay attention to your thoughts and consciously imbue your reality with movement, momentum, and sunshine. This card in a reading is a reassuring sign that things are unfolding beautifully. Know that you are perfect, whole, and loved by the Cosmos, and it may be time to deal with any feelings of inadequacy or not-enoughness in order to find your shiny confidence. The Sun is on its way to illuminate the corners of your heart and to set your world ablaze with opportunity and inspiration.

I am WHOLE. I am more than ENOUGH AND I shine Like the SUN when I am HAPPY.

QUESTIONS FOR THE SEER
- Who makes you laugh 'til you cry? How can you bring more of that energy into your world?
- What were you doing the last time you felt true joy? Imagine it. Describe it.
- If exuberant joy had a color, what would it be?
- In what situations, and with whom, do you douse your flame, hide your essence, or cloud your vibrancy?

"Come into your own miracle through the cheerful blossoming of a life well-danced."

Beautiful Sun,
ILLUMINATE MY PATH

Place the Sun card here.

Spend a few minutes in meditation with the sun's rays on your face. (Or simply imagine basking in the sun.) Feel the sun's radiating love before pulling your cards.

How can I bring more joy into my life?

JOY

CLARITY

A bright message for clarity and understanding

HEALING WITH THE SUN

raises frequency of the body, the ability to move, systemic function and recovery, circulation and regeneration, Vitamin D deficiencies, joy, serotonin, depression, skin conditions, self-identity, eyes, seasonal depression (SAD), over-idealization or idolization

114

LIGHTS FROM ABOVE:
Spirit, Source,
epiphanies, Downloads,
Spiritual awakenings

SOUL DANCING/ TAKING
FLIGHT:

Rebirth, Answering
the CALL of the
HIGHER SELF/ the COSMOS,
UNDERSTANDING,
NEW MEANING after
challenging times,
the growth that
comes after self-
awareness and self-
judgement. the
shedding of OLD
WAYS of BEING.

HEAD BACK with
eyes CLOSED:
IN SURRENDER,
REVERENCE,
TRANSFORNATION.
(I always
imagine her as →
kneeling AND praying)

SEEING HER SOUL:
MAJOR SHIFTS
and NEW ways
of UNDERSTANDING
SPIRIT, LIFE PATH
and PURPOSE

"Face the music with your true voice and find the clearest of harmonies."

20. Judgement

LIGHT SEER: self-realization and understanding, spiritual awakening, redemption, knowing your motives and your heart to be true, total transparency, soul-searching, a glorious unveiling of Spirit, an epiphany

SHADOW SEER: self-doubt, hiding behind many masks, a reckoning, a need to let go of a shadow aspect of your story, denying yourself and your loved ones the experience of your true nature or essence, harsh self-judgement

A JUDGEMENT STORY

When the call sounded, it was unmistakably hers. Harmonic, vibrating, magnetic—she heard it resounding through her soul, beckoning her with its emotion and truth. There was nothing she could do but to stand up to listen. *Nothing could keep her from meeting this part of herself. It was time.* The call asked her to listen deep within and to find her sacred why. It beckoned her to truly dedicate herself to its path. She's known what it's like to live a life based on fear—and to live inside of that box, that category—an illusion. She walked that path for so long that it felt like other people's ideas of who she was became more important than her own sense of self. But she has finally seen how far she strayed from her true nature. Here, she witnesses herself . . . her *true* self, for the very first time. *Light and shadow revealed.* And in the shadows of this reckoning lies the profound wisdom of Judgement—she could never push the truth down so far that it would truly disappear, and that all of those past actions, thoughts, and decisions remained bundled inside of her sense of self . . . and that it was up to her to decide their meaning. Her honest self-evaluation called her toward new levels of self-realization and ignited her purpose. And when she awakened to her true nature, she realized that the only form of acceptance that actually affects our ascension is that which lives inside of our own hearts.

JUDGEMENT'S MESSAGE

You have known Judgement in the past, both as one who judges and one who has been judged, and you are now at a place where the only awareness that really matters is that which you bestow upon your own actions. To truly raise your vibration, you must send healing approval to your own heart from a place of deep compassion and integrity. When you are being completely honest, are you doing your best with others and with yourself? It's time to shed any negative facades that you have been holding on to and to drop the masks behind the masks. *No more faking it.* It may feel risky, yet this profound act of self-acceptance will unleash your absolute essence in a brilliant display of authenticity. You are, sweet Light Seer, stardust and life—you are light, shadow, matter, and consciousness, *and you are a miracle.* Why, then, do you keep your true nature hidden away from the world? If you are holding on to any disdain or doubt about your Divine nature, there is no way to really understand your full potential until you are open and honest with your own heart. To expand and evolve requires a colossal forgiveness of the self. *Forgive your beautiful soul. Accept your beautiful heart.* As you do, you consciously answer the call of your Highest Self, and the vastness of your horizon will make itself available to you.

Hello Essence... I invite you to show up every day. I invite my soul to shine, unapologetically

QUESTIONS FOR THE SEER
- What needs to be forgiven?
- How is it that you really want people to see you?
  And how do you want to see yourself?
- If it were up to you to judge your life at the end of your days,
  what would you say to yourself?
- When you listen to the deepest callings within your heart,
  what do you hear?
- What part of you needs to be accepted in order to feel whole?

ESSENCE & MAGIC

A spread for awakening your true nature

③

YOUR HIGHER MAGIC

Keys to awakening your highest potential and expediting your magic and your higher calling

Key areas in your life to reassess that would help your personal transformation. These could be patterns of behavior, attitudes, beliefs, etc.

①

SELF REFLECTION

②

SELF FORGIVENESS

What do you need to release and forgive? What regrets or burdens can you release?

HEALING WITH JUDGEMENT

guilt, circulatory organs, physical healing linked to emotional states, repressed memories, fatigue and lethargy, respiratory organs, blocked intuition, self-judgement

OUROBOROS WREATH:
CONTINUOUS Change AND CYCLES.
Victory, COMPLETION, END of one
          Journey and the START of
                    ANOTHER

SEED of LIFE:
SACRED GEOMETRY
RELATED to CREATION,
Genesis of LIFE.
(7 circles: 7 days,
7 chakras, 7 major
notes, 7 metals
   in alchemy, etc.)
- Same symbol
  is seen in
  the FOOL CARD

21. the World

Rainbow
DRESS:
LIGHT, JOY,
SUCCESS,
CHAKRAS
ALIGNED

stepping
into a
new
Journey

CORNER SYMBOLS:
SACRED GEOMETRIC PLATONIC SOLIDS.
(REPLACING 4 SYMBOLS of FIXED ZODIAC)
  TOP LEFT : OCTOHEDRON (AIR)
  TOP RIGHT: ICOSAHEDRON (WATER)
  BOTTOM LEFT: HEXAHEDRON / CUBE (EARTH)
  BOTTOM RIGHT: TETRAHEDRON (FIRE) ← inside of
                                       MERKABAH

21. the World

LIGHT SEER: completion, joy, wholeness, achievement, happy endings, abundance, success, new levels of consciousness, finishing a large project, goals met, literally traveling the world

SHADOW SEER: taking shortcuts, a need for closure, a need to follow through, staying focused in order to complete an unfinished task, a delay in plans, unmet dreams

A WORLD STORY

The World steps into her ouroboros ring, ready to celebrate her achievements. As she steps up, the ring begins to ascend. Light shines down from above and floods her senses with the soft hum of her illuminations: *Success. Completion. You did it!* It carries her higher, and she feels her whole body begin to vibrate with this upgrade of consciousness. She senses the union of her spiritual and earthly selves, and her reality shifts as her inner spiritual landscape merges with her outer reality. She remembers that moment when, long ago, she first stepped off the edge of the cliff and into the Fool card, falling right into a sacred geometric lesson with all of her innocence in tow. Back then she had no idea how to stay afloat. Now, inside of that very same sacred geometric ring, she climbs effortlessly. She has mastered this level of awareness, and her experiences have become an integral part of who she is. She holds the rings lovingly. In them, she senses a support system, a teacher, a mentor, a friend . . . as all of the wisdom she has gained on her journey abides within them. She learned, she tried, she fell, she stood up again . . . and now, she has finally *arrived.* Celebrating this joyous moment, every cell falls into resonance with the Universe around it. **And she rises.** She knows that the end of one cycle signifies the beginning of another, and it fills her heart with joy to know that she will jump back into the position of the Fool and begin a new journey soon. But for now, the sweetness of success awaits, and it's time to celebrate this win!

THE WORLD'S MESSAGE

The World brings one of the most positive and abundant messages in the tarot! Congratulations, sweet seer! You've come so far! A large project or period in your life is coming to a successful conclusion, and it's time to revel in the sweet afterglow of your success. Feel into all the feels, because it's time for fruition and abundance! If you're not quite there yet, take this card as a sign that you're on the right path. You are close. If you're feeling a sense of lack around any part of your successful journey, consciously let go of the little imperfections. They, too, are a part of you. And they are beautiful. As you reach this stage of fruition, remain focused. Don't slacken your resolve as you glimpse the magic at the end of the long journey, because the energy that you put into the endings is just as important as the energy of beginnings. It's time to follow through! If there is something that you've left unfinished, move ahead with determination and conviction, and take your final steps and complete the cycle! You've got the world at your fingertips, ready to help you. If your dreams are not being met, perhaps there are some steps along the way that you have missed? Check in with your original intention, and smile with a happy heart, because even in shadow, the World is a positive card that signals bliss and happy endings. You've got oodles of positive energy and joy on the way!

I accept This GIFT of COMPLETION, AND I ascend to new Levels of AWARENESS and WHOLENESS. I am LOVE.

QUESTIONS FOR THE SEER
- What is the most important thing you learned on this journey?
- What is the biggest lesson you have taken with you?
- Next step: Another journey! Another Fool card. Where to next, my love?
- Are you stopping for long enough to notice your progress?
- How are you celebrating your successes?

"The sweetness of completion reminds us that it's time to the be the Fool once more."

JOYFUL COMPLETION SPREAD

Place the world here, and ask her to show you where you are in your current cycle of completion.

② ACHIEVED

What lessons must I remember about the success I am achieving?

What comes next? Where to?

③ TO BE CONCEIVED

HEALING WITH THE WORLD

fear of success or fear of completion, difficulty moving on, existential anxiety, feeling disconnected or alienated from the world at large, endocrine disorders

the MINOR Arcana

The Minor Arcana cards are the nuanced, minor energies of the deck and they relate to day-to-day situations and circumstances. These 56 cards share the ups and downs of life, the light and the shadow, and all the energies of a journey well-travelled.

WANDS

ELEMENT: Fire

ASSOCIATED WITH:

creativity, action, illumination, inspiration, passion,
manifestation, energy, willpower

Ace of Wands

LIGHT SEER: new ideas, the seed of potential, the arrival of inspiration, illumination, intense creativity, the mirrorlike nature of consciousness, the interconnectedness of all things, the ability to manifest incredible things

SHADOW SEER: feeling uninspired, creative blocks, the mind needing rest, unfocused energy resulting in burnout, not trusting your ideas, a time to bolster your faith in yourself

A WANDS STORY

The Ace of Wands pulsates with bright inspiration. Within her Cosmic mind are *all the sparks* for every brilliant new idea that exists, and her mind flashes perpetually. Her creativity and wisdom are connected to a Universal consciousness that creates a delightfully magical soup from which ideas and inspiration can emerge. You may see her magic as being the Akashic Records, the genesis of the imagination, or even the Creative Muse herself. Or you may simply notice the jeweled beads that weave their way in and out of her great sea of ideations. These beads are from Indra's Net, which, according to Vedic and Buddhist philosophy, is a connected set of jewels that line the Cosmos. Each node is a mirrored bead that contains and reflects all the information of *all the other beads* within the holographic Universe. There is a pure and illuminated conscious creativity here, and a reminder of the interconnectedness of all things. One idea seeds the next, just as one spark of inspiration ignites your actions. When one invents, others see (and mirror) what's possible. The Ace of Wands interrupts you with a giggle and a *tsssssk*. Your very cerebral process of trying to define her creative mojo is slowing her down. She opens her eyes and breathes her most important secret out into the ether: *"Connected sparks. How will you use the inspiration that you have been gifted?"*

MESSAGE FROM THE ACE OF WANDS

New ideas. They are yours for the taking if you listen closely. A flame burns here that is meant for you, but it hasn't been put to use yet. Its intensity speaks to the potential that this new spark holds for you. *What will you create with this boundless potential?* Stay open to receive inspiration and insight! You may be shown new information about your Divine purpose or soul path, or you may even feel compelled to put something completely new into the world. If it feels good, it probably is good, and even though this Ace can only predict the inception of something new, it also suggests that all the energy needed to bring this project, idea, or feeling to a successful completion is available to you. Open your heart to this new beginning and enjoy this influx of creator energy.

I seed my BRILLIANT future with the ROOTS of CREATIVITY AND INSPIRATION

QUESTIONS FOR THE SEER

• Where do your interests lie? What new passions are on the horizon right now?
• How are you stoking the fires of passion and creativity?
• Where does your creativity come from? From within or without? And how do you find it?
• How are sparks of genius or creativity different than intuition?

126

FLAME: SPARK of IDEAS, CREATIVITY AND sacral energy.

← CONNECTED BEADS: FROM 'INDRA'S NET', (A VEDIC PHILOSOPHY OF ONENESS.)

SEED of LIFE: INCEPTION, SEEDS of IDEAS

the cosmos of CREATIVITY eyes closed imagining

SHE IS THE PERSONIFICATION OF The Collective Unconscious, The 'field', The holographic Universe, The Muse, ... WHERE IDEAS COME FROM.

DREAMing of the future

wands: one pointing home, the other to future adventure. (CHOICES)

BUS AND GLOBE: DREAMS, PLANS, TRAVEL.

LIGHTS → SEEM TO POINT TO FUTURE OPPORTUNITY OUTSIDE WINDOW

YELLOW SKY
○ SUNNY
○ HEART CHAKRA (DESIRES)
↑ Potential, Happiness POSITIVITY

2 of Wands

LIGHT SEER: planning your future, making progress, activation, possibilities, the choice between your comfort zone and new adventures, leaving home

SHADOW SEER: insecurities, the fear of taking the next step, being stuck in your past, feeling worried about your abilities, opportunities for alignment

A WANDS STORY

She sits in the same window as always, looking out over the endless possibilities that **could** be. The twos in tarot often hold a choice, a duality: *Should she stay, or should she go?* With her fiery passion to experience the mysteries of new places, she dreams up possible futures. Sometimes she feels like she's watching her life happen instead of experiencing it, especially when she witnesses others bring *their dreams* to life while she merely imagines her new adventures. What would change if she took a chance on this dream? Could she really bring this idea to fruition? One wand points outward to the horizon with a definite yes. It reminds her that you only live once: "*YOLO, sweet light . . . life is yours for the taking, and if you want that thing, you'll need to go for it.*" The other wand is tucked quietly into the corner and is rooted in place. It's cozy, secure, and consistent. It already knows exactly what it's like to be right here, and believes they could likely be contented here, forever. "*It would be so easy to just . . . stay.*"

MESSAGE FROM THE 2 OF WANDS

It's time to choose between the Wand that seems happily settled or the one that leans in to exciting new possibilities. Take a deep breath, because self-initiated change can be scary! Sometimes there are unexpected bumps on the road toward change, and there's nothing better to mitigate those roadblocks than an honest-to-goodness plan and some inspired action that allows you to leap right over them. You can dream it and envision it, or you can begin to *live it*. It's time to explore options and to discover what's available to you. Outline the steps to make it happen! Planning and imagining without action are not enough right now. As you observe your dream, you may only be taking half-steps forward, and this could be sending mixed signals to the Universe. *It's time to leave the nest and claim your future.* If you're feeling stuck, it could be the energy of your "comfort zone" that's got you there. The fear of the unknown can be riddled with insecurities, yet we cannot expand when we play it overly safe. If the excitement of adventure outweighs your fear, then it's time to shift and take strides toward your future. Learn that thing. Call that contact. Make that decision. Know that inaction won't get you there, and if you're feeling the angst of dreaming the dream instead of walking the talk, perhaps you've outgrown your complacency, sweet dreamer. Use the fire energy of the Wands to initiate your shift!

The WORLD is FULL of OPPORTUNITIES FOR ADVENTURE, and I welcome THEM into my LIFE WITH PLANNED ACTION

QUESTIONS FOR THE SEER
- Should you stay or should you go? How badly do you want this dream?
- What is it that lies just beyond your comfort zone that would improve your situation?
- The life you have vs. the life you want: Sometimes, we think the grass is greener in someone else's pasture, when it's actually not. Are you romanticizing the future? Or do you have a clear picture of where you're headed and what's to come?

3 of Wands

LIGHT SEER: energy manifested, waiting for the results of your effort, the arrival of opportunities, career and business wins, understanding your ambitions, continuous improvement and moving in the right direction, progress

SHADOW SEER: not dreaming big enough, fear coming up to block your movement, delays, expectations falling through

A WANDS STORY

She waits for her big wave. She sees three coming in, signaling that she won't have to wait much longer. She remembers staring out of the window in the 2 of Wands, hoping for and dreaming about this moment. She's taken the steps and practiced . . . she's committed to doing the challenging things. She has learned what she intended to. And after putting so much energy into this moment, she is on the cusp of manifesting something incredible. Not only that, but she feels confident that when her wave rolls in, she will catch it. She *can* find stability in that rolling sea. Her big energy is on the way, and she keeps an open mind about exactly when and where it will roll up. And all the while, mindset strong, she seeks proof of this magical energy on the horizon.

MESSAGE FROM THE 3 OF WANDS

You've been doing the work, Light Seer. Visioning. Planning. Seeing. Learning. And it's almost time to see your rewards trickle in. Watch for the signs that your dream is on the way because they *are* everywhere! Take pride in the progress you've made, for your past efforts have created the momentum that you needed to get the ball rolling. Today, you are moving through energy you created in the past, and being here, ready and waiting, is a milestone that you should recognize as a success! While there is still work to be done, know that you are headed in the right direction and that you will see waves of opportunity coming in soon. In shadow, you may be holding back or not planning for a better future. Take time to plot your direction in order to avoid delays. When your wave arrives, you may not know exactly how to ride it, but you will be ready to learn. Look for that new relationship, the new client, or that lucky break on the horizon, for its arrival is imminent.

I am expectant and optimistic AND I know that my dream is on the way.

QUESTIONS FOR THE SEER

- Are you open to the new opportunities that are showing up?
- What energy did you call into your life that is here now?
  What lessons did it bring? And what energy are you calling in for the future?
- What steps can you take today to move you closer to your goals?

Balancing DREAMS AND ACTION TAKEN

WANDS WITH FLAMES: MOTIVATION, MOVEMENT, GROWTH

3 of Wands

SURFBOARD: practice needed to bring dreams to Life

3 waves on the horizon:
· opportunities arriving
· past work / training coming to fruition

— standing at CLIFF: vantage point, steady focus on the future

POSSIBLE: Travel or overseas connections

TENT for SPECIAL EVENT: SHELTER, safety, time with FRIENDS AND Family

4 of Wands

TAMBOURINE: Traditional instrument, traditions & family events

Peace FLAGS: a Time of celebration and Relaxation

CONTAGIOUS LIGHT ENERGY

EVERYTHING IS ROSE-COLORED. A PERFECT MOMENT.

4 of Wands

LIGHT SEER: celebration, prosperity, an important event or milestone, gathering of souls, people coming together for a common goal, kindreds, stability in home and relationships, sometimes signifies marriage

SHADOW SEER: forgetting the importance of the simple things, getting caught up in drama, lack of harmony, unmet expectations, feeling disconnected

A WANDS STORY

Bring the noise! They shuffle and sway, finding their natural rhythm among the celebrating guests. The crowd dances with laughter, for this is a day of festivity! Major milestones have been hit, which need to be savored and recognized. The dancers enjoy every moment of this pure communal bliss, and everything feels right and safe and solid: the company, the energy, the music, the sunset. Even the ups and downs of regular life seem to have fallen away, and a sense of contented peace falls over their hearts, bringing together a community of connected souls. *Full gratitude.* They've been planning and waiting for this big occasion, and it's time to breathe it in with as much life and spirit as their lungs will allow, wishing it would never end.

MESSAGE FROM THE 4 OF WANDS

It's time to kick back in joyful elation! You've been building relationships and foundations, and after a period of massive shifting, it's time to enjoy some well-deserved celebratory time! If you've been through a cycle of rapid expansion and awakening, this card marks a transition into a more harmonic and stable state. You will look back and remember this energy as being a wonderful interlude along the way. You have reached new levels of consciousness, and it's the perfect time to enjoy a milestone event and celebrate with the people who love you. And *psst*, sometimes this card signifies a marriage

or another significant occasion! While connecting with friends and family, make sure you relax, release, and allow your body to integrate all the lessons you've been working through. Enjoy this warm vibe of community and success—happiness and harmony are yours to be had. In shadow, this card can signify a lack of harmony in your life, or feelings of vulnerability around your safety and your stability. Take some time to make sure that you are not allowing your passions to blow things out of proportion. It's also a good time to make a point of connecting with others and to work on loving them *as they are*. Bring all of your peeps closer at this time, and shower your community with as much good energy as you can. This will bring you into a more harmonious state with the world. *Also, when was the last time you danced?*

I am Devoted to Connectedness.

QUESTIONS FOR THE SEER
- You've come a long way. How are you celebrating your wins?
- What role do events or gatherings play in your life? Is there one coming up that you could pay more attention to?
- Sometimes the 4 of Wands shows up to remind us that we feel more in harmony with our environment when we can just let loose and be ourselves. Are there aspects of yourself that you tend to keep hidden?
- Who makes you feel totally at home?

5 of Wands

LIGHT SEER: competition, conflict, ambition, challenge, being pushed by others to excel, brainstorming, mental jousting, adrenaline and aggression, surpassing limits, dynamic energy, leveling up

SHADOW SEER: an opportunity to collaborate, not following the rules, in-group fighting or arguments, a tendency to avoid conflict to your detriment, being overly competitive, lack of connection

A WANDS STORY

1. 2. 3. Go! The 5 competitors push and pull their way up the tilting scaffold of Wands in order to reach the light. First to reach it . . . *takes all?* No, wait. First to reach it, shares. Were those the rules? In the thrill of the moment, they can't remember, so they create something new as they go. They've moved beyond the stability of the 4 of Wands, and they scuffle and skip their way up the ladder with the adrenaline of competition in their veins. There is one motive in their equally ambitious hearts: to win. A few experience the rush of friendly competition and they push themselves to excel in this environment. Others feel more aggressive, and the challenge suddenly feels more like a serious conflict. They all desperately want to be seen and heard amid the chaos and the commotion. Yet, just as they didn't really listen to the rules, no one is really listening to anyone else's opinions or ideas on how to scale this mountain of Wands together. Everyone is pushing forward. In their frenzy to be first, they miss the fact that *none of them* will ever reach the light unless they stop pushing against one another and choose to collaborate.

MESSAGE FROM THE 5 OF WANDS

A little rivalry can be a good thing. It can push us to become the very best version of ourselves and to move quicker than we would if we were alone. Allow opposition and challenge to help you to evolve your methods and to push beyond your self-imposed limitations. If competition becomes unhealthy, and you are experiencing the shadow side of conflict or ambition, it's time to take a step back and retreat from any energies that are hindering your progress. Look for healthy collaboration or competition that is inspiring and motivating. Seek harmonious relationships that *add* to your happiness instead of draining it. Others are on their own unique trajectory, so if you are experiencing conflicts with others, take a deep breath and re-examine your own path. Sometimes the need to be right, or personal feelings around being questioned or challenged, can interfere with the ability to see your own goals clearly. You may need to fly solo for a bit in order to re-evaluate your options. While it's true that egos can clash and slow everything down, they can also hone skills and help you to succeed. Use this jousting to improve and to become a better version of yourself! Choose to excel! Learn from others and use competing energies as a way to enrich your experience.

I support others and they support me, and we rise together in accelerated harmony.

QUESTIONS FOR THE SEER
- What challenges are currently holding you back?
- Does competition bring out your negative or positive qualities? Are you motivated by the successes of others?
- What do you need to learn about working with others?

5 of Wands

— REACHING TOGETHER FOR THE WIN

△ FIRE SYMBOL ON WANDS

✗ WANDS CROSSED IN GEBO RUNES (X)
(PARTNERSHIPS, RECIPROCITY, HONOR, GIVING GIFTS)

SAME CLOTHING: A COMPETITIVE EVENT (SAME TEAM?)

MOUNTAINS IN BACKGROUND = OBSTACLES

LIGHTS: Limelight, Success

LAUREL WREATH: → victory, success

HANDS: Recognition, → Achievement

6 of Wands

White Sweater: PURITY OF INTENTIONS and ACTIONS

IN THE ORIGINAL R.W.S. TAROT, WREATHS APPEAR IN THE CHARIOT, THE WORLD, THE 4 OF WANDS and THE 6 OF WANDS.

6 of Wands

LIGHT SEER: leadership, success, accomplishments, being seen, becoming influential, victory, optimism, inspiring others

SHADOW SEER: not seeing eye-to-eye, pessimism, resentment and self-doubt, a desire for acknowledgment, comparisons, feelings of failure, falling from grace

A WANDS STORY

After a long journey, she has finally made it. She returns to the city she once called home with the victory wreath in her hand. She has been doing the work and tirelessly pushing for this moment. The word success whispers itself in her heart, and she knows that this homecoming is going to be special. She knows her people will be here tonight. Her friends. Her family. Her biggest fans. She steps onto the stage and the cheers erupt. *They see her.* She feels bathed in the energy of the crowd, and they celebrate her and the long battle that she has overcome. She allows all the feelings to bubble up: the gratitude, the joy. *Is it finally real?* She wants to pinch herself, hearing the echo of the mic as she steps up to it. *Feeling seen* is integral to her understanding of her own success. Her joy has been amplified by the recognition she feels in this moment. She takes a deep breath of gratitude in, and clearing her throat, she gets ready to begin. Her voice is steady as she begins: "We did it."

MESSAGE FROM THE 6 OF WANDS

Relish the sweetness of this victory! Something that you've been working toward is finally coming to fruition, and it's time to celebrate your wins, beautiful seer. After giving your energy, stretching your mindset, and building this success—lesson by lesson—gift yourself permission to bask in the warm glow of accomplishment. Allow the supportive community around you to witness and appreciate the progress you've made. Taking time to see your own radiance is as important as making the next move on your journey, because acknowledging your evolution will seed more of it. And don't be afraid to truly showcase your skills and show up to share as an influential leader. Others will be looking to you for more wisdom now, so step up and share your brilliance! In shadow, this card speaks to shying away from public attention and hiding your light from the world. Worrying about a marred reputation or a lack of recognition for past accomplishments may be blocking your progress. Receive this message wholeheartedly: *you are worthy of your success.* Turn to your own inner compass to gauge your growth, as the need for external validation can be a self-esteem killer. It may be time to consciously boost your self-confidence and look for ways to feel proud of your progress. Remember that no one else in the world has your magic, and that the most important person to impress, wholeheartedly, is yourself.

I am WORTHY OF
THIS SUCCESS and
I am grateful
that I am seen.

QUESTIONS FOR THE SEER
- What feelings emerge when you think about being recognized and seen, publicly?
- How do you feel about your dreams when important people in your life don't understand them?
- Are you able to accept praise and recognition easily? If not, why is this the case?

7 of Wands

LIGHT SEER: challenge, grounding and protecting yourself, movement, growth, creative innovation, remaining ahead, feeling vulnerable, a sign to continue to share your ideas, self-expression

SHADOW SEER: defending yourself, being attacked, being slandered, being misunderstood, a need to erect energetic boundaries, a lack of preparation, giving up

A WANDS STORY

Haters. As soon as she climbed to her current perch, they started whipping out their Wands and challenging her position. She's been here for what, *maybe* five minutes (?!), and there's already someone who didn't like what she had to say, another someone who disliked what she ate, someone else who aggressively demanded she explain her background, and a whole set of Wands pointing at her flaws. Some people dislike anyone who they perceive as "successful." Others want what she has. Some are just angry at the world, and they attack her because she is visible. She takes a pause, remembering that she has the experience to be at the top and rooting into the unshakeable certainty that she is deserving of this success. She realizes that her only option is to defend herself if she wants to stay put. But while they use violence and aggression to tempt her into losing her composure, she chooses a different route and draws on her integrity, her energy, and her love. *This, too, is a lesson that will serve her well.* Taking a deep breath in, she draws down light from the Universe, and she forms an energetic bubble around herself. She casts a protective shield as she imagines the rune of protection streaming down into her sheltering sphere. Consciously—mindfully—she brings feelings of peace and well-being into her body. *And so it is.*

MESSAGE FROM THE 7 OF WANDS

It's time to show your determination and tenacity, especially if you are being asked to defend your accomplishments to others. Remain confident in your abilities and remember that you deserve this success! You've earned it. Draw on your integrity, your love, and your positive energy, and stand up for your beliefs and intentions. Sometimes, competition emerges as a result of shining brightly in the world. If you are feeling attacked after sharing your magic, it is important to remember that others likely want what you have, so stand up bravely and continue to do your beautiful thing. You are at a place where others may envy your status and are hoping to knock you off your pedestal. It's important to remember that you don't have to accept their opinions as truth, especially when they are vying for your position. Check in with your integrity and make sure you are acting in a way that is aligned with your highest values, and when you know you are, don't let anyone stop you from achieving your dreams! Be persistent and defend what's yours. If you are feeling criticized, unaccepted, or misunderstood, this card is a reminder that standing up for yourself and clearly radiating your truest message will convey self-confidence *and backbone*, so continue courageously. Maintain your flow. Set up healthy boundaries. And bolster your belief. Remaining synchronized and aligned with your bright vision will help you to avoid sinking into any confrontational or negative states that others may be pushing.

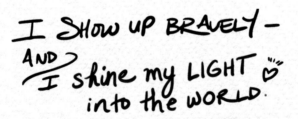

I SHOW UP BRAVELY —
AND
I shine my LIGHT
into the WORLD.

QUESTIONS FOR THE SEER
- How much do the opinions of others affect you?
- Is it time to be firmer with your energetic boundaries?
- How would your perspective change if you were on their side of the situation?
- What would it look like if you showed up in your most vibrant form?

Energetic Bubble
of Protection
is her own Private
Sanctuary of Peace.

Divine Protection

ALGIZ RUNE:
PROTECTION and DEFENSE,
Connection to the DIVINE,
Expansion of consciousness
to HIGHER Realms.

LIGHT from her
SOLAR PLEXUS CHAKRA:
Personal power,
identity, self-confidence

7 of Wands

7 wands
attacking
Her from
Below

8 of Wands

FAST ENERGY:
Speeding toward the
Light —
the velocity sparks the
tips on fire

ALL ENERGY
POINTING in
the same
Direction,
Timelines and
OPPORTUNITIES
CONVERGE.

— GALAXIES AND
STARS:
The Cosmos Are
aligned and
Ready to move.
(may be
TRAVEL!)

8 of Wands

LIGHT SEER: speed, velocity, travel, making split-second decisions, an upcoming positive resolution, haste, good news

SHADOW SEER: instability, delays, unfocused energy and lack of direction, burnout, a tendency to hesitate, cancelled plans

A WANDS STORY

Light speed! Eight Wands hurtle their way through the Universe, gathering the momentum and the energy they need as they go. What started out as one Wand quickly became two, then three . . . and then all the Wands joined the flight in quick succession. They're in a rush because there's still so much that they need to convey and so many experiences to bring forth! They draw inspiration from the galaxies they dart past. Star after star, their energies collide and merge, and they move faster and faster until the velocity causes their tips to ignite. They push ahead because they want to arrive before they burn out! *Friction?* They blow past it. *Hurdles? Barriers?* Gone! They have such great news to deliver, and so much traveling to do! And in the blink of an eye, they have passed by like shooting stars, leaving only the change that they came to enact and their echoed sentiment of *Go!*

MESSAGE FROM THE 8 OF WANDS

Now is a time for swift movement and action. It may be in the form of travel or in the form of energies taking shape. If you have a gut feeling that needs to be acted upon, listen to it! You know those moments in life that feel like a sprint? This type of speedy energy is at play. It's inspirational. It's fiery. It's positive. And it's now. Sometimes these Wands indicate the progression of creative ideas or that a particular piece of news that is traveling quickly. With all this movement, avoid being swept along with an unpredictable tide by having clarity about your desires and direction. When you know where you are headed, you can harness this beautiful window of swift opportunity and cover a lot of ground! In shadow, the 8 of Wands suggests there is some sticky energy influencing your situation. Plans may be cancelled. Dates may be shifted. Your Wands may be stalled out. You want to move, but ack . . . if your foot's not stuck in the mud, then you've locked your keys in the car, *amiright?!* Your timing might be off. If you're fluctuating between *sometimes hesitating* and *sometimes running so fast that you're burning out*, it's time to bring some balanced momentum into your propulsion. Consistent movement that feels right in your heart is the best place to start.

IT'S GO TIME!
I FALL into the flow
of this QUICKENING
ENERGY.

QUESTIONS FOR THE SEER
- What are you waiting for?
- If you could go in any direction with the knowledge that it would be successful, which way would you go?
- And are the stories you are telling yourself about where you *should be* affecting your current situation? (Think: *too late, too old, too young, too early, too slow, etc.*)
- Priorities and quick, short-term goals. What's your list look like these days?

9 of Wands

LIGHT SEER: determination, resilience, defiance, a last defense, the final push, rewards, excitement for what's to come, finding motivation in the face of difficulties, victory

SHADOW SEER: the need to open up and trust people, holding on to old stories, the need to let go of old battles, the need to follow through and finish what you started, trapped by your own boundaries, giving up

A WANDS STORY

Brazenly, the 9 of Wands stands guard, poised and ready to take on anything that comes her way. She has been defending this place for so long that she can't remember what it's like to not be guarding her fence of wands. She *can* remember, however, that it feels like the battle has already been won, and that it was won through resilience, effort, and defiance. The others have already left their posts to rejoice in their newly found peace, but she's not quite ready. Not yet. She wants to make sure that they are truly safe, and she feels like this one last stand is required of her. Is it residual fear? A needed action? She's not sure. But somewhere in her heart, she knows that it's almost time to let go and relax. Underneath battle scars, she wants nothing more than to feel the security blanket of rest. She leans on her most intimidating wand and wrestles with the sedating weariness that creeps into her bones. She promises herself that this will be the last midnight watch she'll take—one final push to complete this task—and tomorrow, yes tomorrow, she will retreat.

MESSAGE FROM THE 9 OF WANDS

Don't give up now! You're almost there! As you round the corner of success, something may surface that threatens your feelings of security and achievement. It's important to remember how far you've come. Don't see this minor deceleration as a symbol of failure. Find your resistance and take this one final step, as attainment and completion are in store for those who are determined and tenacious enough to continue. You've got this! In shadow, this card suggests you are making things harder than necessary or being overly defensive about your situation. You may even be inadvertently choosing the more difficult path because you believe, on some level, that healing and ascension should be difficult. Sometimes we become so enamored with our own stories of rising up that our shadows become romantic notions that we defend. When you take a break from the monotony of being overprotective, it becomes easy to see that you no longer need to hold that sticky, guarded energy close to your heart. Let go of any ideas you have about navigating specific lessons on the path. Turn away from any shadows that are rooting in as excuses or from any old battles that are becoming your raison d'être. Your time to relax into security and success is on the horizon.

I PUSH BEYOND my own PERCEIVED LIMITATIONS, and I Remain open and TRUSTING as I DO.

QUESTIONS FOR THE SEER
- What could you do to make your life easier?
- Are you being overprotective in your current situation?
- Sometimes, as Light and Shadow Seers, we choose the more difficult path because we believe we are making progress when we are battling our shadows—fighting when we could be healing. Or holding on to old lessons when we could be letting go. Are you romanticizing the idea of your painful lessons?
- What have you learned about yourself while overcoming so much?
- What one last thing must be accomplished before you can totally relax and release?

PROTECTIVE LIGHT

WHITE TORN SHIRT:
PURE INTENTIONS, SHE IS A
LITTLE BATTERED FROM BATTLE

RUNES
ON WAND

ᛉ ALGIZ (PROTECTION)

ᛚ LAGUZ REVERSED
(OUT OF FLOW)

FENCE MADE WITH RUNES:

ᚺ HAGALAZ: CHANGE, A FORCED
PAUSE, INTEGRATION
OF LESSONS, PREPARATION
FOR RENEWAL, BREAKING
OF ILLUSIONS.

ᛁ ISA: A STANDSTILL, A PAUSE,
REFLECTION

9 of Wands

10 of Wands

WIND MOVES
HER ALONG
(help from
the universe)

CARRYING 7
WANDS
(PRIORITIZING)

3
WANDS
LEFT BEHIND
SHOWING BURDENS
DROPPED

DUSK: THE END OF
A LONG JOURNEY

HILL: OBSTACLES
almost BEHIND HER

SHERPA: ASKING FOR
and RECEIVING HELP
WITH TASKS AND
RESPONSIBILITIES

SUITCASE: TRAVELLING LIGHTLY INSTEAD
OF TAKING ON TOO MUCH.

10 of Wands

LIGHT SEER: taking on too much, an opportunity to free yourself from heavy burdens, the need to prioritize, finding yourself close to a successful outcome, obligations, a message to keep going

SHADOW SEER: divided attentions, clinging to responsibilities, difficulty asking for help, the oppression of martyrdom, letting go of someone else's expectations of you, a need to stand up for yourself

A WANDS STORY

The 10 of Wands looks up at the last mountain she has to cross, and she winces. Her back is sore, her boots are killing her, and she has been carrying her stack of Wands for days. One look at the top of that mountain, and she realizes that she must do something about her heavy load. She's overwhelmed with these stupid sticks. And even though she loves most of them, she's just *so done* with carrying everything by herself right now. They have become complicated burdens to lug around, and she's seriously overextended her muscular prowess. But gah! The finish line is so close! And these Wands absolutely (positively) need to get there before sundown. She considers her options. She could struggle all the way up. Or she could leave some behind and come back for them later. *It wouldn't be a bad idea, right?* She even considers leaving some for good, because she's probably taking on too much, and it's probably time to cull her collection. *Also, not a bad idea.* As her foot throbs, a friendly little yak comes around the bend just in time. *Salvation!* "How much?" she asks, hoping he'll agree to alleviate some of her strain. "Sweet child" he smiles—"I would love to help. All you had to do was ask."

MESSAGE FROM THE 10 OF WANDS

All. Of those. Responsibilities. Do you really need to carry all of those Wands—all by yourself—all at the same time? The 10 of Wands is telling you it's time to streamline, because you are so, so close yet so overburdened. Prioritize. Get help. Organize. Systematizing your life right now will help you to reach your goals much faster, and it will bring relief to any overwhelm or molasses energy that you may be feeling. Drop the nonessentials, and any heaviness that is weighing you down, and look for ways to bring levity and ease to your day. Sometimes, this means letting go of a learned behavior or a limiting belief, and sometimes it means deleting a task on your calendar. Whether your burdens are material, spiritual, literal, or energetic, it's clear that you've got some extra baggage right now. You may even be missing the breadcrumbs of serendipity because you are so intensely focused on what you already have to carry. Let it go! Release it. And enjoy your last steps to the finish line!

I release my burdens to the ethers knowing that the universe will help me tend to the essentials.

QUESTIONS FOR THE SEER
- If you could drop everything else, what would you choose to focus on?
- If you're taking on too much, what could you drop, knowing that things would likely be just fine without you? (Hint: Others are more capable than you think!)
- How much time are you dedicating to your own growth? Your rest? Your happiness?
- What are your priorities in life? And are you giving them the focus they need?

Page of Wands

LIGHT SEER: explosive creativity and infectious enthusiasm, imagination, creative beginnings, honing a new skill or passion, a newly found inspiration, curiosity and trying new things, gifting yourself permission to dream, a youthful spark, creative ideation and brainstorming

SHADOW SEER: limiting beliefs, creator angst, blocked ideas, a need to establish and ground your energy, feeling eager to start something new but confronted by obstacles, hotheadedness, being rebellious

A WANDS STORY

Everyone asks the Page of Wands why she never stops fidgeting. She says it's because she's always dreaming, but the Universe knows that it's just the way she embodies her boundless creativity. Every time the Page gets a new idea, she says thank you to the salamanders on her printed pants, does a little dance, and then tosses her wand in the air to let off a tiny bit of creator steam. (Did you know that salamanders are magical fire creatures that can bestow so much magic into the world? This Page does, and so she keeps them close.) Some days, her intense imagination keeps her wound like a top, when she desires to produce but can't decide how to start. And when she starts, it's usually more complicated than she imagined, so she goes right back to envisioning. *This Page, you see, gets inspired all the time.* She's so inspired, in fact, that her thoughts lead her from one idea to the next, leaving little space in between to do anything else but imagine. As a result, she never seems to stop throwing that wand of hers around. She has the potential to manifest incredible realities, but she'll need to bring that baton down to earth and stake her idea into the ground first. But for now, she dances through her fertile landscape, and with a little patience and maturity, her creative genius will sprout.

MESSAGE FROM THE PAGE OF WANDS

This Page is a free spirit who carries infectious enthusiasm with her. Delight in this youthful, raw, and exuberant creative energy, and pay attention to any new ideas that are bubbling to the surface of your awareness. You will find flashes of inspiration now . . . impulses that come bundled with massive potential. If you are feeling the creator angst of not having any solid plans to bring your insights to life, let go of your need to formalize your plans right now. If you give your ideas the space they need to develop before sharing them prematurely, you will allow their wings to fully form. Their potency is limitless, so let them breathe! In shadow, this card can suggest that even though you have a million different solutions, it's equally as important to figure out how to implement them. Passions and lofty ambitions are only the spark—you may need to ask for help with the next steps. Spend any extra time in the pursuit of the imagination, and if you are feeling any lack of ambition or drive, or feeling devoid of the ingenuity that this card illuminates, know that you will find this fire when you allow yourself to dream.

as THE DReameR of my DReam,
I SPONTANEOUSLY AND PASSIONATELY
IGNITE THIS FLAME

QUESTIONS FOR THE SEER

- How are you capturing your creative energy? Are you embodying, logging, or cultivating this magical flow of ideas?
- What are you feeling frustrated about right now? What experience do you want but haven't had yet? How can you move this stuck energy in a positive direction?
- Where does your motivation come from? How does it feel in your body?

A NOTE ON SALAMADERS

CONSIDERED TO BE a FIRE
ELEMENTAL (A mythical creature
associated with FIRE) they show
up in THE SUIT OF WANDS.
IT WAS ONCE BELIEVED that the
creatures were "developed in
the fire" AND that they could
SURVIVE the flames, hence their
magical association with FIRE.
THEIR ability to REGROW Limbs
has also Linked them to
transformation and REGENERATION.

SPINNING WAND:
Playful, Creative
NATURE

Page of Wands

DESERT:
New
Landscapes
to
Explore

SALAMANDER
PRINT ON
PANTS

her energy is contagious

Knight of Wands

Expressive
nature,
CHARISMA

Ready to
Gallop toward
goals AND
adventures,
DREAM CHASER.

Knight of Wands

LIGHT SEER: charisma, passion, spontaneity, pursuing your dreams, fast energy, enthusiasm, courage, taking inspired action, the pursuit of adventure, getting things done, someone who enters your life quickly

SHADOW SEER: unfocused energy, impulsivity, recklessness, self-sabotage with fiery emotions, the need for more self-awareness, being cocky

A WANDS STORY

The Knight of Wands gallops across the sand on her stallion, charging full steam ahead toward that passion project that she's been dreaming about. But wait, what is that in the distance? A campfire? A beach party? *Full stop.* She's nothing if not spontaneous, and whatever it is, it looks like an adventure waiting to happen. (Which is indeed the thing that she craves most.) The possible dangers of the situation don't cross her mind, nor does she notice that she's veering off the map. She simply jumps off her horse and joins the party, grabbing a borrowed djembe and an impromptu beat. Her passionate, fiery energy is magnetic, and since she's got charisma in spades, she quickly becomes the life of the party. After a few laughs, she remembers that her scattered energy is often the cause of frustrating delays in her life, and the very thought of setting herself back again has her quickly annoyed by her own fiery unpredictability. She remembers that she has a mission to accomplish, and as quickly as she arrived, she's off again—chasing her dream and becoming her most vibrant expression of self.

MESSAGE FROM THE KNIGHT OF WANDS

What have you been dreaming about? The Knight of Wands gallops in and out of your reading with messages of adventure, of impulsivity, and of bravely pursuing the things that inspire you the most. *That passion project you've been tinkering with?*

That drum circle you've always wanted to join but usually hold yourself back from? Allow spontaneity into your choices and gift yourself the freedom to shift your reality to match your desires. It's okay to crave new things and to run with the wind when you are feeling charged up about an idea. Ardently pursue your curiosities and your interests. Go with it! Allow this high-spirited energy to rush in and incite a wildfire of positive momentum. It will animate new adventures and enthusiasm in your world. In shadow, this card counsels against recklessness and heated outbursts. Make sure you're acting in a way that you won't regret later. You don't want all that pent-up creative energy to spontaneously combust! Fan the flame of inspiration, leaving some reserves for the long haul. Make your passions work *for* you, while whooshing yourself toward long-term success.

IN the PURSUIT of the IMAGINED,
I manifest THIS fire with the
INFECTIOUS FEELINGS of INSPIRATION.

QUESTIONS FOR THE SEER
- What are you continuously optimistic about?
- Are you spontaneous? What area of your life could use some more passionate, spontaneous energy?
- What character trait keeps you sidetracked from your dreams?
- The Knight of Wands lives in and on purpose. What is your sacred reason for living?
- What new passions are blooming in your life? What's making you want to grow? Move? Work? Learn? Or run toward it?

Queen of Wands

LIGHT SEER: confidence, bold expression, joy, warmth, creativity, passion, power, determination, helping others as you build your queendom, intensity

SHADOW SEER: jealousy, being afraid to take a risk, not being totally honest with yourself, an optimal time to build your self-confidence and to let go of what other people think, waning passions

A WANDS STORY

The Queen of Wands exudes an intoxicating brand of confidence and determination. She's incredibly captivating and charming, and she brings her intense creativity and passion with her wherever she goes. When she enters a room, her smile is only overshadowed by her warmhearted laughter and her ability to share her legendary stories. She steps comfortably into her role as Queen—self-assured and assertive as she leads. Today, she sits on her desert throne, surrounded by her dreams and her memories, her irresistible energy, and her people. She understands the power of deep connection and the lengths that people will go to when they are cared for and when their efforts go noticed and appreciated. Even though she knows there have been times when her emotions blazed too hot, her bright heart always burns fearlessly, and she remains deeply loved by everyone around her. She has built her long-term happiness by nurturing her optimism, her positivity, and her passion over her fear and her fury. With a fierce conviction for creative expression, she is a powerfully inspirational character who radiates love, enthusiasm, strength, and warmth.

MESSAGE FROM THE QUEEN OF WANDS

You are capable and fierce. It's time to claim the magic you've been looking for and to boldly step into the limelight of your life. Don't be afraid to be the center of attention, and for Goddess's sake, stop acting small in order to make those around you feel more comfortable! It's not your role to make others feel larger than you in your presence—it's your role to make them feel loved. Allow your powerful presence to fill the room, inciting deep respect while also lighting the way for others by bravely sharing your fire. Potent connections of love will ensue, so it's a perfect time to put yourself in situations where you will have a chance to meet new people and socialize. There is, of course, shadow cast in the wake of all of this light, so don't push it down so deeply that you can't find it again. Sometimes this Queen shows up to indicate jealous or manipulative tendencies, especially when you let that stubborn streak grow hotter than your common sense. *Always go back to love.* Know that it's okay to be healing . . . and still want to heal others. It's okay to be vulnerable and imperfect, and still lead. Make sure your fiery bursts of productivity are accompanied by laughter and gratitude, and refuse to be defined by any perceived failures that have held you back. Transmute that shadow! Sit with it briefly and then light it on fire because you don't need it anymore. You are luminous, so allow your generous and brave heart to express its fierce love enthusiastically!

I FILL MY WORLD with AN INTENSE LIGHT THAT CONNECTS AND INCITES PASSIONS.

QUESTIONS FOR THE SEER
- How does your intensity show up in your life?
- What part of you desires to be seen? What part of you wants to lead?
- When do you feel most powerful?
- Have you pushed shadow parts of you so far away that you have a hard time accessing their lessons? If you could illuminate them, what would they whisper?

← △ Fire Symbol earrings

LIGHT &
SPARKLES:
Charisma,
Power,
MAGIC,
WARMTH

BLACK CAT: the OCCULT, MYSTERY,
PROTECTION, connection to
magic, psychic abilities

CANDLES: REVERED by
OTHERS, WARMTH, SURROUNDED
BY many

SPIRAL energy: GROWTH,
evolution AND
CHARISMA (Hypnotic)

Queen of Wands

King of Wands

LION AND LION CREST
TATTOO: STRENGTH,
AUTHORITY, COURAGE,
INSPIRATION

GECKO/
SALAMANDER ON
SHIRT: FIRE
ELEMENTAL,
magic AND
TRANSFORMATION

Runes on WAND
‹ KENAZ:
Torch,
illumination,
guide, WISDOM,
CREATIVITY

⚡ SOWELO:
Sun, Light,
truth, Power

King of Wands

LIGHT SEER: an entrepreneurial spirit, a natural-born leader, fearlessness, ideas that could be ultra-successful, a creative visionary, determination, timelessness, success, heat

SHADOW SEER: being overly ambitious, a need for compassion, egomania, being too assertive, explosive emotions, impatience, misguided vision

A WANDS STORY

This fiery guy. He's a charismatic, natural-born leader, and his vitality emanates through his laughter and his obsession with creating a life well-lived. Embodying a perpetual zest for joy, his optimistic nature makes him highly influential. When you step into his sphere, you may feel a surge of entrepreneurial energy . . . his enthusiasm is highly infectious and you may even find yourself wanting to support his vision. His belief in his dream is magnetic. A revolutionary who constantly pushes the limitations of what's possible, his desire to make the world a better place keeps him innovating and creating. His goals are boundless, and he doesn't allow rumination or daydreaming to get in his way. He simply imagines a new possibility and takes action to bring it to life, quickly. Because of this, he isn't afraid of a little risk. He constantly expands his potential by stepping out of his comfort zone and onto exciting new trajectories. He challenges the status quo in many ways—he may even keep strange company, but only because he loves offbeat thinking! This is a part of his visionary magic, and he does whatever it takes to move in the direction of his brightly lit future. Keeping his eye on the prize, he runs toward the fulfillment of his ever-evolving dream.

MESSAGE FROM THE KING OF WANDS

The card of moguls, masterpieces, and soul-inspiration, the King of Wands asks you where you are headed and pushes you to the edge of your epic success. It's time to unleash that offbeat weirdo that you've got inside, being unapologetic in your pursuit of the stellar. Spark your vision through the wildly novel expression of big ideas—yes, yours!—and if you find yourself getting tripped up by the minutiae of the everyday, recruit help and map out the broader picture. Recharge your energy by taking time to appreciate awe, beauty, and wonder, and then go take a chance on your dream! You can only create something this epic by being at the helm of your extraordinary story, so holler passionately and invite others to see exactly what you envision for the future. If it feels like your perspectives seem curiously avant-garde or unique, invite others to partake in your momentum. The shadow side of this energy is that you may not perceive your own limitations because of an overzealous ambition. Keep arrogance and unrealistic expectations at bay, and work out the kinks first, before charging ahead with your intensely vibrant heart. Love, career, health . . . it all gets a positive boost within the fire of the King of Wands' passionate energy. Ignite your mission!

PASSIONATE AND HEART-FUELED
WE BUILD THIS EMPIRE
of LIGHT TOGETHER

QUESTIONS FOR THE SEER

- Are you living inside the dream you envisioned for your life?
  Or are you living inside someone else's dream?
- As you run toward your goals, what small details keep tripping you up?
  And can you work out a better way to deal with the little things?
- What mission or purpose are you igniting? And which three steps could
  you take toward it now?
- Who could help you with your current challenge? Share your vision and enlist help.
- What would an intensely creative and inspired life look like to you?

CUPS

ELEMENT: Water

ASSOCIATED WITH:

emotions, relationships, love, intuition,
compassion, empathy, feelings, healing

ace of Cups

LIGHT SEER: new connections, new romantic relationships, friendships, seeds of love and hope, newfound emotions, awakening the heart, joy, positive outcomes, Oneness, bliss, creativity

SHADOW SEER: a time to nurture more self-love, making sure you aren't repressing your emotions, opening up to the possibility of love

A CUPS STORY

The origins of love are rooted deeply within the primordial Universe. Our human systems have evolved over the eons, and we have gone from starseeds and energetic dust to fully fledged keepers of consciousness. We have blossomed into custodians of life and guardians of Source energy. Our energetic systems, alongside our biology, are fine-tuned and delicately primed to sense the imminent arrival of love in our lives. It kicks up the old dust and turns it into hormones, mindsets, and beliefs that penetrate every cell of our being—as if our very biology drinks it in. We hum to life in its presence. Love penetrates us. It moves our souls. It grows in leaps and bounds. It transcends. It flows forth from every splitting cell and every coming together of two lights entangled, and it springs forth from deep within the Cup of the old Universe, flowing right into your waking life today. *What, sweet light, will you use it for?*

MESSAGE FROM THE ACE OF CUPS

An extremely positive message of vibrant beginnings, the Ace of Cups marks the genesis of relationships, emotional connections, and deep feelings of love and friendship. Unions are blossoming in your life, and it's time to cultivate an expansive, optimistic perspective as you allow new feelings to emerge. Consciously love the world, and your awakening heart magic will become a powerful beacon for adventures, romance, and

for the effusive joy that you are manifesting in your life. Your emotions are powerful magic, and tuning in to the language of the heart will unlock powerful creativity and intuition at this time. This Ace of Cups energy is both ancient and Divine, and it has had millennia to vibrate at just the right pitch to connect your body and your spirit with its bright light. You are likely receiving new guidance from the Cosmos, and it's important to pay attention to any new desires or passions that are arising from the unconscious mind. As your capacity for love expands, check in and make sure you aren't repressing your ability to connect with others as a result of being overly protective of a tender heart. In shadow, notice that the Cup, even when overturned, is still full. There is nothing that you can do that will render yourself unworthy or incapable of love. It is always there. It permeates everything. Mindfully extend any love you feel for others to your own heart as well. Forgive yourself for past mistakes, and discover a fountainhead of deep healing within your heart. With copious amounts of self-acceptance, get ready to expand! Exciting affinities are surfacing, and it's time to open up and give yourself permission to deepen your kinship with the life and love around you.

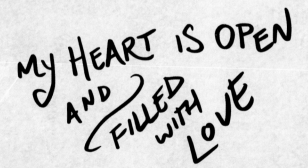

My HEART IS OPEN AND FILLED WITH LOVE

QUESTIONS FOR THE SEER
- What vague new ideas or feelings are starting to stir?
- Creativity flows when emotions flood your system. Is there something you are called to create? Or something that you are called to feel?
- In challenging times, loving the world is a profound skillset. Get started by listing the things you love. The people . . . places . . . feelings. The foods, colors . . . experiences. List anything and everything that comes to mind.

Rainbow bracelet: ———
(Love is Love)

Prism water has all the
colors of light (all the
potential), magic created
by the emotion of love.

green + red bowls:
heart chakra ↙   ↘ Root chakra
(Love)   (safety)

wedding
Ring

new
horizons,
sun =
joy

2 of Cups

magic
Lights:
dreams,
hopes
AND
WISHES

EVOLUTION
HUBBLE → The old Universe,
DEEP FIELD   the beginning of
GALAXIES: time AND love.

— Heart: creating love
— whirlpool: pulls everything
   in, emotions
      spill out.
         (water =
            emotions)

hands in PRAYER
at heart chakra:
calling in new Love

ace of Cups

2 of Cups

LIGHT SEER: romantic partners, soulmates, friendships, connected hearts, passion, kindred spirits, joyful connection and cooperation, union, sometimes marriage, duality, love consciousness

SHADOW SEER: emotional blocks, not being open to receive love, disharmony, unions disrupted, separation, healing past trauma, a need to rethink a relationship

A CUPS STORY

Love at first sight? *Possibly.* Attraction at first millisecond? *Definitely.* Like matter and anti-matter, day and night, Yin and Yang . . . some things are primed to complement each other. Our whole Universe shines with examples of charged opposites that are drawn into each other's gravitational pull. And sometimes, when the moon is ripe and the stars align, these opposites find their match, and they are able to sustain this beautiful alchemy without fizzling or draining each other. In such moments, like the moment when two souls unite, an outpouring of magic spills forth. Ideas flow and manifest in every color of the light spectrum. Conversations expand and vibrate at a frequency beyond the sum of the two parts. Work becomes purpose. Kindreds become soul family. There is nothing to do except to witness, embody, and delight in this intoxicating partnership.

MESSAGE FROM THE TWO OF CUPS

When you share your joy with those around you, you will attract deep and meaningful ties with others. This card whispers of romance and love, bliss and attraction, and the unity of the like-hearted. Sometimes it signifies the beginning of a new friendship or a business partnership, while at other times it marks a profound romantic union. This perfect pairing of matched souls has the potential to develop into the magical and intoxicating entanglement of souls mating or the merging of paths that will be forever united or changed. If you are single, look for the arrival of a romantic companion who will be a profoundly passionate and devoted lover. In shadow, this card is a reminder that the love hormone oxytocin is emitted when we experience feelings of love *or* jealousy—and that we can be addicted to either feeling. Choose to consciously remain on the side that serves up doses of love. Sometimes this card suggests a breakup, a falling out, or a need to consciously work on a partnership. Are you putting enough energy into your relationships? How you see yourself as one half of a committed pair will deepen and shift as the effervescent magic of the 2 of Cups bubbles into your life. It will serve as a sacred reflection for who you really are—shadow and light—with an intermingling of spirit, emotion, love, harmony, and balance. Remember that soul ties can illuminate our deepest growth opportunities and our most exquisite idiosyncrasies, and your flourishing involvement with another will grant you a gateway to your own highest evolution.

I THRIVE IN PARTNERSHIPS AND I REVEL IN THIS SACRED MAGIC of CONNECTION

QUESTIONS FOR THE SEER
- Are you open to making new soul connections?
- People often say, "When I find love, I will be happy," or "When I have money," or "When I have that job," etc. Remember that when you are happy, you will attract all of those things into your life. Are you waiting on external things to feel fulfilled and whole? How can you stop waiting and start living?

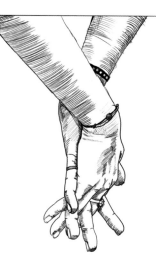

3 of Cups

LIGHT SEER: friendships, abundance, cooperation, community, sisterhood, brotherhood and siblinghood, joy, communication, celebration, soul contracts, soul family

SHADOW SEER: a need to see the value you bring to a relationship, disputes or miscommunication, feeling left out, a love triangle, a need to make amends

A CUPS STORY

Sister soul-journeyer, sacred kin, thank you for being here with me on the path. When one is happy, the other two are happy for her, and when another needs help, the other two rush to her side, no questions asked. Their bonds are richer than blood, for they know that they have been here before, *at a different time and in a different place,* supporting one another through their own evolutionary cycles. The bonds of time and light and soul-family have helped them to find one another again and again, with every subsequent birth. And every year when the timing is right, they take a weekend away to celebrate their deep bonds of friendship and love. They take an oath now to always remain a part of one another's lives, and as they do, they look up at the stars and they smile. *All is well in the world.* The seven sisters of the Pleiades shine down on them, winking at the interconnectedness of life and blessing them with the knowledge that they will always have a home together, anchored among the stars.

MESSAGE FROM THE 3 OF CUPS

Deep friendships are the family we choose. Our sisters, our brothers, and our siblings are not always defined by blood, and the packs that you run with and the kindred connections that you forge are your living and breathing support system. These sacred connections are to be cherished, nurtured, and celebrated! *Go have fun!* In the best and worst of times, your companions serve as mirrors, allowing you to see who you really are through their eyes. Who do you need to reach out to? What connections are waiting to support you? It's time to call in your besties and enjoy the laughter and warmth that come from a powerful soul group. Chosen family should offer a mutually loving and beneficial bond, and the opportunity to bring out the best in one another. The vibrational attraction is often ancient or energizing, and any setbacks that arise from miscommunication or disharmony with others may be old wounds or patterns that are resurfacing to be healed. If you are feeling disconnected or left out, commit more energy to cultivating trust and connection. And if an important connection has gone awry, it may be time to make amends. Trust your heart to lead you, knowing that your soul family is waiting to support you.

I CONNECT INTO THIS SACRED SIBLINGHOOD AND INTO THIS EXPANSIVE EXPERIENCE of WITNESSING THROUGH TIME

QUESTIONS FOR THE SEER
- What person comes to mind as a kindred spirit who could lend a hand or some much-appreciated advice right now?
- How much time do you dedicate to your friends and to your inner circle? Make a list of the people you'd like to spend more time with.
- Do you see old wounds or repeating patterns playing out in many different relationships? What steps can you take to heal some of these imbalances?
- How do you react to feeling left out? And how does your reaction help or hinder your ability to jump in and join the party?

PLEIADES STAR CLUSTER
· Known as the 7 SISTERS
· ancient Kin, STARSEEDS.

TRISKELE:
Sacred Pre-Celtic
Trinity Spiral

STANDING IN THE
SHAPE of "AWEN"

AWEN
- inspiring
friendships
- essence
of Life

DREAMY SKY for
daydreaming or
meditation

3 different
Clans,
1 SOUL
Family

3 of Cups

Lavender
· LOVE and FRIENDSHIP
· PURIFICATION
· calming, protection
· connected to triple-
bodied goddess
HECATE, the
"one who works
from afar"

FIELDS of
ABUNDANCE

4 of Cups

Fancy MEDITATION
CUSHION, yet she
remains unsatisfied
or uncomfortable

MISSED OPPORTUNITY
· unappreciated/UNSEEN
magical handout

4 of Cups

LIGHT SEER: missing opportunities, a time to meditate, a time to find gratitude, frustration and boredom, being a brat, not appreciating what you have, apathy, introspection, fantasizing

SHADOW SEER: focusing on the negative, pessimism, lack or scarcity thinking, a time to practice gratitude, a gentle nudge to stop complaining

A CUPS STORY

"Ack. This meditation thing just isn't working. Breathe in. Boredom. A million and one flippin' thoughts." She sits, fidgeting. Restless and insecure. She wants it and she wants it now. Privileged in every single way, she's ready to give up, because clearly, she's not made for this. *"Why does everyone else seem to be able to do it? And why on earth do they like it?"* Some days she's angry with the world because it's never lived up to the expectations she had. *"Lightworkers and rainbows of energy, pffft."* Some days she's just angry with herself for not being able to crack this ascension thing that people keep talking about. *"Manifesting? Rubbish."* She squirms. *"This is not my dimension, clearly. And this stupid pillow is way too hard. I've wasted a week doing this."* She is so focused on the things she doesn't have in her life that, even as she attempts to attract the things she does want, she can't shift her perspective to see the sparkling opportunities at her fingertips. Everything looks tiresome because she's been seeking lackluster gray.

MESSAGE FROM THE 4 OF CUPS

If you are finding yourself bored, unsatisfied, or frustrated with your current situation, know that you are likely missing the vibrant landscapes that are present. They lie just beyond your peripheral vision! Often, we become so focused on our desires and

our internal landscapes that our *feelings* about a situation prevent us from noticing the arrival of extraordinary opportunities and remarkable things. If you remain open to shifting your perspective (ever so slightly!) you will see your situation in a fantastic new light, for the present moment is filled with the most dynamic magic! Put on your rainbow-and-rose-colored glasses for a moment. You are being offered a chance to change your habitual thinking—your patterns of seeing—so that they will work magic for you. Instead of focusing on what you don't have, focus on what you do—or even better—spend energy focusing your thoughts on the experiences that you will create in the future. If you are feeling disconnected from your emotions, or disinterested in the vibrancy of life, make a commitment to find a way out of this rut. *Know that it's not forever,* and remember that any disillusionment that you have experienced doesn't need to be a part of your future. Taking time to meditate and slow your mind will show you that life is so much better than it seems. Take a good honest look at your attitude. With a little determination, positivity, daydreaming, and focus, you can shift onto one of the abundant and fortuitous timelines that's available to you right now.

I SEE THE FULLNESS AND RICHNESS of MY LIFE

QUESTIONS FOR THE SEER

- Are you feeling like the grass is greener on the other side?
- How would a total pessimist see your situation? And how would a total optimist view it? And where do you sit?
- Are you rejecting the sacred gifts that the Universe is offering?

5 of Cups

LIGHT SEER: grieving, disillusion, disappointment, betrayal, bitterness, wallowing, self-pity, can signify a broken heart, acceptance, moving on

SHADOW SEER: not letting go of past trauma, crying over spilled milk, rooting deeply into shadow work without healing and letting go, old stories that become a part of us, callousness, becoming jaded

A CUPS STORY

Empty. She had five full Cups. *"Five."* She wallows in her empty Cups, and they overtake her mind and her heart. *"Gone. Empty. Spilled. My loves."* Her grief consumes her, and soon enough she feels totally indifferent to the one Cup that still sits, sparkling with joy and possibility. *"Lies!"* she screams into the night and picks up the last Cup. *"I don't want to feel this anymore. Why are you there looking so shiny and happy?"* In her grief and confusion she detaches. *"And what right does anyone have to pretend that there is life here? Vitality? Options?"* Sinking deeper, she pushes her foot into the sand and tips the last of her joy into the thirsty earth. *"There it goes."* She watches her life force drain slowly. Now she has every excuse to let it all go down the hole, as she has made sure there is nothing left here to strive for.

MESSAGE FROM THE 5 OF CUPS

The illusion is lifting, and when life doesn't go the way we expect it to, we can suddenly feel hit with a reality that is both painful and disappointing. If your dark night of the soul was a result of someone else's deception or betrayal, you will need to find the seeds of forgiveness in order to avoid a calloused heart. Our wounds are temporary when we allow them to heal. Release yourself from any guilt you may feel about the situation. You didn't have all the information. When we realize that the career, relationship, solution, or direction we were working toward is no longer an option, it's easy to focus on the loss and allow our energy to stagnate and spiral into self-pity. *Don't allow your life force to drain away with the things you once loved.* Allow your tender heart to navigate toward the curative magic of acceptance and possibility and have faith that wonderful new experiences are coming your way. Be willing to see the lessons in this. If you are having a hard time letting go (and losing your ability to dream as a result!) then it's time to untether your heart from your fragmented expectations and give yourself permission to envision a brighter future. Dismantle your grief, reclaim your happiness, and consciously step back onto a path filled with hope.

MY TENDER HEART HELPS ME TO ~ NaVIGaTe ~ TOWARDS MY BRIGHT FUTURE

QUESTIONS FOR THE SEER

- Sweet spark, what would happen if you gathered all your life-force energy and brought it close to your heart? If you said no to allowing it to slip away? If you plugged the draining energy and actively reclaimed it all?
- Taking the time you need to grieve losses can be difficult. Are you finding time in this fast-paced world to process, integrate, and grow?
- Actively look for your bright future. Make a list of the things you love to do and the people you love to be with. Is there anything on this list that has clues to your next steps?

DAWN —
· Sun is on the way

RAINBOW CUP OF HEALING and POTENTIAL

→ THE PATH BACK HOME IS EASY TO SEE

— SPIRIT / ESSENCE (she allows it to drain)

— cracks in soil (situation dried up)

— BLACK AND WHITE WELL (Seeing things in absolutes, YIN/YANG duality. eventually darkness turns to Light)

5 of Cups

COSMOS / DREAMS, The Universe changing timelines

PLAID SHIRTS
· Remembering past, HERITAGE (tartans)

CHILDHOOD MEMORIES
· cuddles AND puppies

Rainbow cups
· possibilities, magic sent from past or future

GOLD CUP
current timeline

NOTES FROM the PAST

INNER CHILD and FUTURE SELF

6 of Cups

6 of Cups

LIGHT SEER: nostalgia, memories, reconnecting with people from the past, harmony, themes of your life, inner child and future self

SHADOW SEER: living in the past, lamenting decisions and actions, a need to forgive others, a reminder to forgive yourself, letting people in, a need to deal with regret, sadness and guilt

A CUPS STORY

He sits with the timeline of his life stretching before him. The past lovers, friendships, the family—the wounds. He stares into the past, wonders about the future, and contemplates, silently, *How does it all connect*? He remembers a special childhood friend he once loved. The old flame. He misses his younger self for a moment. Life was simpler then. *But wait, isn't that old version still alive inside of him?* Isn't that carefree, easy life still available to him now? He knows, on some level, that he is revisiting old stories because they hold a lesson for him. They offer a perspective or an idea he could use today. He glimpses his repeating patterns, and he sees both where he has stumbled and the progress he's made, and he finds a newfound compassion for his inner child. His dog, with its gift of living fully in the moment, nudges him as if to say, *"Hey friend, we are here in the present."* Too much energy spent reminiscing about the past or imagining the future will only keep him from enjoying the time he has right now, so he gathers all the teachings, blesses the memories, and comes back to embody presence. *It's good to be here.*

MESSAGE FROM THE 6 OF CUPS

Your past is likely coming into focus, and you may be feeling nostalgic about days gone by. What lessons do they hold for you today? Who you were will highlight how far you've come, and that growth can shine beauty on where you are headed next. The

6 of Cups reminds you that it's time to forgive yourself by releasing any residual guilt that you still carry from past relationships, traumas, or previous actions. Accepting your humanness is the best place to start! Give yourself permission to stop lamenting the decisions that you've made up until now, as fresh slates and new beginnings are always available to you. Focus on cherishing the kind and joyful moments that have shaped you, for time is a beautiful thing. *Contemplate the needs of your inner child or listen to advice from your future self.* These versions of you are profound gateways to healing and will offer wise guidance on things that need to be forgiven and understood. Our inner child usually wants us to play more, to lighten up and find our laughter! Sometimes this card is a literal message that someone from your past—an old friend, partner, colleague, or even an old challenge—is going to re-enter your life. It may be the perfect moment to reconnect and reminisce. Sometimes, remembering our roots is the only way to remain grounded in a rapidly changing world. And sometimes, only when we connect with all the moments on our timeline (past, present, and future) can we truly find our wholeness.

I am at Peace with my Past, It Has Brought me where I am meant To Be

QUESTIONS FOR THE SEER
- What memories are coming into your mind? Can you connect them to your present situation?
- Write your inner child a letter explaining how wonderful things will be and at what stages they will need to grow, learn, and persevere.
- Can you look back and, instead of seeing the missteps and things you would change, recognize how far you have come?

7 of Cups

LIGHT SEER: choices, wishful thinking, fantasies and illusions, the allure of temptation on the path, needing to move forward without knowing the full picture, options and opportunities

SHADOW SEER: feeling blocked by indecision, fear of making the wrong choice, overwhelm

A CUPS STORY

Carefully, oh so carefully, he tries to keep his eye on his Cup as the Universe shuffles them around. Where did he place his lucky talisman again? Underneath one of these Cups is the path he selected for his best future, if only he could remember which one he placed it under. Which was the one that leads to success? Which one looks like it leads that way, *but actually doesn't?* He tries to remember if he preferred the Cup with the spiritual focus or the one that was filled with diamonds and riches, pondering over the Cup that looks like it may include both. Like the Cup memory game, even when he tries to keep his eye on the prize, the Cups shift and evolve, and it's hard to remember where his original intentions lie. He realizes there is nothing to do but get back to his center and let go of what he thought he wanted. He must pay attention to where he is right now and make a choice from that perspective. The rest is just an illusion.

MESSAGE FROM THE 7 OF CUPS

When you daydream your way into the future, the options that you have in front of you can feel both under- and overwhelming. The path from A to Z is often nebulous, and life can present itself like a game of chutes and ladders that brings you down only to lift you up again. Your desire to choose the correct path—the perfect path— can further complicate and muddle your decision, because there is no way to know

everything that will spill forth from the Cup you choose! Use your intuition to decide—remembering that the temptation of shiny things can be illusory, while challenging paths will often hold unexpected opportunity and lead to incredible experiences, growth, or wisdom. Ask your discerning heart what options honestly stand in front of you today, as this card shows up when there are *many* possibilities waiting to be seen and reflected upon. In shadow, you may feel some confusion around where you're headed. It's time to see past any distraction or fantastical notions and move purposefully ahead with a plan. If you feel swayed by the opinions of others, give preference to your own inner voice, and then decide. Even if things are not exactly as they seem, choosing what you truly desire will offer the most useful stepping stone right now. Move in the direction of that which feels expansive.

My wildest imagination is a tool that I can use to inform my future in a down-to-earth way

QUESTIONS FOR THE SEER

- This card often shows up when it's time to make a move. What are the pros and cons of each of the options before you? Which one is your best choice right now?
- Are you taking inspired action toward that dream you want? Or are you pouring too much energy simply deciding and dreaming of what could be?
- All the gifts you could ever desire lay hidden under those Cups. You get to select one to move toward today. Which thing would you choose above all others?

SKULL on CUP: · victory over death

7 of Cups

LADDERS: option to Rise / elevate

7 HIDDEN CHOICES

DRAGON WING : Power, magic or inner demons

LAUREL WREATH : Victory, success

MASK : the veil, things we can't see, mysticism

CRYSTALS : an ORACLE, spiritual Lessons

PEARLS : wealth, money

SNAKE : Rebirth AND transformation

CASTLE : home, safety, goals, achievements

~ HOW TO ~
BOWL BURNING CEREMONY

· Write down the things you want to LET GO OF AND BURN THEM

8 of Cups

- SUNRISE : (a new life on the way!)

7 OTHER CUPS (OR THEIR SHADOWS): IN THE WATER, ALREADY SINKING

8 of Cups

LIGHT SEER: letting go, releasing that which no longer serves you, a ritual releasing, moving stuck energy, walking away, leaving your old reality to pursue a new one, abandonment, disappointment

SHADOW SEER: walking away and then regretting your choice, feeling stuck in your current reality, fears that block your momentum. feeling caged, escapism, avoidance

A CUPS STORY

She has released her eighth and final Cup into the sea, and her Burning Bowl ceremony has come to a close. There were seven bowls before this one: seven days and nights to build her new vision for her life, and seven ceremonies to let go of old habits, feelings, beliefs, and ideas. And while she's not totally sure that she's quite there yet, she knows she feels more empowered than she ever has before. These rituals have cleansed her heart and spirit, and she understands that she deserves much more than she's been settling for lately. She feels so powerful in this moment that she doesn't even feel compelled to watch that last bowl dip its way into the sea. She knows what fate has in store for it: a complete submerging and then washing away. She knows the water will cleanse any sign of its presence, and the only thing that will remain is her memory of it. Her muscles tend to store the things she remembers, so she vows to actively create new experiences to recall—reflections to be called upon and enjoyed. She will look back on this moment for years to come—the moment when her past held so little power over her that she walked away before the burning was even complete. She no longer needs this purification, and she now chooses her own path. She is already growing beyond this current version of herself.

MESSAGE FROM THE 8 OF CUPS

Is it time to walk away from something in your life? Choosing your sacred dream—especially when you're feeling disappointed—is one of the biggest acts of self-love that you can enact. When you take that very first step, you begin to choose yourself, and there is nothing more healing or more powerful! Find your resolve and untether any anchors that are holding you back. Though your disillusioned heart may require some TLC, you can realign your path by shedding outgrown expectations, hopes, people, ideas, beliefs, guilt, or ways of being. If you find yourself exhausted or confused—or jumping from thing to thing—know that you are entering a mystical period of intense shifting and that releasing old stories will help you to travel lightly. Electrifying new futures are waiting to be discovered! Go in the direction of epic dreams, happiness, and greater meaning. True fulfilment can only be found when you take a chance on your dream . . . and on yourself.

I walk away from negativity and choose myself in a rebellious act of self love

QUESTIONS FOR THE SEER

• How often do your place your needs ahead of others?

• Do you hold on to things long after your time with them has come to an end?

• Imagine your life as an epic adventure, and the closing credits have you walking off into a sunset. What have you just accomplished? Who are you with?

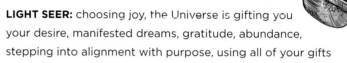

9 of Cups

LIGHT SEER: choosing joy, the Universe is gifting you your desire, manifested dreams, gratitude, abundance, stepping into alignment with purpose, using all of your gifts

SHADOW SEER: delayed gratification, unfulfilled desires, unmanifested dreams, greed blocking your path, wheeling and dealing, not appreciating the simple things in life, smugness

A CUPS STORY

Floating in her visionary dream state, she sees nine Cups in front of her carrying all the things she's been dreaming of. Bliss. Transcendence. Wealth. Love. Her heart explodes with emotion, and its energy spills into the nine beautiful vessels. *All the gifts. All the love.* She used to believe that these Cups were guarded by the Universe and that she would have to choose between them. She used to believe that she could only have some of these things, some of the time. But now she sees that they were all created by her, for her, and through her. She recognizes her love in all of them—her own heartbeat vibrates in their carved surfaces, and her own joy is embedded among the jewels. Her creator nature has generated these sacred gifts, and it is her own essence that allows them to flourish—or not. She realizes that her choice today is more about priorities, focus, and clear intention than it is about choosing one thing over another. She realizes that the world really is her oyster, and that she is being gifted the opportunity to choose which gift she wants to experience *first.*

MESSAGE FROM THE 9 OF CUPS

Yes! Those dreams you've been dreaming? Those aspirations you've been envisioning? They are headed your way, and you will be able to enjoy their blessings as a result. What have you been yearning for? This is a card of abundance and happiness, and is often, fittingly, called "the wish card." Do a happy dance, because the Universe is granting wishes and bestowing contentment! Allow yourself to experience how fulfilling this journey can be, and infuse your life with all the laughter and bliss needed to lift you into the next phase of your prosperity. Take stock of all of the feelings that are surfacing, and remember to practice gratitude for the manifestation of your dreams. While the appearance of this card in your spread is an auspicious message of harmony and getting what you desire, sometimes it may point to smugness or to having too much focus on material gain. If you are experiencing any dissatisfaction, frustration, or feeling unfulfilled, be sure that you are not missing out on opportunities to connect from your heart. Remember that true joy stems from connection. Nurture relationships, and find your 9 of Cups of joy by sharing yourself and your gifts with others. Even in shadow, this auspicious card suggests that good things are on the way. Open your heart to receive them!

I open my GRATEFUL HEART to THE GIFTS THAT ARE COMING MY WAY

QUESTIONS FOR THE SEER

- If a magic lamp came into your life to grant one wish, what would you ask for?
- Start keeping track of the proof that your dream is coming to you. What signs of its arrival have you recently received?
- Daily gratitude will guide you to this 9 of Cups place. How is your relationship with gratitude? If it's "been there, done that" or if you're just not feeling it, what's getting in the way of your thankfulness?
- If you've been knocking on the door of gratitude and the door's not opening, reflect on your approach. Are you saying, "I am grateful, but . . ."? How can you express gratitude without caveat or complaint?

9 CUPS of JOY

COLORS

YELLOW: JOY, HAPPINESS, SUCCESS, Positive emotions.

● BLUE: WISDOM, TRUTH, STABILITY, SERENITY. BLUE HAIR: AUTHENTIC EXPRESSION

○ SHIMMERING DRESS: FULL of LIGHT, a BRIGHT aura

◐ GOLD: SUCCESS, SPIRITUAL ATTAINMENT

WATER = REALM of the EMOTIONS

HEART CHAKRA energy

TREASURE CHEST abundance AND WISHES GRANTED

9 of Cups

} THIS JOY CAN BE CULTIVATED!

10 CUPS of LOVE

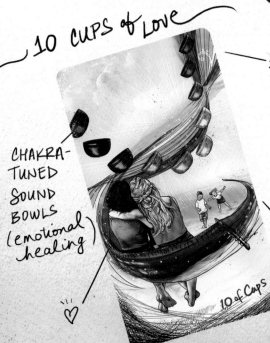

CHAKRA-TUNED SOUND BOWLS (emotional healing)

♡

10 of Cups

BASS CLEF HAMMOCK
· the Bass is the LOWER Part of a song that HOLDS the RHYTHMIC and HARMONIC foundations together. It also creates emotional impact.
(Love, harmony)

RAINBOW:
JOY, LOVE, DIVERSE types of families. Relationships AND DREAMS

10 of Cups

LIGHT SEER: community, love, soulmates, harmony in relationships and family, Divine connections, heart opening and expansion, wholeness, completion

SHADOW SEER: disharmony or disputes, miscommunication, struggling relationships, unrealistic expectations, not feeling worthy of love, a delay

A CUPS STORY

She breathes in acceptance. Total and utter acceptance. Her fears of rejection have long since washed away. She relaxes into her rainbow hammock and notices that she is living one of *those* moments. Her heart fills with gratitude. Right now, everything feels absolutely perfect. She opens her awareness to her surroundings. The sun is shining at just the right angle, and the rays of light are playing tricks with the sand and the dust. There are magical shimmers of the Divine everywhere she looks. "This is it," she tells herself, "I am exactly where I am meant to be." Her children laugh in the distance. Her partner's unwavering devotion wraps her in warmth. Her feelings about herself and the things she wants are aligned and clear . . . and everything falls into place. She smiles and pushes her feet in the sand, rocking the hammock lazily. "I love you," she whispers in her partner's ear, and leans into this moment, hoping to commit it to memory forever. The Universe beams love.

MESSAGE FROM THE 10 OF CUPS

What a time of harmony and wholeness! This card has the powerful energy of connected hearts, giant love, and devoted acceptance. Often seen as the "one big happy family" card, it's a giant **yes** for relationships and love, and it predicts your fairy-tale ending. (And hey, you get to decide what this soulmates-and-unicorns ending looks like!) When seeking alignment—or realignment—within relationships, let your common values guide your heart's expansion, and watch the energy flow with abundance and ease. Allow your heart's energy to pour into all your connections, including those with your community. In shadow, this card suggests that you need to look at how you feel about yourself within your relationships. If you are looking for a "white picket fence" in order to find happiness, remember that your joy will come only from the inside out. By waiting for other people (or better things!) to create your happiness for you, you undermine your own power to create feelings of emotional fulfilment. And you, sweet light, are *more than capable* of bringing these feelings to your life daily. Welcome gratitude and generosity. Every. Single. Day. Spend time focusing on those you love, and gift them your heart energy through time, kindness, and loving service to find your truest joy. *Are you ready to walk into the sunset with your favs?*

I LIVE IN a STATE of ONENESS BY BRINGING HARMONY AND love to my relationships.

QUESTIONS FOR THE SEER
- What does your happy ending look like?
- Do you have true clarity on the types of relationships that you desire to nurture?
- What can you do to make your current relationships flow a little more smoothly? How can you bring more love into your daily interactions? What attitude can you adopt (or disown) as a way to make things resound a little more joyously?

Page of Cups

LIGHT SEER: new unexpected trajectories, a dreamer, serendipity, creativity, magic and synchronicity, an open and joyful heart, sensitivity and naivete in romance, being motivated by innovative ideas

SHADOW SEER: missing the signs, being overly sensitive, displaying childish emotions, blocked creativity

A CUPS STORY

He sits at his favorite thinking spot, allowing his imagination to drift. He has a crush on everything. All the styles. All the ideas. All of his dreams. And that girl he saw skipping while reading comic books? He has a crush on her too. Life is such a fascinating journey with so many things to be enamored by. He is in a dreamy flow with his Universe, and because of this flow he manifests easily. His fast fruition makes it easy-peasy to not become overly attached to specific outcomes, so he is often gifted with unexpected and delightful surprises in his life. He knows that a new love may pop into his life at any moment, and that the miraculous will always happen in the most unexpected of ways. He imagines his future timeline as a beautiful symphony of delightful tales, and looking across dimensions he calls forth the experience that he would like to explore. He knows the world is offering them, so *why wouldn't they be meant for him too?* He hops down from his spot, ready for whatever unexpected adventure crosses his path next. His heart waxes poetic with all the possibilities, and inspiration floods his emotions once again.

MESSAGE FROM THE PAGE OF CUPS

There is serendipity and magic here. Like the first breath of hope or a very first kiss, anything is possible at this time. Be open to wildly wonderful miracles. This is the "when-pigs-fly card," and holding it in your hands is a sign that unforeseen (yet fortuitous!) events are coming your way. Cultivate your childlike enthusiasm for the unknown and welcome any unexpected twists on your journey. Don't be surprised if you find yourself drawn to the unique, the quirky, and the eclectic! Be open to inspiration from the strangest of places, and pay attention to the intuitive musings that arrive—for they will give your creativity wings. As you enjoy this time of strangely unique thinking, ensure that you are not being overly sensitive or allowing immature emotional reactions to sabotage your flow. (Temper tantrums? You're better off without them.) Allow your emotions to follow the breadcrumbs of joy. And don't block your own flow because you are trying to control the process. Play a little more. Do something silly. Stay curious and brave in the face of unknown endings, and note any feelings of wonder and awe. It's time for your inner sensitive dreamer to dream! Embracing magic, have faith in the fact that you can attract miracles.

The WORLD IS MY MAGICKAL OYSTER AND I'M EXCITED TO SEE WHAT FLOURISHES NEXT

QUESTIONS FOR THE SEER

- When the pig flies or the fish jumps, do you stare in disbelief? Or do you claim it as a sign from the Universe and run with the magical coincidence?
- In what situations are you less emotionally mature than you'd like? What triggers this response? How could you better handle things?
- Are you being overly sensitive about your current situation?
- Serendipity knocks. Do you recognize the stirrings of magic when the Universe sends it your way? Start to log it! Take note of all the subtle magic in your life.
- What sign—if you received it in the next few weeks—would help you to really believe in the miracle of synchronicity or manifestation?

"WHEN PIGS FLY"
The pig is flying!
- A highly favorable time for miracles

COLORFUL WILD HAIR:
- expression AND creativity

MAGICAL SYMBOLS: ☆
- positive thoughts
- dreams and wishes
- magical outcomes likely

SPLIT LEGS: MANIFESTING TIMELINE AND PERSPECTIVE SHIFTS

POSSIBILITY of NEW CONNECTIONS AND LOVE

atomic Quantum leaps or a celtic knot

NEWS, MAGIC

B O T H   M E S S E N G E R S

PROPOSALS

Roses AND CHAMPAGNE: a classic Romantic

HERMES WINGS ON SHOES:
- swift communication
- connection
- moving between Realms

Page of Cups

Knight of Cups

DANCING: HORSE EXPRESSION!

INVITATION ON THE WAY!

Knight of Cups

LIGHT SEER: a classic romantic, a passionate soul, artistic tendencies, creativity, wearing your heart on your sleeve, seeking connection, being in love with the idea of love, chivalry, an unexpected invitation or message

SHADOW SEER: missing the signs, protecting your heart, not being open to love, a player, a jealous partner, moodiness, sulking, negative emotions blocking your progress, disappointment

A CUPS STORY

Poem? *Check.* Wine? *Check.* Strawberries? *Yep.* He wants this to be perfect. It's not every day that you declare your undying love to someone. Intuitively, he loves this idea. This picnic and setting. This beautiful feeling that is falling in love. And oh boy, is he falling! He's head over heels, and so excited about the future. He feels a little nervous, but in his heart, he knows that she will melt with this gesture. Part of him worries, however, that she may think it's too soon for this sort of overture—and for this level of commitment. He knows that he has given his heart away too quickly in the past and that some people have seen him as too needy or emotionally starved. *"None of which are true, of course,"* he reminds himself, shaking his head. *"I am like this with all kinds of love, not just ones that involve people. I feel this passion deeply for my ideas, my desires, and my dreams."* Contrary to what society would expect of him, he doesn't restrain his feelings. And today, on this perfectly romantic afternoon, he is in love with being in love.

MESSAGE FROM THE KNIGHT OF CUPS

This classic romantic invites you to step into a world of roses, bubble baths, and champagne, and is fully devoted to you for today. And maybe for every day! This card heralds romance and embodies the graceful movement of a slow dance. Enjoy this flirtation and be present to connect. This Knight is intuitive and totally in touch with his emotions. As such, he knows what he wants, and he has no problem wearing his heart on his sleeve. This card often signifies someone who is passionate and expressive, and who is in love with the idea of love itself. It can also signify a passion or hobby. Sometimes this energy comes bundled with unrealistic expectations that are difficult to meet, and sometimes, it is an invitation to step into a more artistic and expressive life. Proposals are likely, so listen to your heart and respond with both diplomacy and authenticity. Are you ready to be swept off your feet and to allow deep honesty and vulnerability to flow freely in your life? Do you believe in this type of true love? Get ready to take inspiration and run with it—to make art, music, and love, and your veritable masterpiece of life.

I AM IN TOUCH WITH MY EMOTIONS

QUESTIONS FOR THE SEER

- Do you trust love when the opportunity presents itself? Do you believe in true love? How do you feel about the deep honesty and vulnerability that accompanies love?
- When are you the most guarded? And when are you not guarded enough?
- What are the telltale signs of a player or of someone who is not the right partner in your current circumstance? And what are the telltale signs of someone who *is* right?

Queen of Cups

LIGHT SEER: extremely intuitive, sensitivity, strength, a highly attuned emotional intelligence, love and compassion, leading with your heart, empathy, healing

SHADOW SEER: controlling or suppressing emotions, feeling insecure, a need to listen more, emotional blackmail, being melodramatic, irrationality, an opportunity to be responsible for your own emotions

A CUPS STORY

The Queen sits floating in the water, halfway between her intuitive mind and her emotional body. She sits listening to the cues from her heart and channels its wisdom to heal the kingdom around her. She has always been a masterful healer, as healing is a natural result of the way she loves and connects so deeply. She floats, attuned to the messages from Spirit. There are so many ways of seeing and feeling, and while her third eye is aligned and alive, she knows that her most important nudges arrive from deep within the heart chakra. As her telepathic heart begins to expand, her red dress ripples out around her, seeming to move in time with the rhythm of her heartbeat. The waves and fish respond to her benevolent and compassionate frequency, and she closes her eyes softly, tuning in to *your* heart so that she can sense your innermost feelings. As a true empath, she will mirror them back to you while she nurtures and supports your dreams. She has always navigated the world based on what has felt right to her, trusting her own emotional sensitivities. Her gentle empathy and loving kindness have always steered her in the truest direction.

MESSAGE FROM THE QUEEN OF CUPS

The Queen of Cups is one of the most intuitive characters of the tarot, drifting in her dreamlike state of spiritual connection. She asks you how well your emotions have been serving you lately and reminds you that you have the ability to connect with your environment on a much deeper level: *Emotionally. Intuitively. Spiritually. Lovingly.* Step into flow and resonance, and begin engaging with the world in unprecedented ways! Choose to feel and accept your emotional intuition, consciously remaining present to your reality. This will allow you to lead the vibration that emanates from your heart center, *always in charge of your emotional charge*, regardless of the state of others. Listen deeply to hear what is truly going on and ensure that other people feel seen and heard by devoting time to their emotional cues. There is Divine beauty in all of life's experiences with the senses . . . it takes both sun and shadow to make the ocean floor sparkle, so allow yourself to feel all your feelings. In shadow, this card can indicate that you may be out of touch with your emotions, or that you are suppressing your feelings while refusing to see the obvious. If you sense any insecurities about openly connecting with others, grow into a better partner by vulnerably sharing your own tender heart. Your unconditional and pure expressions of love will bring you new opportunities to connect, lead, and expand.

My INTUITIVE HEART openLY expResses Deep Love AND compassion

QUESTIONS FOR THE SEER

- How tuned in is your emotional intelligence? In what ways does it guide your steps, your path, and your life? In what specific situations does it falter?
- Does your intuition come from your head? Or your heart? From deep inside you or from outside of yourself in signs and synchronicities? Can you sense the difference between intuition that stems from your third eye and intuition that arises from the heart?
- If you had an opportunity to listen to your heart chakra, what would it say?

—the UNDINE—

This Queen was inspired by the "UNDINES"— mythical water elementals who resides in lakes, oceans, AND rivers. They purify and energetically charge water, and they can help us with emotional healing, love, and opening up our intuition.

WATER SYMBOL ON FOREHEAD

RED emotions, HEART

PURPLE intuition, CROWN CHAKRA

Queen of Cups

meditation: energy healing hands

VIBRATING HEART
• Heart waves radiating love and in a state of COHERENCE.

PLAYING SOUND BOWL: sharing healing frequencies —

FISH: SPIRITUALITY, PEACE, ADAPTABILITY

DEEP OCEAN (depth of his emotions and WISDOM)

King of Cups

—EVEN WITH STORMY SEAS HE REMAINS CALM

STARFISH navigation, INTUITION, REGENERATIVE HEALING

King of Cups

LIGHT SEER: love, generosity, emotional intelligence, being nurturing, patience, experience, stability and balance, creativity, diplomacy, someone supportive, a wise leader

SHADOW SEER: a drama king, withdrawn, not in touch with emotions, being triggered, temperamental, an opportunity to work with the subconscious mind and dive into self-care, manipulation and moodiness

A CUPS STORY

He softens his gaze and reaches for his singing bowl. When something unexpected comes into the King of Cups' awareness—something that might shake another person's composure and send them into a state of stress or anger—he regulates his emotional state with his calm, practiced, mature, and meditative energy. Warm. Cheerful. Devoted. He consciously fills his heart with the energy of compassion, and he smiles. He has been practicing holding this state a little longer every day for years. He closes his eyes with a deep breath, and his heart softens into peace. He knows that his emotions are the key to his intuition, and that his intuition is the key to his successful leadership. He shepherds others with a gentle hand, choosing to guide with a loving heart and modelling the way through being and doing. From his deep wisdom comes the breadth of his experience, and he finds balance and tranquility in daily life, even when tumultuous energies arise, which allows him to lead from a place of inner stillness.

MESSAGE FROM THE KING OF CUPS

Finding the sweet spot between your empathic heart and your intelligent mind is the key to this card's wisdom. Allow your emotional intelligence to guide you as you seek to marry logic, kindness, and love. You may be called to lead others at this time. Stepping successfully into this role will require relaxed flexibility and your ability to assert your ideas in a peaceful, nonconfrontational way. If you are in a situation that asks you to navigate turbulent energies, find your serenity by calmly choosing care and diplomacy over force. You are being asked to flow around obstacles and employ compassionate and influential energy. What do you need to do to find this type of peace? Mindful practices? Getting to yoga class or spending some time among the trees? Even time with trusted companions can help to bring that consistent stream of laughter and peace into your world. In shadow, this King can suggest that you may be feeling withdrawn, moody, or temperamental—or you may be losing touch with how others are feeling at this time. Stay clear of situations that feel emotionally manipulative, and rethink relationships that are not filling your Cup with energy, love, or joy. Instead, seek to understand others through empathy, tolerance, and compassion . . . and emotional fulfillment will be yours. Know that the things you cannot change may simply not be meant for you at this time. The Cosmos likely has something even more heartwarming and blissful in store for you, so move in the direction of your positive emotions. If old wounds are resurfacing to be healed, be gentle with yourself and take all the time you need as you listen for the loving nudges of your magnificent heart. They *will* guide you in the right direction.

My heart holds deep wisdom and Love, and I use it to CONNECT AND LeaD

QUESTIONS FOR THE SEER
- What does your heart's intelligence tell you about your situation? Ask it. Listen. And write it down.
- Who embodies this King's wisdom, compassion, loving kindness, or unconditional, nurturing guidance in your life?
- What gestures demonstrate the regulated, resilient energy of this card? Which of these can you share with others?
- What is your leadership style? How can you invite more King of Cups wisdom into your actions?

Swords

ELEMENT: Air

ASSOCIATED WITH:

communication, thought, observation and perception,
logic, strategy, the mind, psychology, ideas,
awareness, challenges

$$\phi = \frac{1}{\sqrt{2}}\begin{pmatrix} \phi^1 + i\phi^2 \\ \phi^0 + i\phi^3 \end{pmatrix}$$

Ace of Swords

LIGHT SEER: new ideas, clarity, an "aha" moment, truth revealed, awareness and heightened states of consciousness, memory or thought, communication, victory, success and triumph, a stroke of genius

SHADOW SEER: overanalyzing, getting stalled out or stuck, clouded judgement, keeping truth inside

A SWORDS STORY

For the Ace of Swords, there is nothing that can compete with the fierce rays of wisdom and truth. She sits quietly at the bottom of the golden spiral staircase, waiting for clarity to arrive. *An illumination.* It will arrive quickly, because insight and higher thinking flow naturally here, in her brightly spiraling Fibonacci gateway. This is the entry point where creative solutions arrive, and where she experiences colossal Divine downloads. Here, all of her systems align, and the secrets of the Universe flow through. She sees glimpses of her Higher Self, and she is granted access to the Akashic Records in full waking consciousness. With rapidly fluttering eyelids, she begins to see through all distraction while her neurons fire transmissions of intuition, intelligence, and truth. When she is in this state, her logical mind feels totally activated and alive, assembling data together in visionary ways that feel transformative. Her ability to receive information is mirrored by the widening of her throat chakra. She will soon translate and clearly communicate this as well. Light begins to shine out to the world, and thought emerges swiftly. She feels a smile form, and her brain begins to buzz, *understanding.*

MESSAGE FROM THE ACE OF SWORDS

Massive clarity is on the way. A new door is opening for you, often unveiling a life-changing idea or a significant spiritual breakthrough. Expect "aha" moments of lucidity to pierce your awareness and to reveal a totally fresh vision for the future. Trust this clarity to propel you forward. The Ace of Swords illuminates deep truths with laser-like precision, and this improved thinking may significantly shift your paradigm. As this essence spirals into comprehension, use this time to see things as they really are and to tune in to new beginnings. The quiet insight of the unconscious mind is being made available for you, so you may experience a rapid expansion as your conscious mind integrates this newfound information. Is your thinking mind helping you achieve your goals? Have you been waiting for an answer? Know that it's on the way! Nothing can compete with the fierce rays of wisdom and truth, so if you are finding yourself with clouded judgement or with stalled thinking, it's time to seek the brightly lit energy of honesty. Gather your discernment, your intellect, your logic, and your insight, and clearly communicate the truth that is bubbling up to be witnessed.

I EXPERIENCE BRILLIANT MOMENTS of CLARITY

QUESTIONS FOR THE SEER
- In what areas of your life do you obscure your own clarity? And why?
- Clarity happens when you better understand yourself and the way you connect with the world. If you were to draw a set of lines between you and those around you, and make a note of how you see others and how they see you, what would you notice? What roles are you playing? And do they serve your desires?
- This card signals a big lightbulb moment is coming to you. What will you do to ground it and make it real?

SUMBOLS for THE MIND

ALCHEMIST'S 3 PRIMES
(WHICH EVERYTHING IS MADE OF)

🜍   ☿   🜔

SULFUR   MERCURY   SALT
(SOUL)   (SPIRIT)   (BODY)

TREE of LIFE · SPIRITUAL JOURNEY

CHAOS STAR · MAGICK UNDERLYING PATTERNS IN RANDOMNESS

$\phi = \frac{1}{\sqrt{2}}\left(\begin{smallmatrix}\phi^1 + i\phi^2 \\ \phi^0 + i\phi^3\end{smallmatrix}\right)$ EQUATION · PART OF THE HIGG'S FIELD CALCULATIONS (THE GOD PARTICLE)

GOLDEN RATIO STAIRS for EVOLUTION IN PERFECT FORM and TIMING

Ace of Swords

THE GOD ODIN'S TWO RAVEN ANIMAL GUIDES PULL HER IN TWO DIFFERENT DIRECTIONS

Named 'Huginn' (THOUGHT)

Named 'Muninn' (MEMORY)

2 of Swords

TATTOO: 2 AIR SYMBOLS CROSSED, TROUBLE ACESSING the MIND and THINKING

DIVINATION WITH SAND DOESN'T SHOW A CLEAR DIRECTION

2 of Swords

LIGHT SEER: stalemate, a crossroads, making a difficult choice, opposing ideas or options, choosing the best route of action, memory and thought

SHADOW SEER: the angst of the unknown, between a rock and a hard place, fear of commitment

A SWORDS STORY

Which way do I go? She stands at the crossroads of two paths, totally unsure of the future. The two choices take her in vastly different directions, and she needs to figure out which road is the right one to travel. Normally, this feels easier, but these paths look like they lead to two options that are equally as wonderful . . . *or was that equally as difficult?* She sways, confused, and feels the rising pressure of her decision. Night is creeping in, and she must get off this road before dark. Looking back and forth at the barren landscape, she calls out to the elements to help guide her. *"Dear Universe, Help me choose."* She struggles to hear the whispers in the wind. There are no clues to be found in the sand. There is no answer from her intuition except for its growing silence. When the wind finally stirs, it brings with it two crows, and she is reminded of Odin's familiars, Huginn and Muninn. The pair would bring him daily accounts of their bird's eye view of the landscape. One crow brings her memories to the surface and pulls her to the east. The other brings her logical thoughts to the surface and pulls her to the west. Feeling even more stuck, blocked, and confused, the two opposing crows remind her that she is the only one who can make this decision. They whisper that *whatever she chooses will be the right decision for her.* Because this is how the Universe works.

MESSAGE FROM THE 2 OF SWORDS

Decide. Decide now. You know that feeling of not knowing? It's time to make a choice, even if it seems like you are between a rock and hard place. If you can't decide which way to go, it's likely because you can't see the bigger picture . . . yet. The 2 of Swords is whispering that you must choose to move in one direction. If outside opinions are pulling to you toward different paths, close your eyes and listen to your internal guidance system for your map. And if your intuition has fallen unusually silent, it's asking you to trust yourself and your ability to discern and decide. In shadow, this card counsels to take your time weighing your options . . . *but not too much time.* Even blindfolded, you already know the best way forward! By avoiding this decision, you are only able to react to the shifting landscape around you, instead of taking a role in steering and guiding it. Plot your path with the information you have and commit to taking those first few steps. As you begin to move, the bigger picture will reveal itself to you. Have faith that the Universe is serving you the right experience, and that it will help you move forward safely. At the crossroads of duality, your analysis and overthinking will just get you buried in the quicksand of a million possible endings, so find peace of mind by trusting your judgement.

WHen BLINDED BY THE UNKNOWN, I TRUST myself To find the LIGHT

QUESTIONS FOR THE SEER
- Are you stuck between options? When you write a list of pros and cons, and then add your lists of wants, needs, and loves, what happens?
- Do you trust yourself when your intuition feels like it's offline?

3 of Swords

LIGHT SEER: painful separation, loss, heartbreak, an opportunity to heal, shadows coming to light, finding inspiration again

SHADOW SEER: not accepting loss, a need to heal, being stuck in your grief or sadness, not seeing the part you played in your circumstances

A SWORDS STORY

Heartbroken, she falls to her knees and screams to the Universe for a second chance. *What happened? Why did she have this taken from her?* Her heart aches, and she cycles through the emotions that surface. Sadness, anger, guilt, shame, grief . . . she looks up at the gray sky that answers back only with hollow gusts of wind. *Empty.* She watches the branches that have dropped their leaves, noticing that the birds have long since left. Following the roots down into the earth, she wonders if the roots are still alive. She wonders if they will ever bloom again. *Someday, maybe. When the Spring arrives?* Reaching out for the earth, she pleads for healing. . . *Will I, too, feel better by Spring? Please relieve me of these memories. This feeling. A moment of reprieve . . . of peace.* A gentle pulse pushes up through her palms and beckons her to feel. **Healing happens now.** She surrenders to the warmth of the earth and tethers herself to her broken heart, remembering for the first time in a long time that it *will* mend. It always does. And when it does, it will lead her to the peace that she desires.

MESSAGE FROM THE 3 OF SWORDS

Separation can come in many forms. From the loss of a relationship or identity, to the painful disintegration of belief, purpose, or goals, to separation from what we thought we once had can mark painful moments in our lives. If you find yourself amid wavering realities and losing something that feels near and dear to your heart, know that this, too, shall pass. This severing, although painful, is a necessary part of the process. Despite all proof to the contrary, your brightly lit future will arrive in spite of this experience. Sometimes it arrives *as a result* of this experience, and with more vibrance and light, because contrast is a powerful teacher. Sometimes, a conscious mental shift and a new direction will need to be taken in order to grow and evolve with this energy. Stitch yourself to your light and prepare to spend some time nurturing your tender spirit. These shadowy times are always opportunities to become stronger and more resilient, so give yourself time to heal, process, and evolve. And know that you will love, thrive, and find inspiration again soon.

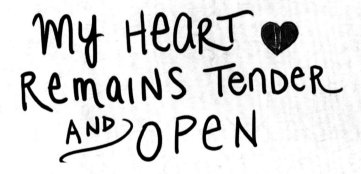

QUESTIONS FOR THE SEER

- Beautiful seer, it's time to purge those emotions. Drum. Dance. Scream. Write it. Burn it. What will you do to make sure these feelings move through your body and that they don't settle in for the long haul?
- Painful punches to the gut can have you blaming everyone and everything else for what happened. Gently ask your heart, What have you contributed to your current situation?
- How will you remain open for connection as you knit together these wounds?
- Have you been responsible for someone else's 3 of Swords moment? Maybe it's time to send an apology. Sometimes our deepest wounds lie in someone else's pain.

BARREN
Landscape
AND TREE

3 BIRDS IN the
DISTANCE
• something Lost

• feelings of
DESPAIR,
Loneliness

• a SITUATION
WILL BEAR
NO FRUIT

STORMY SKY
• challenges,
obstacles

TIED TO HER HEART
• challenging emotions,
grief

3 of Swords

Same RED
THREADS
that sewed
her heart
in the 3 of
swords now
stitches a place
of deep rest.

(her heart is
almost
healed)

NEST- Sheltered
Rest

↳ INGUZ
(INGWAZ)
Rune
• a period of
gestation
• growth
• NEW LIFE
phase
• Peace

4 of Swords

4 of Swords

LIGHT SEER: time of deep rest, transmutation of shadow, healing from burnout, taking a brief holiday from your reality, a sanctuary, healing, self-love, introspection, renewal, self-love

SHADOW SEER: exhaustion, not recognizing the dangers of burnout, working too hard, recovery, not stopping long enough to recover, long-term effects of stress

A SWORDS STORY

She pushed so hard. So far. For so long. And when she couldn't go any further, she fell into a deep healing rest. During this time, the world will shift and change around her. Her hope will be restored, and her body will recover. She will release old wounds that she's carried with her for so many moons, and her hardships from old trauma will be alleviated. As she rests, her magical love will be replenished, and she will burrow down peacefully in long moments of stillness. Silent. Watching. Blinking. She will feel her life force energy slowly mending as it begins to stitch together the fragmented parts of her heart and spirit. She finally has the energy for this deep healing, and in her resting state her anxious mind begins to slow down and *trust*. Her heart beats calmly, strongly . . . truthfully . . . every pulse weaving a tale that comes from deep within her soul. It pulses to her unique timing. It moves to her unique purpose. After the visceral pain of the 3 of Swords, the vitality of her Spirit pulses again, and in the quiet, she heals.

MESSAGE FROM THE 4 OF SWORDS

It's time to rest. This period in your life marks a moment of intentional healing and self-care—a critical pause. More than just integral to your wellness, it is integral to your being at this time—body, mind, and spirit. How you heal is your choice, and you can find quiet regeneration through sleep or other restorative practices like meditation, journaling, dreamwork, energy healing, etc. Consciously decide to slow down and process before sprinting ahead. The hustle of life can be tumultuous and demanding, and the only person who can really direct your own radical recovery is you. Tend to your wounds, as you may be on the verge of burnout—this is a very real message that you need to slow down. Your nest will grow around you as you sleep, and the landscape of your life will shift beautifully as you fall into your own rejuvenating energy. In your dream state, you will transmute and transform your experiences, and emerge renewed, whole, and ready to rise. But first you must rest. Sweet dreams, sweet chickadee.

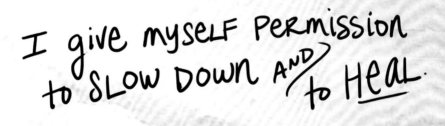

I give myself permission to slow down and to heal.

QUESTIONS FOR THE SEER
- What needs to heal? And how much time will you devote to this healing?
- Lessons require a period of integration. Are you integrating something?
- Can you take a mindful pause from the busy world? Plan your weekend of deep rest.
- Sometimes, we rest and relax our psyche through social fun, binging a favorite show and watching fluffy things that make us laugh. Are you laughing enough lately? And are you balancing this levity with more consciously directed healing time?

5 of Swords

LIGHT SEER: conflict, unfair advantage, experiencing loss, the need to build your skills and your confidence, hollow victories, headaches

SHADOW SEER: deceitful strategies and feeling guilty about your win, winning at all costs, resentment, a desire for peace, psychic attack

A SWORDS STORY

He shakes his head—and tries to get his bearings. *"How did that happen?"* He was outsmarted and out-jousted, and totally overpowered. He lost four of his birds in the chaos, and nothing seems fair about his situation. He was promised a fair fight but certainly wasn't given one. The outcome was determined the moment he agreed to this competition because it was rigged, dishonest, and he was never strong enough to overcome this adversary. He watches his opponent celebrate his advantage and his win. Even through loss, his loyal crow—his cherished companion—remains. The bird waits for a moment and then whispers, "You came with your integrity, and you left with it. You did your best. You still have the higher ground on this higher road." Head in his hand, he knows he will recover, and realizes he has actually learned more than he has lost. He was defeated only to win three important things: pride in his values and in his actions, clarity around what's needed to succeed next time, and an understanding of the type of person he is *and who he is not.*

MESSAGE FROM THE 5 OF SWORDS

You may have experienced a defeat that has left you a little bit sore. Sometimes life isn't fair, and these unexpected losses or inequities can drain our energy for much longer than they need to. Often, it's the fear of failure that does most of the draining, or it's our own thoughts about another person's actions that destabilize our peace long after the moment has passed. Wins and losses are a part of the human experience, and the keys to self-improvement lie dormant inside the difficulties. Learn from your own shortcomings and boost your consciousness. Upgrade your skills and build on this experience. In shadow, we learn that winning isn't everything, especially when deceit is a part of the strategy. The obsessive desire to win can have us stopping at nothing to feel victorious, and in the long run we risk everything we've built along the way. You may find yourself a few steps backward after winning if you are not bringing your integrity to the games. If someone else's negative energy has got you down, send them some fierce love (for real!) and move on with your day. Don't let them derail you. Stay true to your heart and what you know to be right. Live and learn, lovely seer!

THE LESSONS move me aHeaD, ALWAYS.

QUESTIONS FOR THE SEER
- Have you won fairly? Justly? Honorably?
- What steps are you taking to right any injustices in the world? How can you help those whom society has marginalized? How can you spread the love?
- If you were wronged or defeated by someone, what insights did you gain that fortified your strength? Did you use the loss as a powerful instigator of your internal magic?
- In adversity, integrity and grit are beautiful allies. How could you lean on them a little bit more?

ONE CROW
Remains
(NOT all
is lost)
- can
symbolize
close
friends
OR
family
you can
count on.

5 of Swords

THERE IS
LIGHT IN
EVERY SITUATION

WINNER
CELEBRATES BUT IS
also HURT

RED SCARF

Red for emotions
(heart)
and Sacral
chakra
(MOVING
TOWARDS)
SAFETY

WIND PUSHES
HER TO
Sunny SHORE
(Help from the
Universe)

STAR
(HOPE)

3 CROWS
Help from
Strangers or
Unexpected Places

6 of
Swords

SHORE
New Beginnings,
New OPPORTUNITIES

LIGHT SEER: transitions, help arriving at the perfect time, rites of passage, healing, moving beyond trauma or shadows of the past, support from others, personal evolution, a spiritual transition or journey

SHADOW SEER: difficulties accepting help, resistance to change, arduous transitions, carrying baggage and weight from your past

A SWORDS STORY

She stumbles through the fog, unsure of where she's headed. She's lost. Lonely. Confused. Nothing ever remains the same, yet—how could she be so far away from what she imagined for herself? She has nothing but the clothes on her back, and she realizes she needs some help. Looking up at the dark sky, she sends a silent prayer to the heavens. "Help. Please." She approaches the shoreline and arrives at a little dingy with a simple note that says **Passage for the Lost.** "Lost. Lost." She nods silently—this is her ride. Feeling numb, she steps inside the vessel. The wind picks up, and the boat begins to move through the water. Even though she can't see where she is going, she surrenders to the rocking of the sea. She notices a small suitcase with clothes *(in just her size!)* on the seat. Bird calls pierce the air and, when the clouds break, a ray of sunshine highlights a new shore in the distance. She notices that her unlikely winged friends have been captaining her vessel, pulling her toward a new beach—a new day—and a totally new life. Grateful for help coming from the most unusual of allies, she turns her face toward the sun, dries her cheeks, and breathes in the fresh air of possibility.

MESSAGE FROM THE 6 OF SWORDS

You are moving through a period of realignment, and things can feel turbulent during these times of transition. Trust that a better future awaits you on the other side of this change. Maybe you're going through a rite of passage or an intense spiritual transformation. These experiences are profoundly personal, and you may feel very alone right now. Even when it is difficult to accept assistance from others, remain open to receiving help from unexpected places. Allow the gentle support of the Universe to move you through this ocean of evolution, for it is directing the gusting winds of adjustment in the right direction! Lean toward the silver linings on the horizon. (More sunshine? Yes, please!)

Sometimes we find ourselves adrift because we think we are ready to move on, but our heart is still anchored to the past. If you are finding it difficult to move forward, it's time to consider the heavy emotions that you are still carrying with you. What old chapter needs to be closed before you can move forward unburdened? Chase guidance in the form of renewed hope and get ready to explore fresh beginnings on a new shoreline.

I accept HeLp as I easily CRoss THIS TRansition

QUESTIONS FOR THE SEER
- Are you able to ask for help when you need it? And are you able to accept help when it's offered?
- Are you going through the growing pains of growth and realignment?
- What's your relationship with helping others like? Do you offer help so often that you enable those around you? Or, conversely, do you accept help so often that it enables *you*?

7 of Swords

LIGHT SEER: deception or betrayal, taking only what's needed, the Universe bearing witness to true intentions, trickery, being strategic, getting away with something, being grateful for the resources you have, moving silently and quickly

SHADOW SEER: lying to yourself or to others, a need for perspective and honesty, secrets, something stolen, taking more than your fair share, being held back by impostor syndrome

A SWORDS STORY

Stealth. He lands silently in the snow, having taken what he needed from the crow's nest. Sometimes, others steal these feathers for wealth, or for their own personal gain. Sometimes the desire for these feathers causes deceit and dishonest intentions, but right now—here—he knows that he has taken only what he really needed, and nothing more. The crow screams, assuming the worst—enraged at the loss. Crouched, he holds his breath, waiting to see if anyone else has heard the bird's alarm call. She settles when she realizes that her chicks are safe, and she settles into her nest once more. When he is sure that he is safe, he dares move ahead toward his destination. He pauses for a moment to look at the moon and offers a silent prayer of gratitude. The Universe will bear witness to his truest intentions, as it does to all who were here before him. Regardless of being caught or not caught, the Universe always sees the truth. With a lightness of heart, and clarity of purpose, he continues.

MESSAGE FROM THE 7 OF SWORDS

Grace. Determination. Deception. Traditionally, this card warns us that we must be on the lookout for illusion, thievery, and betrayal. If someone's actions feel off to you, trust your instincts. Betrayal can come in many forms, and while we sometimes find ourselves the victim of someone else's deceitful actions, this card also serves as a nudge to act in alignment with our own highest morality. Integrity and honor are called for at this time. Sometimes we pretend that we are doing the best we can, or that everything is okay, even when it's not. Sometimes this shows up as recklessness or as avoidance of responsibilities. Take only what's needed and remember that no excuse outweighs your ability to act from a place of love and integrity. You cannot deceive your own heart, and the Universe will always notice your motivations and your truest intentions. It's an important time to pay attention to your surroundings and to the potential outcomes of your choices. This may mean mulling over long-term consequences or, quite possibly, considering when to be discreet. There are times when it's wise to keep our thoughts to ourselves. And when standing alone and vulnerable under the light of the full moon, the only thing that matters is the truth. Move forward with the lightness of conscience to guide you.

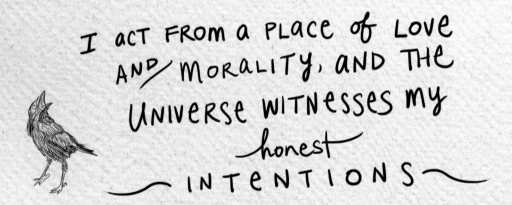

I act from a place of love and morality, and the Universe witnesses my *honest* INTENTIONS

QUESTIONS FOR THE SEER
- Are those around you being completely honest with you?
- Are you getting away with something you shouldn't be?
- Are others misreading your actions or intentions?
- The Universe will always see our motives.
  How aligned are your intentions and your actions?
- Are your motives as altruistic as you tell yourself they are?
- How often do you take only what is needed?

Perspectives...
are the BIRDS TYING HER UP...
or are they HELPING to set her free?

MIRROR: THE way we see ourselves
and our circumstances,
a TIME FOR SELF
REFLECTION

BINDINGS: FEELINGS of BEING
TRAPPED (ILLUSIONS)

STARS: THE universe's
magic is always
PRESENT.

SHE
CAN →
SEE
THE way

8 of Swords

The
moon:
TRUE
Intentions
WILL BE
Illuminated

STOLEN FEATHERS:
He took what was
needed without
causing Damage

CROW'S CRY: →
foul play,
a WARNING,
a thief

7 of Swords

SAFE BIRDS

LIGHT SEER: feeling stuck, a time to open your eyes to unveil the truth, having more options than you thought, an opportunity to let go of an old story

SHADOW SEER: being a victim, feeling helpless, refusal to see the truth, pessimism, using your "stories" or past experiences as excuses to remain shackled

A SWORDS STORY

She is stuck. Bound. Impossibly anchored down. And from where she's sitting, there are no options. Even the Universe seems to conspire against her, with every twist and squirm. *Why does everyone and everything keep me down? Why am I so unlucky? Why it is always me that's targeted?* Every time she tries to move, she stumbles. Every step is painful, and she feels her bindings tighten, becoming more ensnared as she struggles. The ties convince her that the world is out to get her. Breathing deeply, she realizes that she has been here for a really long time. She will not escape unless she makes some serious improvements to the way she sees her position. She wonders, *What would life be like if I was one of those people who believed that the Universe was working in my favor? What if I began to see opportunity instead of blockades? Lessons instead of failures? Old stories instead of oppressions? What if I stopped believing in my own bad luck?* She thought about the blame she was continually doling out, and on the past scenarios that she clung to in order to corroborate her thinking. Teachers from grade school. Old bosses. That family member. A romance gone sour. She closed her eyes and saw that she was allowing them to bind her power, even now. And she realized that she had a choice: to change her perception. And the moment she saw beyond the blindfold of her stories was the moment she saw her bindings were figments and illusions.

MESSAGE FROM THE 8 OF SWORDS

This card is a gentle reminder that you create your reality. Look beyond the veil of illusion that your current limitations are projecting. If you are feeling trapped with no path forward, remember that this is a mindset that can be lifted. When you choose sovereignty over victimhood, you become the fierce wielder of choice. You can free yourself from your shackles and shift your outcome *dramatically* by accepting that you are the one person who is responsible for your happiness. Create infinite portals of possibility by becoming your own solution. *For we are never really stuck.* Nurture your soul and spend the time you need to transmute any feelings of frustration or helplessness. While we can't control every experience that is put on our path, we can definitely work on how we respond to each one. With self-reflection and self-sovereignty, you will find your way out of this predicament! Be ever vigilant of any wallowing, low-vibe thoughts and judgements that you may be holding on to. See if you can reframe your experiences as lessons to be processed and choose to heal.

I am free to choose my HEALING AND my LIGHT.

QUESTIONS FOR THE SEER
- In which areas of your life do you feel impossibly bound?
- The illusion of being stuck often keeps us in one place for too long. With zero baggage and zero restrictions, where would you go and what would you do?
- Sweet light, what stories are holding you back? And how can you release them?

9 of Swords

LIGHT SEER: nightmares, insomnia, worry, depression or anxiety, fear, an opportunity to find courage, a time to focus on safety and the things that are going well in your life

SHADOW SEER: paranoia, deeply anchored fears, inability to think clearly, inner turmoil, negative self-talk affecting self-esteem, disturbing thoughts, an opportunity to actively begin the healing journey

A SWORDS STORY

They keep flapping, with their wings, beady eyes, beaks, and talons. They swoop down and send her over the edge. Her heart thunders as they peck and poke, assailing her through echoing caws. Her thoughts race, immediately going to the worst of the worst of the worst-case scenarios. She feels cornered, blocked from making an escape. She's shaking and panicked as if her anxiety is attacking her from within and from without. There's nothing to do but to protect herself as she freezes and then falls. If only she would calmly look to her side, she would see the shadow of her bed and the soft pillow at her side. If only she could open her eyes and let the light in, the imaginary attackers would begin to dissipate. Maybe she would notice the dove cooing softly outside of her window and realize that she was safe all along. With her root chakra rooted and her eyes open, she would see her night terrors for what they really are: symbolic representations of the stress of her waking life. She would notice that her hallucinations were not real, and she could fall back to sleep, lulled by the refuge of her warm bed, and held by the wings of love and safety. But she is the only one who can pull herself out of these nightmares, and until then, she is trapped inside of her own illusions.

MESSAGE FROM THE 9 OF SWORDS

What's keeping you up at night, sweet seer? This card suggests a time in your life when your negative thoughts are gaining momentum, and when you may find yourself spending too much energy worrying about the future. Pay attention to the stressors you are stimulating with the energies of fear and rumination. If a pessimistic mindset spirals wildly out of control, it can lead to anxiety, stress, or depression—even when your thoughts carry no truth. Are you imagining the worst instead of activating the best? Or working through the looping-swooping thoughts of a frantic nervous system? Know that this situation is not permanent, and that your perception is everything right now—so don't allow negative self-talk to trip you up! Flip your script and send nurturing, loving thoughts to your heart in order to overcome any disturbing feelings. Look toward the light in your situation and notice that even the tiniest window of brightness can keep fear at bay. Instead of focusing on things that could go wrong, allow the light to illuminate the many ways you are safe, held, and looked after. As you allow any worries to soften, you will expose the illusions and bad dreams for what they really are, and you will leave room for tranquility, hope, and optimism in their place.

I see my FeaRS as the ILLUsions THaT THeY aRe.

QUESTIONS FOR THE SEER
- What fears cause you to freeze and hold you back?
- Perspective check: Are you seeing illusions and imagining an unhappy ending before you even begin?
- If depression and anxiety have got you hiding, know that you are not alone. If it's time to reach out for help, do you have someone you can call, beautiful soul?
- Does your nervous system register the difference between fear and danger in your body?
- If you focus on the light and allow your fear to dissipate, what's left in its place?

ONE GHOST BIRD: SPIRIT,
A GLIMPSE OF THE ILLUSION

RAYS OF LIGHT: FAITH, HOPE

RAIN:
TUMULTUOUS INTERNAL ENVIRONMENT

BED OUTLINE: DREAMS, NIGHTMARES

9 of Swords

DAWN:
ENDINGS AND
Beginnings

BRAVELY
FACING HER
SHADOWS

BIRDS (FROM
R.W.S. PAGE OF
SWORDS): GUIDING
her toward
the LIGHT
(and into the
next CARD)

DEPRESSION
IN SAND
WHERE SHE
WAS LAYING
IN DEFEAT

10 of Swords

10 of Swords

LIGHT SEER: painful endings, crisis, being stabbed in the back, psychological wounds, an opportunity to find deep healing, an opportunity to find hope and resiliency, change

SHADOW SEER: failed attempts, resisting the inevitable, rock bottom, not wanting to let go of negative emotions, a narrative rooted in lack and helplessness, devastating loss, recovery

A SWORDS STORY

Picking herself up off the cold ground, she watches the first signs of dawn tickle the landscape. She longs to feel the sun's warmth on her skin. After that devastating ending, she is beginning to heal, and she is finally coming to terms with everything that happened. Her thoughts—once muddled and knotted—feel clearer now. "Processing is a process," she whispers, and continues reciting her mantra in her mind: *No more swords. Just healing. No more swords. Just healing.* She remembers the painful betrayal and the deceit, the ugly truth, and the harm it caused her. This will always be a part of her story, but one that she will no longer be defined by. She is stronger than this, and she recognizes her courage and her resiliency in her ability to rise above her past and to thrive. She longs to share her healed wounds with the Sun—to bathe them in its hopeful, curative energy. She shakes out her dress and walks toward the horizon . . . vulnerable, whole, and totally alive. She is free from that horror, free from her pain, and her scars are vivid markers of her tenacious, resilient spirit. With her heart ready to love, and her soul ready to shine, she walks calmly toward the light.

MESSAGE FROM THE 10 OF SWORDS

     The 10 of Swords comes to us in times of blinding truth, when disillusion is lifted. Sometimes the truth is painful and jarring, filled with stories of backstabbing or personal loss. This card can mark an abrupt end to our current path and a distressing resolution in the form of a broken partnership, a fractured dream, a detour in a career path, or a discontinued story. While these endings feel severe in the moment, the most potent seeds of hope are always planted in their place. If you are going through a period of deep transformation and closure, know that you must allow yourself space to heal from past trauma, and that you will become stronger and more resilient with time. Remember that our wounds teach us about our greatest strengths and remind us of our innate ability to heal. Your dark night of the soul will be met with a beautiful new dawn that is filled with more light than you've ever experienced. Remain open to love and joy as you process this ending and look to the sunlight that awaits. Watching the sun peek over the horizon is the highest task of a bruised heart.

I Transform and Heal
every Day.

QUESTIONS FOR THE SEER

• Our wounds often heal stronger than before and give rise to some of our greatest traits. The wound itself, however, is not who we are. Have you been able to remain malleable and soft through your challenge and transformation?

• When something in life comes to an end, it leaves space for something new. What is that new thing that is arriving? Name it, and claim it as your own.

Page of Swords

LIGHT SEER: restless energy, curiosity, a thirst for information, learning new things, tests or exams, an apprentice or student, intellectual pursuits, ideas and reasoning, a messenger

SHADOW SEER: arrogance, gossip, rumors, nervous energy, being all talk and no action, white lies, dishonesty arrogance, gossip, rumors (a little birdie told me), nervous energy, being all talk and no action, white lies, dishonesty

A SWORDS STORY

She hops along: *Skip, skip, study. Study, study, think.* Curious and intelligent, this Page has a thirst for knowledge that seems unquenchable, and you will often find her skipping and studying down the paths of those who have gone before her. She's a quick-witted and eager communicator who feels compelled to share her many ideas or messages with others, and at times, she's so talkative and intense that it becomes too much for others to process. Her frenetic energy can come across as unsettled or even nervous. She carries her ideas proudly, carting around her big "aha" lightbulb moments for others to see, for she strongly self-identifies with her intellect. Observant and analytical, she's the type of person you'd find reading a particle physics textbook as they attempt to understand the essence of life. Today, her inquisitive nature has her listening closely to those little birds as they tweet cheerfully and answer her millions of questions. In their birdsong they set goals and share dreams, and they tell her far-fetched and epic tales (as if they were much bigger birds!) She chatters with them, welcoming the distraction, yet also suspecting that what they are sharing is a little far-fetched. What those little birdies told her may be slightly misinterpreted truths, so she commits to learning the truth to avoid being swayed by their dizzying narratives.

MESSAGE FROM THE PAGE OF SWORDS

You may be actively seeking answers right now. *Where am I going? How does this thing work? What will I learn when I arrive?* It's exciting to begin new things, isn't it? This Page of Swords energy asks you to look at how you are perceiving your reality. Over-identification with your mind may have you believe that everything you are thinking is real. Be open to the lessons the Universe is sending your way, and if you've accidentally been lulled into assuming your truth is the *only* truth, this is a perfect time to try on another's point of view. Learn to synthesize facts in a new way! This curious Page suggests using an air of inventiveness in your current pursuit. Your goals will be met by walking a path of honest discovery, especially where others are concerned. Keep the lightbulbs of curiosity turned on, and cultivate a beginner's mindset as you learn new things! Avoid falling into gossip or even arrogance with your communication. In shadow, this Page can be all talk and no action. Make sure you are striving for *less know-it-all* and *more proven track record*. Remember that everyone who crosses your path has something specific to teach you, and that sacred mirrors for learning are all around. Remain open to unexpected lessons, share truthfully, and delight in every interaction.

I learn, and I expand my consciousness and I open new opportunities for my life.

QUESTIONS FOR THE SEER

- This ambitious and intelligent energy suggests you are ready to expand. How can you use your communication to get you there?
- How can you tell the truth *and* do good instead of harm with your voice?
- All of that curiosity! What are you are excited to learn about?

LIGHTBULBS: IDEAS, A-HA's, IDENTIFYING with one's MIND OR INTELLIGENCE.

BIRDS: "a LITTLE BIRDIE TOLD me", Gossip OR chatter.

BOOK: Studiousness, Always Learning, Curiosity

WHIRLWIND: Frenetic and UNSETTLED ENERGY

SWORD: BALANCING new things with the LIFE we LIVE.

Page of Swords

← Lead by thoughts, signs, patterns.

MOTORBIKE INSTEAD of HORSE: Velocity, Dedication to best option.

CROSSBOW: aiming HIGH, Focus, being mechanical

01011010
BINARY CODE on SOLES of SHOES: Being Logical/Analytical, DUALITY, SPEED, PROBLEM SOLVING.

Knight of Swords

Knight of Swords

LIGHT SEER: haste, streamlined decision-making, intelligence, wit, determination, saving the day, the pursuit of excellence, ambition, being assertive, success, conquests, autonomy and willpower

SHADOW SEER: unfocused and scattered energy, acting too quickly, impatience, the need for a logical solution, feeling held back, stalling, unpredictability, ruthlessness, a cutthroat, being hard-edged and emotionally unavailable

A SWORDS STORY

This knight has one thing on the brain, and it's running toward success. He's kind of a superhero. Someone in trouble? A blip in the proverbial matrix? He's on it. He's determined and ambitious, articulate, and intelligent, and he has an intensity that is hard to grasp. When something needs to be solved, he doesn't wait for an answer; he just gets to fixing it. He sees every solution in probabilities, percentages, and time frames. His analytical reasoning is so fast that everything else seems to slow down when he finds himself running against the clock. Strapping on his crossbow he runs to his destination, and it's impossible to stop him once he has identified his target. All this energy comes with a certain amount of impatience, especially when needing to course correct or when he feels that others are slowing him down. He used to have a sword and horse like everyone else, but they were just so *tedious*. And slow. He's since traded up, and he'll hop on his motorcycle until he finds a plane to fly. *Whatever will get him there faster*. With the grace and speed of an athlete, he turns on a dime, and since he has no doubt in his sound logic, he succeeds.

MESSAGE FROM THE KNIGHT OF SWORDS

On purpose, and on time, this Knight charges into your reading with calculated energy worth learning from. There's a competitive resoluteness here, and if you follow his decisive lead, you will invite a lot more strategic momentum to your world. The rush toward positive outcomes usually accompanies this knight when he shows up! How assertive are you being? How much innate drive do you feel? Are you determined to accomplish everything you set out to do, or are you letting things slide? Strive for excellence every single day in order to bring some of his speedy magic into your life. Be brave and move quickly! As with all powerful energies, you may run the risk of being overly forceful or domineering. While it's important to make swift and rational conclusions, be careful not to hurt others with your impatience to win. The results may not be worth it if you charge straight into unfavorable circumstances with others. If you are feeling scattered, distracted, or blocked, spend time organizing your thoughts, and make sure that all your energy is hurtling in the same direction. Take decisive actions toward speedy success!

> I move QUICKLY to HELP OTHERS AND, AS I DO, my SUCCESS EXPANDS.

QUESTIONS FOR THE SEER
- What is your biggest goal right now, and what will it look like when you achieve it?
- This knight brings hero energy to the spread. How could you become your own hero right now, and swoop into your situation and move it in the right direction?
- Do you need to communicate something with more clarity and precision in order to be understood?
- Sometimes this Knight charges ahead without paying enough attention to his direction. Do you have clarity on where you are headed?

Queen of Swords

LIGHT SEER: a thought leader, unbiased decision-making, an excellent communicator, wise and logical counsel, trustworthiness and honesty, being perceptive, intelligence, being direct, seeking truth

SHADOW SEER: sharp and sometimes cold communication, being overly "mean" or "emotional," indifference, a message to use your head more and your heart less, aloofness, bitterness

A SWORDS STORY

She takes a deep breath in. "Ahhhh. Clarity." Highly astute, intellectual, and honest, the Queen of Swords sits calmly, overlooking her kingdom. She finds it easier to reign when she can see the bigger picture from this bird's eye view. From up here, she can remain laser-focused on the future of her kingdom, with only the gentle winds of insight accompanying her many thoughts. She knows she appears aloof to some, but she is simply tuning out the low-vibe drama that is clamoring for her attention. Sometimes she is judged to be too sharp and strict, yet underneath her cool exterior she knows how deeply she cares for those around her. And—*oh how she cares about the state of the world!* So much so, that she is always seeking the truth that lies hidden behind the masks of people, places, and structures of power. She seeks integrity in her relationships, communication, and actions. She loves to communicate, and she is a witty conversationalist who speaks authentically and remains guided by her principles—avoiding the gossip and small talk that others may want to engage in. Leading with her head does not make her cold-hearted, just logical. She prefers the clean air of strategy and clarity, for there is great power in truth, and so much light hidden within it.

MESSAGE FROM THE QUEEN OF SWORDS

It's a time for direct communication and straightforward interpretations in your situation. This powerful Queen asks you to be genuine in your relationships, honest in your speech, and to bring your clearheaded, unbiased reasoning to the table. The truth is incorruptible, so make use of your finely tuned rubbish detector as you objectively consider the facts. What do you know to be true? And where are you filling in the gaps and making-it-up based on your assumptions? With principled justness and morality, you will be able to cut through the noise and *you will thrive*. While this card suggests a time for radical authenticity, openness, and candor, this communication style can sometimes come across as overly direct. Or worse—cold and cutting, even. If you are having trouble communicating something that is difficult for another person to hear, know that you can always dip your toe into the cup of empathy and compassion to help with your delivery. Sharp analysis and careful consideration are always intelligent moves, as is being able to clearly connect with others in a way that is easily accepted and understood. A clear heart and clear mind will allow you to speak your truth, always.

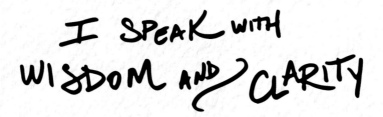

QUESTIONS FOR THE SEER

- What truth needs to be spoken? How can you deliver the message with love?
- The Queen of Swords can represent independence and not needing approval from others. This can be healthy, but in excess, this can be a defense mechanism that hides insecurities under the guise of "I don't care what people think of me." Where do you sit with this?

HEAD ON HAND: Thinking, Logic, analysis.

● PURPLE SHIRT / HAIR: CROWN CHAKRA

△: AIR SYMBOL IN BLUE FLAG

⬡ BLUE FLAG: AIR
⬡ YELLOW FLAG: EARTH
● RED FLAG: FIRE

WATER IS IN THE CUP

The cup is locked away, yet kept close to her... She has access to her emotions (suit of cups) but prefers to use her mind.

Queen of Swords

△ WINGED THINGS AND WISPS OF WIND: This CARD SHOWS THE movement of "SYLPHS": INVISIBLE, MYTHICAL creatures that embody the magic of the element of AIR. SYLPH ENERGY HELPS WITH HEALING, THOUGHT AND CLARITY and CONNECTION WITH SPIRIT.

SWORDS: Sharp wit, Intelligence

2 feathers from animal familiar: BRAVERY, PROTECTION, SPIRITUAL Communication

King of Swords

🦇 BAT: EXTRA PERCEPTION
OWL: WISDOM
DRAGONFLY: Self-Realization, inner transformation, messages from SPIRIT

King of Swords

LIGHT SEER: intelligence, logic, rules and law, clear thinking, a strong communicator and leader, truth and proof, blending mental and spiritual pursuits, bravery and courage

SHADOW SEER: manipulation and conceit, showing off your intelligence, can indicate a rigidness in thinking, tendencies to overcontrol, irrationality, being cold and calculating

A SWORDS STORY

Highly intelligent and diplomatic, this King leads with facts, rationale, scientific principles, and the logical mind. He is inventive and resourceful, and always seeks proof and data to back up his beliefs and ideas. To some, he may appear cool or detached, but he is simply operating from a different facet of his brain when he thinks about the logistics of leadership. *Impact. Solutions. The best action to take.* Shrewd judgement and thoughtful perception are necessary for his ability to lead. Even though he always seeks data and proof, he also knows that blending experience with inventiveness—or blending intelligence with emotional and spiritual energies—allows for well-rounded success. When faced with a challenge, his favorite perspective is one of unbiased and open-minded fact, for clarity in decisions are what will propel his kingdom forward. In moments of contemplation, he calls to the wind from the top of his mountain, and all the winged things join him there. They share his affinity for observing the world from a distance, quietly, while remaining objectively aware, and *present.*

MESSAGE FROM THE KING OF SWORDS

Be courageous in the pursuit of your path, and find your own methodical, confident authority by knowing the way rather than just feeling the way. This King has an affinity for rules, ethics and thought, and he suggests finding impartial clarity before you take your next step. Draw on your experience or on the experience of others, and welcome level-headed solutions and an honest examination of the facts into your decision-making process. Sometimes, this King is seen as stern, yet in truth he remains flexible, so be open to receiving new information that may change your point of view. Lean heavily on your moral compass to guide your next actions, knowing that integrity and fairness will always point you in the right direction. When you tap into his articulate, analytical energy, you will be able to share your thoughts confidently; your clear and logical explanations will be well received. In shadow, this card can suggest using knowledge to take advantage of others. With truthful communication, it's time to help others in a way that is honest rather than manipulative or crafty. There is no need to demonstrate superior intelligence or class . . . you will only make others feel like they are out-of-the-loop or *less than*. Share your wisdom and experience gracefully, and seek to become the success engineer of your life. With confident communication and clear thinking, you will find your victory.

I make intelligent AND WISE DECISIONS about my future.

QUESTIONS FOR THE SEER
- Seeking the clarity of truth is your highest goal. Have your own stories become clouded by excuses, shadows, or insecurities?
- How do you perceive the facts? What layer of truth do your emotions add to the situation? What complications do they add?
- Pathworking visualization: In your mind's eye, take a walk up the mountain. The winds, the birds, the dragonflies . . . all the winged things are here. As you rise above any chaos or confusion, you get a bird's eye view of your path. Looking three years into the future, where do your options lead? Which path is the best one for you today? What subtle messages do your companions whisper?

Pentacles

ELEMENT: Earth

ASSOCIATED WITH:

health, wealth, physical security, the material world,
comfort, responsibilities, manifesting, and
bringing things to earth

Ace of Pentacles

LIGHT SEER: the beginning of a new venture or task, new ideas, planting seeds for the future, great potential for success, manifesting power, positive outcomes, ambitions, an inheritance, a material gift, prosperity

SHADOW SEER: the need to create strong foundations to support your dream, risk of financial loss, the need to prioritize, missed opportunities, being overly greedy and missing the bigger picture

A PENTACLES STORY

He holds the Pentacle in his hands and admires its new roots, suffused with potential. Thrilled for this chance to begin anew, he thanks this seed for the gifts it will bring. It glows softly in response, sending a low hum up through his hands. The vibration moves through his body and into the earth. He feels deeply connected to the soil beneath him, and for a moment he swears he can hear the stories of the trees and the mycelium in barely audible whispers. He knows it is time to bury his seed. Reverently, excitedly, he takes a breath . . . prays a wish . . . and then plants the seed in this magical soil. He knows that it will root and grow and bloom forth all the security and warmth that he has been longing for. He knows there is unprecedented potential in this moment. *Steady. Calm. Every seed that is planted here flourishes, you see.* The secret to this earth magic is knowing exactly what he is planting—so he envisions the things that he wants to anchor and bring forth: *Prosperity. And comfort. And joy.* As he packs the earth lovingly around his freshly planted future, he reminds himself that this will also require his action, patience, and a growth mindset. He must be open and ready to nurture such gifts.

MESSAGE FROM THE ACE OF PENTACLES

Freshly rooted beginnings! This Ace is a powerhouse of possibility and reveals the materialization of earthly ambitions and all the wonderful things. When you seed your future by planting your very first intentions, things feel so exciting, raw, and possible, don't they? Hold on to those feelings of optimism and success, for the new start that you are welcoming in to your life right now has **incredible** potential to thrive. Your Ace initiates a timeline where your future wealth, health, and material abundance are ushered in. By figuring out your soil conditions, your watering schedule, and the needs of this unique seed, you will be able to see it through to fruition. Bring your determination and dedication, and see your abundance spring to life in the form of successful outcomes, material and financial wins, and soul-satisfying well-being. With this wonderful message for good things to come, it's time to visualize, attract, prioritize, and act.

I PLANT MY GOALS with INTENTION, DIRECT FOCUS AND Faith.

QUESTIONS FOR THE SEER
- In what areas of your life would you like to root more wealth?
- You have the opportunity to align the material and spiritual. What does that look like for you?
- What abundance do you already have that you may be overlooking at this time?

MANDALAS AS PENTACLES:
• WHOLENESS, manifestation and CREATION. MATERIALIZATION OF DESIRES THROUGH WORK, GOALS COMING to FRUITION, SUCCESS, the SPIRITUAL IN THE MATERIAL FORM.

← PLANTING NEW SEEDS for the FUTURE

← THE ROOTS OF PROSPERITY and ABUNDANCE

Ace of Pentacles

Mandala MOON: INTUITION/ SPIRIT

MANDALA PURSE: THE EARTHLY/ the MATERIAL

(Juggling PRIORITIES)

2 of Pentacles

LANDSCAPE:
← WATER RUSHING OR STANDING IN A RIVER, TRYING TO MAINTAIN BALANCE. COULD ALSO BE A BARREN LANDSCAPE... A TIME WHEN THE CHOICES MADE WILL CHANGE HER ENVIRONMENT.

2 of Pentacles

LIGHT SEER: a need to balance many aspects of self, juggling obligations, equilibrium, managing the ups and downs of life, seeking harmony, competing circumstances

SHADOW SEER: being out of balance, disharmony, committing to too many things, a need to prioritize, a time to slow down

A PENTACLES STORY

Somewhere between asleep and awake, and somewhere between the forest and the sea . . . in this in-between place where everything is perfectly counter-balanced, she is able to feel the pull and the weight of it all. She has so many responsibilities, tasks, and dreams that she needs to keep afloat. Her mind wanders to the moon, and she wants to give her full attention to its mysterious and ethereal beauty. But her other arm tugs her toward her family and her relationships, and she also strives to give that her undivided presence. And she would have been able to focus, *truly she would* . . . if it weren't for the third obligation that was tugging at her attention from the inside of her purse. She pauses to take a breath. And then for a moment, for the briefest of moments, she can hold them all in a beautiful dance and give each one the energy it requires. She sways to the pull of both the moon and the ocean, and she stabilizes her fluctuating responsibilities, hoping to commit this see-saw balancing act to memory.

MESSAGE FROM THE 2 OF PENTACLES

With all of those roles and responsibilities that you've been juggling, you may be feeling a little imbalanced. *Busy much?* Maybe your calendar is totally overbooked, and you're feeling the stress of being stretched in too many directions. Perhaps you are taking on too many different roles and tasks, or reconfiguring your time to add something new to your life. Balancing too many things will force you to continuously shift in order to remain upright, and this can slowly erode your well-being and inner peace. *Not to mention your sanity!* It's time to better balance the dualities or opposing aspects of your life (your time alone vs. your time with others, or your material life vs. your spiritual life, etc.) Make sure you aren't investing too many resources in one area at the expense of another, especially when both are equally as important. Even though this card suggests that you're likely able to manage it all in the short term, do you really desire this much juggling for your future? Put some of your precious energy into creating a balance that you absolutely love—an equilibrium will not take from your reserves of energy but will add to them. Create a rhythm that frees up time to work, play, love, and create.

I create an equilibrium in my life that allows me to be my best self.

QUESTIONS FOR THE SEER

• What task could you let go of today?

• What opposites or dualities are you holding simultaneously? (i.e., wanting to give your time to family and wanting more time for yourself, or wanting to grow spiritually while also wanting things in your life to remain relatively the same.)

3 of Pentacles

LIGHT SEER: cooperation, community, teaching and learning, mentors, sharing and listening, teamwork, no limit to what you can manifest together

SHADOW SEER: difficulty working with others, a need to listen, selfishness, pushing one's own agenda, not trusting your partner's ability, ego clash

A PENTACLES STORY

Different skills, roles, ideas, and energy, and they come together as a group to create the world of their dreams. Indeed, they are each a unique manifestation of universal consciousness, and their combination of talents and mindsets work beautifully with one another—especially when they open up to the collective magic that they have at their fingertips. Each one adds a piece of love into the fabric of reality that they are weaving, and each one takes on a role of equal importance. *Together, they create wholeness, and love is present here.* While one sees and directs the bigger picture, the other works on the finer details . . . each one the temporary authority of their own small part of the process. *Master and student. Intern and partner.* In flow, they spin their masterpiece to life, and create a beautiful moment that would only work with the unique energy of this specific trio.

MESSAGE FROM THE 3 OF PENTACLES

Working with others can be challenging, yet it gifts us with the opportunity to learn from one another and to blend energies to create something totally new. Look for conscious collaborators—as mentors, apprentices, or both! *How can you offer your skills to those around you?* Co-creating for the good of the whole is powerful magic, and this teamwork and community card calls you forth to add your unique essence to the bigger picture. It's time to reach out, communicate, and plan. Remember that your relationships are the base of your well-being, and if you are having trouble engaging with others, seek to align your goals so that you can cultivate peaceful unions. Mutually beneficial relationships place equal importance on each person's novel wisdom and *way of being in the world,* regardless of the relational hierarchy. Everyone has something distinct and enchanting to bring to the table, and when we allow group dynamics to shift, we can discover new things from both beginners and experts. When life paths are entwined, strive to create harmonic states as you weave your way in and out of one another's days. Prioritize the goals of the group, always remembering that self-respect and self-worth do not need to prove *rightness,* and that wanting to advocate for your ideas—in shadow— can sometimes come across as egotism and rigidity. Think fluidity in forward motion when working with others, and by welcoming people into your heart, you will open doors of possibility that didn't exist before.

I Step INTO the VIBRATION of CONSCIOUS COLLABORATION

QUESTIONS FOR THE SEER

- What part of your unique essence do you share when connecting with others?
- Do you like working in a team? Or are you more of a lone wolf? How easily do you flow between these two ways of being?
- Do you find it easy to direct others and to also follow another person's lead?
- What do people like about you? What part of your personality tends to go missed or unnoticed? And how can you share more of yourself?
- Collaboration over competition? For everything? How does collaborating make you feel?

- WEAVING PROJECTS TOGETHER /
CONSCIOUS COLLABORATION

COLORS : 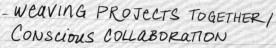 GREEN = HEART CHAKRA,
CONNECTION

RED = ROOT CHAKRA,
SAFETY

YELLOW = SOLAR PLEXUS
CHAKRA, WILL,
ego, personal
ideas

ALSO!
COLORS of A TRAFFIC
LIGHT, KNOWING WHEN TO
STOP, GO or PAUSE.

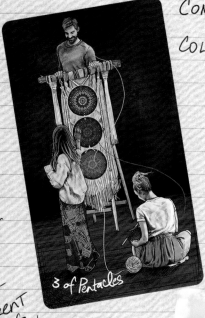

3 of Pentacles

NO
LEFT
HAND -
DIFFERENT
ABILITIES
CAN LEAD /
USING LOGICAL
SIDE of BRAIN

OTHALA RUNE
EARRINGS :
WEALTH, INHERITANCE,
HERITAGE.

4 of Pentacles

CLUTCHING PURSE:
Scarcity mindset,
BEING CHEAP or frugal,
fear around finances.
Could be the need to save money.

community
IN DISTANCE:
a NEED TO
Save and TO
ALSO BE
CHARITABLE

WHITE
PICKET FENCE:
HAVING MORE
MORE WEALTH
THAN SHE MAY
REALIZE.

4 of Pentacles

LIGHT SEER: stability, savings, success, generosity, accepting your worth, being in flow with the Universe, feelings of gratitude, helping others in times of need

SHADOW SEER: hoarding, coveting, over-controlling, a scarcity mindset, placing too much value on money, a need to be more charitable

A PENTACLES STORY

She clasps her pentacles close to her body. "I must hold on to these," she whispers, and she looks over her shoulder at the poor village below, "or else I end up with nothing." She clutches tighter, grasping her purse. She only lessens her grip when her rational mind comes back online. She looks around her and realizes that she is safe, and that what she has made will not be taken from her. She remembers that she can save and earn . . . and squirrel away a little now, *for later.* She opens her heart to the reality that money comes and goes, and that her own generosity of spirit will be the key to making abundance flow into her life with a little more ease. It will be an investment in her future. Looking over her shoulder once more, she gathers her things and gets ready to go to the little village below. She has some gifting to do—an act that is long overdue.

MESSAGE FROM THE 4 OF PENTACLES

You're building your life coin by coin, and you're reaching a moment of stability. Getting here signifies an interval when you can rest, re-evaluate, and take stock. Likely, you are being reminded to double-check those foundations and to save some money for a rainy day. Continue toward your goal without overfocusing on material possessions, and let go of any jealousy or resentfulness derived from another person's position in life.

Ask yourself if you are looking down on others based on how much money they have, or don't have . . . and if you are truly grateful for the things you *do* possess. Are you placing value on the things that *really* matter? Being deeply appreciative will magnetize and draw more abundance into your world, whereas negative feelings around prosperity will breed energy blockages big enough to hold even the most magical of trajectories back. Loosen your grip and step into the flow of wealth and happiness! Let go of any fear that what you have will be taken away. Not sure where to start? Imagine that everything you buy (including the little things, like your morning tea) *also* helps every person whose work depends on that item being sold. There's an energetic loop of transactional productivity, prosperity, and abundance there, so be grateful that you could be a part of it! Every time you pay for something? *Be grateful.* This is a reminder to live generously. Sending wishes of prosperity to others will work miracles for your money mindset! *Actively save and give in the world,* and focus on feeling excited and expansive.

I LIVE an ABUNDANT LIFe
AND I have more than I need.♡

QUESTIONS FOR THE SEER
- What are you clutching too tightly?
- How often do you judge people for the money they have or don't have?
  What does this say about your relationship with saving, giving, hoarding, coveting, or wealth in general?
- Are you trying to over-control your situation?
- Does your need for control keep others away?
- How do you feel about your generosity?

5 of Pentacles

LIGHT SEER: financial or health difficulties, feeling left out or ostracized, worrying about your security, asking for help when you need it, a chance to clear energy blockages

SHADOW SEER: scarcity mindset, feeling helpless, feeling left out, victimhood, inability to move ahead, fear and isolation, resistance to positivity, feelings of low self-worth that keep you from participating in prosperity, a light at the end of the tunnel

A PENTACLES STORY

"I lost it all. Everything." She weeps into her torn sequined scarf, and she no longer has the energy to curse those who did this to her. Her life. Her wealth. Her health. Everything seems to have slipped away, and she can't seem to get things back in order. Petting her bruised knee and wrapping her dirty clothing around her, she settles in for a long, cold night. They won't help her. They have forgotten her. And she is beginning to believe that maybe she isn't worthy of their love. Shame sets in, and she doesn't remember exactly when that rooted . . . this belief of *not enoughness* . . . but it has slowly grown its way up to her heart. Her shoulders shake silently, and she begs the heavens for help. A light shines down and illuminates a key right behind her. She sees the light but knows it isn't meant for her. *Why would it be for her?* The key offers her a warm bed. Fresh sheets. A new start. If only she would believe that it could be hers. If only she would shift her perspective and see the truth—that absolutely everything she wants is within reach.

MESSAGE FROM THE 5 OF PENTACLES

      Things are a little sticky right now, and it's time to squarely address any feelings about safety and security that have you worried about your well-being. Are you stressed about your finances or health, or feeling left out from the prosperity that others seem to enjoy? To counteract these corrosive energetic states, you are being asked to reclaim your personal power. Find your hunger for fierce positivity, and seek opportunity in your current circumstance. *It's hiding in the shadows.* If you've been stagnant for a hot minute, ask yourself if you've been laser-focused on the things that are lacking in your life. Don't allow your inner voice to spew out unnecessary mental and energetic chatter that convinces you that are not deserving of the life you long for. If fear, self-pity, or helplessness try to dictate your reality, flip the script and remember that against all odds, all oppression, all class barriers, all *everything* . . . there is always a choice to move beyond the limitations you are presently encountering. It's time to make the absolute best of your luminous life—you are not locked out from that which you desire. See the keys that will help you get there, and choose to open the door.

DOORS that activate magical opportunities are always opening for me.

QUESTIONS FOR THE SEER
- What story are you holding on to about your wealth (or health) that you'd like to let go of? And what could emerge if you chose to see your reality in a different way?
- Your money relationship: What role have you played in your own circumstance?
- Who or what are you shutting out? And what would happen if you opened the door?

5 CIRCLES: SHAPE of PENTAGRAM = a magical GLYPH SYMBOLIZING 4 ELEMENTS PLUS SPIRIT, HUMANITY's connection to the UNIVERSE AND COSMIC FORCES, PROTECTION, GROWTH

the KEY to OPEN the DOOR to health AND wealth IS PRESENT

5 of Pentacles

6 of Pentacles

ABUNDANCE

giving, generosity

CHARITY

Receiving, gratitude

THE INFINITE FLOW of RESOURCES, elements AND MATERIALS from ONE SOURCE to ANOTHER

the PATH OF manifestation

6 of Pentacles

LIGHT SEER: two-way abundance (giving and receiving), being charitable, a positive and generous mindset, advancement, awakening, inflow, help coming from others

SHADOW SEER: one-way flow of abundance (over-giving or over-receiving), hoarding and holding on to what you have, choosing not to help, being uncharitable, selfishness, judging others, ulterior motives, inability to accept help

A PENTACLES STORY

Like magic, he takes one coin and makes it two. She takes two coins and makes them four. Somehow, somewhere, they acquired this trick, and it has taken them far in life . . . traveling across the globe and seeing the most wonderous of things. And sharing, gifting, and showing their skills. Some witness this pair and immediately see their generous hearts. They see their open minds and their flowing magic. And even though they don't really understand how easily the pair can gift coins to all the people who are willing to listen to them, they appreciate them. Others see them perform, and they judge them as evil and uncharitable, because with those coins they could clearly gift a lot more.

MESSAGE FROM THE 6 OF PENTACLES

Being open to give and receive are states that must be cultivated. This card asks you to experience these energies consciously. How does helping others make you feel? *It feels good, right?* Abundant? Heart-centered? Gifting your time, money, or energy to someone else will open the floodgates of new resources coming your way. Be generous with everything you have learned, and remain conscious of the flow of abundance from the Universe. Consider these sacred dualities: learning and teaching, receiving and giving, and accepting and offering. Open your heart to this sacred balance of energy, and fill in any gaps you have around scarcity and abundance. Trust the benevolence of the community around you, and imbue your life with compassion and generosity, for it will usher in new states of prosperity.

In shadow, this card can suggest selfishness or using a "gift" as a means to control someone or something. Make sure your charitability comes with no *expectations* to receive, and that generosity isn't a mere stepping stone to power, status, or righteousness. *Intentions always matter.* Donate your energetic resources with no strings attached, and your desire to help others will be life-changing for those in need. Choose a cause that moves your soul, and watch your feelings of love and prosperity shift.

I SHOW GRATITUDE FOR MY LIFE ~ THROUGH ~ GENEROSITY AND COMPASSION

QUESTIONS FOR THE SEER
- Where can you give more? And where can you take more? Do you find it just as easy to give as to receive?
- Where could you be more balanced when it comes to your material possessions?
- What would you give to others if you had all the resources in the world?

7 of Pentacles

LIGHT SEER: a pause, a time to re-evaluate and reflect, states of gratitude, waiting to harvest the fruits of your labor, a sign to keep going

SHADOW SEER: giving up too early, impatience, losing faith, not following through, frustration with rewards

A PENTACLES STORY

Inspecting the work, he imagines how fruitful these plants will be. He can't see the magic underneath the soil. He just has a feeling that things are happening under there. And it's a very good feeling.

"It's almost here, right?"

His intuition answers, *"Yes."*

"But I can't see anything yet."

"Have faith."

He puts his hands over the plant and sends it some healing love. Sighing, he understands that there is nothing more he can do right except to continue believing and to consistently nurture this little venture. He realizes he may even be able to sneak away for a short while to rest and to restore his strength. Even though he can't see the immediate effects of his loving effort, he certainly feels it, right away, in his heart.

MESSAGE FROM THE 7 OF PENTACLES

When we watch our fields too closely, they never really seem to grow. But after looking away for a moment, they flourish overnight. This card is a sign that things are happening even if you can't see instant progress. You've been doing the work, and your wildly successful roots are growing. Know that they exist, and that any lack you are feeling is simply residual energy that's being worked through. It's time to fall into faith, and to pause and give thanks. Remember that you've been playing the *long game.* And that you are a living, breathing result of all your memories, hopes, and hard work. *Keep going.* This moment gives you a Divine interlude to revisit your purpose and direction—your arrival is possible only after you pinpoint the destination. Has your journey shifted so much that what you originally germinated is not the thing you desire to harvest? What needs to change to satisfy your deepest intentions? If you are feeling any frustration around your lack of progress, remember that giant dreams are not built in a day! Delays happen. In shadow, this card can sometimes indicate that you have been watering seeds that may never offer the type of harvest you desire. It's time to prioritize and focus, and assess your energetic input vs. the rewards. Does it feel right in your soul? Direct your energy toward a crop that will make your heart sing. Take a moment to breathe and reflect, as these profound sacred breaths will reinvigorate, realign, and rejuvenate . . . while the fruits of your labor bloom.

AS I GIVE THANKS FOR WHAT I AM ABOUT TO HARVEST, I KNOW THAT MY LIFE IS HEADED IN A BEAUTIFUL DIRECTION.

QUESTIONS FOR THE SEER
- How much faith do you have when you can't see the proof?
- Is it time to take up (or revisit) a gratitude practice?
- Amazing things take time. What else can you do while you are waiting for your seeds to blossom?

a PAUSE →

MAGICAL
ROOTS
ALREADY }
GROWING

7 of Pentacles

HEALING ENERGY:
the POWER of focus,
attention, intention,
AND awareness.
(Manifesting)

MANDALA MOON PHASES:
the time it takes to
master a CRAFT, cycles
of LEARNING and GROWTH.

CANDLE: up EARLY
OR late to practice

8 of Pentacles

BOOKS:
training

FEATHER:
writing,
art,
expression

DESK
COLORS

EARTH ↘ FIRE ↘
AIR →   ↖ WATER
SHE ALCHEMIZES the
elements to create
something new

HERBS AND POTIONS:
PRACTICING a
CRAFT,
DEDICATION

8 of Pentacles

LIGHT SEER: mastering a skill, an expert, craftsmanship, the meraki that you put into your work, methodical progress, patience and determination, soul purpose

SHADOW SEER: seeking shortcuts to your detriment, burning out or giving up, not enjoying your work, sporadic output, inexperience, unhealthy perfectionism

A PENTACLES STORY

For many moons and many nights, she has worked on this, learning the herbs and the subtle complexities of this craft. She blends her oils and her potions, and she is so immersed in her love for this field of study that there are days when she finds her flow . . . *full Zen.* When she is in the zone, she is a prolific creator. Some would say she does it with the skill of a master herbalist, yet she knows that her technique is not quite there. *Yet.* She is close, though! She can already train in this field. And make a living. And heal. And bring to manifest so many beautiful things. But that level she desires is—well . . . next level. She smiles, immersed in her art, noticing the subtle nuances and details that few others would. Working late into the night, she breathes in the moonlight and breathes out its magic, charging her crystals and her teas, and gratefully setting up for another day of focused exploration and practice.

MESSAGE FROM THE 8 OF PENTACLES

Patience, determination, and *pride in your progress* are the best ways to ensure your success. Mastering these skills takes time and perseverance, and shortcuts are not the best path forward as you build your proficiency. Remain dedicated to excellence and to developing your unique form. Study, practice, improve, and thrive. Put your meraki (your love, your soul, and your energetic essence) into your work, and bring it in a consistent, methodical way. Perfect your craft and imbue joy into the repetitive things that fill your day. Try to find flow in the details, no matter what it is that you find yourself dedicated to. If you know it's time to move on to something more inspiring, then find your plan and begin your shift.

Consistent action is called for right now, as are time and persistency. *One cannot build a life from one day to the next, just as the moon cannot complete a cycle overnight.* If you are feeling blocked, know that obstacles build right before we expand into new phases. Remember that "perfection" is always an illusion, and as you seek to do your very best work, don't let comparison or impossible standards become the thief of your joy. While striving for perfection can help us to make great strides, don't allow it to become an unhealthy and self-shaming obsession. Seek hobbies and work that light up your days! And as you become the master, finding joy in continuous self-improvement is the energy that will get you there.

WITH LOVING DETERMINATION, I PERSEVERE, and BECOME the PERSON I LONG to BE.

QUESTIONS FOR THE SEER

- How are you showing up consistently in your life (or in your relationships?) Are your actions showing your dedication to your chosen path?
- What are you mastering right now? What skill would help you level up?
- It's okay to be imperfect and learning while you teach, lead, or show up . . . fully. Do you stop yourself from doing what you really want to do because you're *not enough* or still growing?

9 of Pentacles

LIGHT SEER: spiritual and material satisfaction, inner peace, personal achievement, milestones met and celebrated, the energy of a successful harvest, solo performances, contentment

SHADOW SEER: a need to evaluate your relationship with work, can indicate material success while feeling alone, a workaholic, the realization that money alone will never be enough, financial delays, the pressure to appear more successful than you are

A PENTACLES STORY

Looking at her apothecary of life and love, she breathes it all in. Every last plant. Every last light of life. She has done this . . . all of it. From the bottom to the top, she has built something extraordinary with her love for her dreams and her love for herself. She rummages through her study, taking a moment to relish in the sweetness of this success. She envisioned this. Wanted it for so long. Worked for it. Manifested it. And now, finally, she can take a moment alone, and rejoice in this feeling of satisfaction. She reaches up to her plants, her greatest allies, and a bird lands on her hand, reminding her that her connection with the elements is strong. Putting some incense in her cauldron, she congratulates herself, and then she nods to Mama Gaia. With gratitude, she grooves to the hum of the earth and sways to the mysteries of the Divine. Others might say that there was no music playing, but she hears it pouring out of everywhere.

MESSAGE FROM THE 9 OF PENTACLES

You know those moments when everything feels a little bit brighter? When the sun beams so brightly that it feels like little gold kisses are dripping off its rays? You are reaching one of those moments—a culmination of hard work and desire—when you will be stepping into your manifested hopes and dreams. These moments of spiritual and material bliss are highly personal and serve as funnels of glowing success. Look for this feeling as it surges into your heart, and use its power to move mountains, spread love, and to enjoy your harvest. Go ahead and bask—you deserve it! Spending some time alone will help you to process your progress. *Then celebrate!*

In shadow, this card suggests that you may be working too hard and not seeing enough in return. The payoff must always equal your energy expenditure in order for life to remain balanced. If you sense an imbalance, it's time to re-evaluate your self-worth and your personal contributions in order to make amends. While there's no harm in working hard to achieve something spectacular, make sure you haven't become habituated to the appearance of success. Likewise, becoming so addicted to the idea of success that your *busyness* has you missing out on life is a lifestyle worth shifting away from. While it's wonderful to have created all of this on your own, it's also wonderful to share your creations with those you love. Sharing your energy now will bring you the harmony and the harvest you seek, as success shared with others is the sweetest kind.

I am WORTHY of the BLISS AND ABUNDANCE that IS enTerING my LIfe.

QUESTIONS FOR THE SEER
- What brings you moments of great joy?
- Are you able to celebrate your wins alone, without needing to seek external validation from others?
- Do others in your life celebrate and support your successes?
- When was the last time you truly felt proud of your accomplishments? Where were you, and what did you achieve? What lessons does this memory hold for you today?

DRYING HERBS: Effort coming to fruition, a period of PROSPERITY

9 of Pentacles

FALCON: freedom and independence, foresight, control over one's DESTINY or one's WILD NATURE

CUP CAULDRON: Using her MIND, her inspiration and her HEART to create material abundance. (The suit of Pentacles is the last suit. She has mastered the other lessons.)

PEARLS: abundance, RICHES, generational wealth, WISDOM ACQUIRED through past experiences

GRANDPARENTS: Legacy, family

KABBALAH TREE of Life: SPIRITUAL Lessons and GROWTH.

10 of Pentacles

LAMPS AND MANDALA CHANDELIER: a home filled with LIGHT and the energy of LOVE.

YOUNG child BALANCING on Pentacle: Learning how to work with the energy of money.

10 of Pentacles

LIGHT SEER: spiritual and material abundance, community, generosity, wealth and prosperity, building a legacy, traditional wealth creation, positive outcomes

SHADOW SEER: chasing luxury and status, financial loss, negative energy around wealth, finances and greed coming between people

A PENTACLES STORY

They've been co-creating this life for some time. Their place, their family, their friends . . . their life. They've learned along the way that it doesn't have to be "difficult" or "hard" to build abundant lives—even though they used to think that it did. They've learned that the flow of prosperity comes to those who are generous enough to know they deserve it. Over the years, they've figured out that the energy of money can take many forms, and the form that makes them the happiest is the energy of being able to celebrate with those they love. On days like today, when everyone is looked after and the meals are prepared, and when they are all sheltered and warm, they find themselves incredibly grateful for their financial success. It is one of the things which helps to underpin their happiness. Each and every person in their circle is taken care of . . . *no one does without.* They dance beneath their tree-of-life pentacle chandelier, remembering the times that they've grown as a community, and when they built their dream, step-by-step, *together.*

MESSAGE FROM THE 10 OF PENTACLES

Oh baby, this is the big one! All the love, abundance, and joy that you can muster in your heart is coming your way, and it's coming fast! It's time to prepare for its inevitable arrival and to commit to your long-term success. This energy is so big, in fact, that you should be prepared to spread some of it around generously. Bring an abundance of positive energy into your life and watch everything shift. Expect the arrival of success, happiness, and an upbeat and loving network as avenues widen and the right connections click into place. *Remember that perceptions change.* You are one small move away from seeing the bigger picture and from unearthing a legacy of Pentacles *that is already yours.*

The cloudy side of the 10 of Pentacles reminds us that faking status or wealthiness to impress others will only make us feel unworthy, less-than, and dishonest. This energetic facade is one that is rooted in lack and will push your Pentacles farther away. Chasing luxury as if it's the most important goal can leave you feeling empty and alone when you finally achieve it. If you find yourself in disputes over finances, earnings, or inheritances, remember what really matters and where your true joy resides. Even in reverse, this is a card of forthcoming stability, and this Pentacles miracle offers abundance in all forms, not just the material ones. *You deserve this.* Taste the pleasures of life, and embody a state of consciousness that says yes, I am worthy of all of this success.

I am successful and I share my wealth and joy with others.

QUESTIONS FOR THE SEER
- How does wealth affect your feelings of abundance? Do you tend to save more when you acquire more? Or does it make you more generous?
- This card often speaks of conventional wealth. What are your money goals?
- How comfortable are you with the idea of being rich? Are you inadvertently pushing money away because you "dislike" those with it or think it is "evil"?

Page of Pentacles

LIGHT SEER: manifesting new opportunities, beginnings, good news, ambitions, skills and training, financial opportunities, new career paths, new connections, exploration stage, a beginner, earth magic, making plans a reality

SHADOW SEER: being noncommittal, lack of progress, learning from past mistakes, procrastinating, not bringing plans down to earth

A PENTACLES STORY

This Page holds her mandala with a curious heart, and she roots into the bedrock to begin understanding the manifesting essence that we all hold. She knows she has been procrastinating again, and she is determined to become as loyal and hardworking as her brother, the Knight. She looks at the coin, wondering, "How does one bring more of this into one's life?" She grounds her energy as she has been taught, and seeks her answer with an openness for receiving. Quietly, she begins to understand the manifesting power that she holds—*that we all hold.* The power to give life to new ideas, and to activate our magic with our hopes and desires. We need to, however, learn to bring our thoughts into physical form. She wants you to see that progress happens one life stage at a time, and that you must anchor down into the "details" of the work while you simultaneously keep your head in the clouds to dream. Bridging earth and air, she practices calling her ethereal visions down to the material realm, focusing diligently, *and so it is.*

MESSAGE FROM THE PAGE OF PENTACLES

There may be work to do and pieces that still need to fall into place, but that doesn't mean that they aren't going to arrive! Harness this Page's youthful earth energy, and dig into life. (Remember when you thought you could be an astronaut? Go ahead and ground that energy before it dissipates!) Seek confidence and dependability, and know that no matter what age you are, or where you are starting out from, new perspectives and upgrades of consciousness are on the way, so use your plans for the future and expedite its arrival. Progress happens one life stage at a time, and you must anchor into the details while *simultaneously* keeping your head in the clouds to dream. You're in the perfect place to figure out how to make your prosperity a reality. Get ready to activate your practical magic by taking small, simple steps, and see the prosperity in your progress.

In shadow, this card can indicate a lack of commitment or a loss of interest. Are you losing your momentum or excitement? If you've lost your ambition to move ahead, it may mean you haven't found your thing yet. If you find yourself procrastinating because your task feels too big, or if you have giant ambitions without the financial backing, know that you can move ahead slowly. You don't need to make it all happen at the same time. Dedicated and grounded progress will make your plans a reality.

I can be practical and realistic and still run ahead to meet my dreams.

QUESTIONS FOR THE SEER
- You are in a period of new beginnings. Where are you headed? And what progress can you make today?
- 3x3: What would you like to see happen in your life 3 weeks, 3 months, and 3 years from now? Plan your trajectory.
- What would you like to learn? What piques your curiosity?

Page of Pentacles

TREES: EARTH ENERGY, STABILITY, GROWTH... VITALITY AND BEING full of LIFE!

ROOT: WRAPS around foot and enters earth... Reminder to remember your roots AND remain GROUNDED

Mandala on GROUND: SHE IS TAPPING INTO the energy of NATURE and MINDFULLY manifesting.

ONE FOOT: LEARNING the Right balance

MANDALA SHIELD: Being PREPARED, safety, financial SECURITY.

Knight of Pentacles

BAREFOOT: "EARTHING"- connecting to nature.

PLOWED FIELDS: hard work and future harvests, DEDICATION.

PLANTING seeds for future

Knight of Pentacles

LIGHT SEER: diligence and hard work, determination, steadfastness, building material security, safety, being pragmatic, expansion

SHADOW SEER: focusing solely on wealth, workaholic tendencies, being selfish or cold, laziness, boredom, taking harmful shortcuts, stagnation or feeling stuck, being overly conventional

A PENTACLES STORY

He's toiling and tilling his lands, and enjoying every minute of it. He was born to do this. This Knight is a little more practical than the other knights, with his steadfast momentum and his consistent earthbound energy. He's here to improve things, both for himself and for those he loves, and he remains devoted to solidifying his already stellar foundations. He carries his pentacle shield on his back because this knight is into security. Barefoot, he walks his fields, earthing . . . grounding his energy and soaking up the life force that is available to us all when we spend time in nature. He trusts the deep magic that is happening beneath the surface. The roots. The fungi. The worms and the nutrients. All of it hidden, yet flowing in perfect synergy. He has found his zone of peak performance working happily here, in the outdoors. *"Extra care today will multiply your harvest tomorrow,"* he assures himself. Since we know him to be self-sufficient, loyal, and trustworthy, we can accept this as truth.

MESSAGE FROM THE KNIGHT OF PENTACLES

The Knight of Pentacles shows you the way to turn your foundations into castles: through persistent, determined movement and devotion. It's time to display fierce loyalty, pride in your work, and consistency. Tend to your home while getting your

seeds in a row! Find your patience and diligence, and follow through on your plans and promises. Now is not the time to overpromise and underdeliver! Even though it feels somewhat mundane, this archetypal energy is one of infinite expansion in the material realm, and with time and faith, your seeds will take. Sometimes this energy is so stable that it feels repetitive, making it easy to miss how magical the journey actually is. If you are feeling resistance (or if you'd kinda prefer to stay in bed!) find the things that add joy to your day-to-day progress. You are, after all, working toward the fruition of your dreams in *your life!* In shadow, this card can indicate stagnancy. You may be stuck in a routine or acting in a way that is unduly rigid or safe. When life feels like a grind, or when your desire to be efficient becomes extreme conservatism causing boredom, it may be time to seek new adventures. Try something new! You can shake things up and *still* be rooted in your goals. Release any sluggish energy that's blocking you from your dreams, and with a little creative hustle, you can work, laugh, and love all at the same time.

SEED BY SEED I PLANT MY FUTURE with my ROCK-STEADY FOUNDATIONS of FAITH.

QUESTIONS FOR THE SEER

• Step by step, row by row. What foundations are you creating?
• How secure do you feel in your day-to-day life? And if you are feeling vulnerable, what needs to change so that you can relax more into your own natural rhythms?
• When do you find your state of flow? How can you bring more of that into your life?

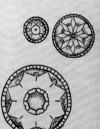

Queen of Pentacles

LIGHT SEER: a healer, a working parent, a self-made person, a kind and nurturing heart, material wealth and abundance, being down-to-earth, strength in family and community, groundedness, generosity, dignity

SHADOW SEER: financial stress, being self-absorbed, smothering others, helicopter parenting, overindulgence, materialism, work-home imbalances,

A PENTACLES STORY

She relaxes down, lifts up her head, and takes a deep breath. This self-made Queen spends a few morning moments here every day, giving thanks to the life she has cultivated. A natural healer, she has always connected to earth energy, drawing peace from the trees, the soils, the mosses . . . and sensing the lush green energy that pulses all around her. They taught her how to step into affluence and into her fairy-tale life by shifting the shadows that she was holding on to around natural wealth. She let go of her stories and everything she was taught. She let go of the things her parents believed. And she created a sanctuary of sacred space that could ground and hold her expressive and nurturing power. With her down-to-earth approach, she built a life that allows her to care for her whole community. Generous, practical, nourishing . . . and everything she touches turns to gold. She is a true Queen of the earthly realm.

MESSAGE FROM THE QUEEN OF PENTACLES

Take some time to create a sense of peace and harmony in your physical surround-ings, and harness the abundance that's available to you. Let go of any scarcity or fear you are holding on to about wealth and security. *You are safe.* Pay attention to your finances to level up your money game, and give yourself permission to rise into the upper ech-elon. *(Pssst. Notice any resistance that you may be feel about that idea.)* What stories are you holding on to about wealth that may be actively holding you back? This is a positive message of creature comforts and happiness, and this earthly medicine announces in a life well lived in the material world. Connect with nature to find your calm, healing, and rooted power, and harness the abundance that's available to you by bringing ground-edness to your situation. Shower others with warm blessings from a charitable heart, as loyalty, family, and community are important themes at this time. Your nurturing and sensible approach will gift stability and support to those in your life. Give . . . but don't overextend your energy, and avoid enabling others by over-mothering them. They must learn to walk on their own. If your supply of nurturing energy feels drained, indulge in some you-time by creating space for self-care and cozy retreats. By looking after your-self, you will be able to give freely to others and to Mama Gaia . . . and when you are recharged, you always make the world a better place. *Pamper yourself.* And then liberate your compassionate guidance and your glorious, powerful love.

I LIVE my DEEPLY CONNECTED Life with WARMTH, ABUNDANCE AND LOVE. ♡

QUESTIONS FOR THE SEER
- How are you supporting your community and your loved ones?
- What steps are you taking to promote your own healing and to ensure that your own self-care is prioritized?
- What could you do today to bring more sacredness into your everyday space?
- How do you feel when you spend time in nature? And how could you ensure that you doing it more?

TREES: vitality, life, energy

BRANCH ANTLERS:
(CONNECTION TO MOTHER EARTH)
This QUEEN is the PERSONIFICATION
of the EARTH "ELEMENTAL":
MYTHICAL CREATURES that EMBODY
EARTH ENERGY called GNOMES or
PLANT DEVAS.

CROWN with HOLLY BERRY:
Life, vitality, abundance,
goodwill.

HALF GLOVES BECAUSE everything
SHE TOUCHES TURNS TO gold.

RED CUSHION: Safety, Comfort

Queen of Pentacles

King of Pentacles

HOLDING PENTACLES: Wealth

LIBRARY: a LIFETIME of
EXPERIENCE AND STUDY, his
LEGACY, Finding Peace after
a LOT of WORK

WOLF DOG FAMILIAR: LOYALTY,
WARMTH, social connections,
Family, safety, protection

King of Pentacles

LIGHT SEER: material abundance, personal growth, patience and determination, a confident and warm leader, expansion, a time to level up

SHADOW SEER: obsessing over riches, overindulgence, a need to balance the material with the spiritual, workaholic tendencies

A PENTACLES STORY

Warmth. This king just exudes it, and he welcomes you into his private study for a heartfelt conversation and a few anecdotal lessons of life. He's worked his fields, met his soulmate, found his financial freedom, and now he looks out the window at his manifested dream. He brings infinite blessings for success, and he counsels you to use all of the elements that are available to you without having a singular focus on life's material things. He knows that well-rounded success makes the most fulfilling life. He smiles, taking a peek at his family in the yard below. They are his most important achievement, and they have been his support along the way. He relied on them, and on his trusted familiar, his logical mind, and his generous heart. He used all of the energies he had access to in order to build this life, and they all led him right here, in his library of experience, where he always knew he wanted to be.

MESSAGE FROM THE KING OF PENTACLES

This card holds one of the tarot's most powerful messages of dreams manifested as well as forthcoming prosperity and ease. You are finally arriving to that place that you have long dreamt of. The most important thing to be done is to enjoy it all, sweet seer. Enjoy every lesson, challenge, failure, and of course, every success. Get clear on where you want to be. Plan and envision it. There is manifesting power in the longing, and so much joyful expansion as you bring your greatest potential into existence. Happiness happens when you do better than the last time, and in the pursuit of personal growth, you can allow yourself the extravagance of desire. The rest is a happy consequence of faith, steady habits, and the courage to cultivate enormous dreams. Work on your rock-solid mindset forged with confidence and determination, and dream your biggest dream. In shadow, this card counsels against being miserly or rooting into a mindset of scarcity. Choose generosity over greed. If you have experienced material loss (or even allowed it to flitter away through gambling or irresponsible spending), it can be turned around quickly when you set your goals and stick to your plan. Remember that success is *a feeling*, not a specific number on a piece of paper, *so feel* into it now to bring more of it into your world. This wealth and happiness card reminds you that earthly abundance is accessible to you right now, and that you're in the right place to find it.

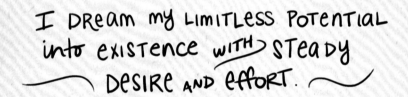

I DREAM MY LIMITLESS POTENTIAL into existence WITH STEADY DESIRE AND effort.

QUESTIONS FOR THE SEER

- One of the keys to this King's success is always finding an excuse to envision his future. Where are you headed? Do you have a clear idea of exactly who you want to be and how you will get there? What do you really want?
- Success doesn't always happen overnight. What action steps are you taking now to create the future you desire?
- What is your definition of success?

TAROT

correspondences

the LIGHT SEER'S AND the RIDER-WAITE-SMITH
SYMBOLS CHART

A chart to peek into some of the most prominent symbolism of
The Light Seer's Tarot (LST) and the traditional *Rider-Waite-Smith Tarot* (RWS)

(Images shown are from the "Pam A" 1910 edition of the RWS tarot.)

RIDER-WAITE-SMITH	THE LIGHT SEER'S TAROT	
0. THE FOOL 		**RWS: Dog**: spirit messenger, companion **White rose**: innocence, purity **Knapsack**: journey ahead, no baggage **Red feather**: message from Spirit, life force, also appears on Sun /Death cards **LST: Amethyst crystal**: companion **Staff/Wand**: protection she needs **Red dots in hair:** from High Priestess's pomegranate (where she is headed) **Seed of Life**: sacred geometry (creation) **Rooted feet**: suggests a need to let go
1. THE MAGICIAN 		**RWS: Lemniscate**: infinity, infinite power **Hand up/down**: connect heaven w/earth **4 suits on table**: having all 4 elements to work with, resources, alchemy **Roses**: alchemy, love, manifestation, connecting the material and spiritual **LST: Metatron's cube**: (Tattoo) Sacred form containing all frequencies of the Universe, map of creation **4 element symbols**: having resources **Golden aura**: pure intention, spiritual power, clean energy field
2. THE HIGH PRIESTESS 		**RWS: Pomegranate**: fertility, Divine feminine, Persephone **B+J Pillars**: Boaz & Jachin pillars from King Solomon's Temple (duality, strength and establishment, between worlds) **Tora Scroll**: esoteric, hidden wisdom **Solar cross**: balance of opposites, duality **Crescent moon**: intuition, subconscious **LST: Scroll earrings**: from Tora scroll **Chakras above head:** connect to Cosmos **Runes**: plurality, esoteric wisdom

RWS: **Wheat**: bountiful abundance and nourishment, growth, being cared for
Waterfall: flow of emotions, love & intuition, source of life
Scepter: power, Divine conduit
Heart Shield with Symbol of Venus: beauty, creativity, love, femininity
Pomegranate dress: fertility, abundance
Crown of 12 stars: zodiac, cycles of life
LST: **Moon scepter**: Divine power
World belly: fertility, creation, Mama Gaia, water (intuition / Divine feminine)

3. THE EMPRESS

RWS: **Ram's heads**: Aries, being ruled by Mars, action, leadership, boldness, determination, stubbornness
Ankh: life, protection, immortality
Orb: the world he dominates
Armor: readiness to defend position
Red: energy and action
Barren mountains: structure and order
LST: **Ankh tattoo**: embodied vitality
Chess piece and floor: strategic mind
Mars: initiative, overcoming confllict
Handkerchief: ready to help others

4. THE EMPEROR

RWS: **Papal cross trinity**: dominion over the three worlds (the conscious, subconscious, and superconscious)
Hand gesture: Divine blessing, bridge between spiritual and material worlds
Crossed Keys: unlocking mysteries
People below initiates: hierarchy
LST: **Spiritual symbols around head**: knowledge of variety of spiritual paths
Stairway: to be walked by initiate
Mandala sun: enlightenment
Simple clothing: non-materialism

5. THE HIEROPHANT

RWS: **Sun**: clarity, joy
Man and Woman: partnership, romance
12 flames: 12 zodiac, tree of life (human nature and experience, moral choices)
Angel: Raphael, healing, protection, Divinity, Divine blessings, fated
Volcano/mountain: passion, obstacles
Tree of knowledge & serpent: choices
Mountains: obstacles and challenges
LST: **Tattoos**: from Hierophant's journey
Merkaba: gateway to the Divine
Spirals: choosing to fall in love

6. THE LOVERS

7. THE CHARIOT

RWS: **Charioteer**: determination, control
Star canopy: celestial influences, spiritual connection to Universe
Square on chest: earth, groundedness
City walls: journey, structure, foundation
Winged sun disk: Ra & Horus, sun deity, power, protection
Red spinning top: dynamic balance
Sphinxes: mastering duality, different directions, positive & negative
LST: **Horses**: movement, duality
Balancing charioteer: harnessing power

8. STRENGTH

RWS: **Maiden and Lion**: purity, innocence, compassion, patience, taming the beast, base instincts, influence, control
Lemniscate: ∞ infinite potential to overcome obstacles and challenges
Flower garland: triumph, connection to natural world, beauty, life
Lion: primal instincts, fears, danger
LST: **Animal Guide**: working with inner guides, self-control, power, triumph
Heart necklace: compassion and control
Lamb: strength to help those in need

9. THE HERMIT

RWS: **Hermit**: solitude, introspection, meditation, sage, guide, wisdom
Lantern: light of knowledge, illumination, star inside often the Seal of Solomon (protection, harmonizing opposites)
Staff: authority, support, spiritual help
Mountain: accomplishments, growth
Robe: shrouds him in secrecy, away from distractions of external world
LST: **Lantern**: guide for most of the way
Mountain: overcoming challenges, pauses, peristence, self-discovery

10. THE WHEEL

RWS: **Wheel**: cycles, change, perpetual motion, ups and downs, success / loss
Hebrew letters: Yod, Heh, Vav, Heh (Divine presence and influence)
ROTA: Latin for wheel (also TARO)
Anubis and Typhon: ascending and descending the wheel, inevitable change, protection and afterlife
Sphinx: knowledge, power needed to remain on top of wheel
LST: **Chaos symbol**: all potentials present
Roulette: chance, luck, timing, fate

RWS: Justice: impartiality, fair distribution of law, equity, clarity of thought
Scales of balance: weighing decisions and actions, balance, fairness
Sword: double edged nature of justice (can condemn or acquit), cut through bias or misinformation to find truth
LST: Justice: calm, clarity, weighing truth
Scales' shadows: not always black or white, truth is often grey, nuance
Shadow figure: choices, cause and effect

11. JUSTICE

RWS: Man: finding serenity in his predicament, legs create upside down #4 (when reversed, can be stability and structure), sacrifice, surrender, a pause
Tree cross: Yggdrasil/world tree, between heavens and earth, renewal, flexibility
Halo: an enlightening truth arriving, spiritual connection and faith
LST: Aerial sling: choosing to surrender, a pause, meditation, acceptance
Runes: esoteric wisdom, knowledge

12. THE HANGED MAN

RWS: Skeleton: death, essential truth, essential nature of life, impermanence
White horse: spiritual purity, strength
White rose: 5-sided hexagram reversed, spiritual rebirth, significant change
Fallen King: endings, transitions
Figures of different stature: equality (death is universal)
Scythe: reaping, harvest, cycles of nature
LST: Reaper's hood: rebirth, new life
Forest: repeating patterns (bottom left and inside hood), renewal and regrowth

13. DEATH

RWS: Angel (often Gabriel): Divine guidance, messenger, sanctity, communication, protection, good news
Right foot: intuitive realm (water)
Left foot: grounded, earthly realm (land)
Two cups: the blending of opposites, wholeness, intuitive decisions (water)
Triangle in square: trinity, balancing different forces, middle path, alchemy
LST: Sun and Moon: balance of opposites
Androgynous angel: balanced energies, strength and ease, Divine guidance

14. TEMPERANCE

15. THE DEVIL

RWS: Devil: temptation, vices, materialism, feeling trapped
Torch: illuminates base desires and shadowy aspects of humanity
Figures in chains: transformative power of indulgence/greed, addiction, bondage, servitude, trapped in the material world, dependency, projections
Pentagram: physical world dominating spiritual, negative forces and influences
LST: Unicursal hexagram: a choice to banish or invoke, self-control, magic

16. THE TOWER

RWS: Lightening: sudden change, Divine intervention, flashes of understanding
Tower: structures, systems, ambitions, beliefs, desires, paradigms
Falling: sense of helplessness or sadness during tumultuous times, confusion
Crown: loss, changes in establishment, overthrowing authority, shifts in power
LST: Flames: also look like monarchs of transformation, change, illusions
Hazelnuts dissipating: loss of security, illusory nature of perceived safety

17. THE STAR

RWS: Naked figure: vulnerability, purity
2 jugs of water: nourishment, conscious/unconscious, inner/outer worlds, emotional/material (duality)
1 foot on land, one foot in water: miracles, "walking on water," practical intuition, duality, liminal spaces
8-pointed star: Spirit, omnipresence
Ibis bird (in tree): Egyptian symbol of Divine wisdom, healing, writing, magic
LST: Holding star cord: connection, guidance from the Cosmos, Spirit, hope

18. THE MOON

RWS: Moon in different phases: cycles of change, intuition, subconscious, dreams
Towers: gateways to the unknown, dualities (safety/danger, conscious/unconscious, etc.)
Dog and Wolf: tamed and wild parts of our mind, needed vs. needless fear
Crayfish: emerging fear, vulnerability vs. shelled exterior
LST: Moon rays: leading the way to the surface, casting light and shadow
Dog and Wolf: light and shadow, instinct

RWS: **Sun**: vitality, positivity, life
Child on horse: innocence, joy, nobility, freedom, simplicity, natural living
Red feather: passion, courage, life force (also on Fool and Death cards)
Red flag: triumph over challenges, spirit
Sunflowers: growing toward light, truth
LST: **Sun**: radiance, life-force energy
Rune on skirt: Sowelu rune (sun), wholeness, success, goals met
Mandala: turning suffering into joy, awakening, light energy

19. THE SUN

RWS: **Angel with trumpet (Gabriel or Metatron)**: calling forth to be judged, a messenger, "face the music", spirituality
Flag: St. George, triumph, chivalry
Resurrecting figures: rebirth, spiritual awakening, redemption, renewal
Mountains: obstacles, cannot avoid being judged, challenge

LST: **Spirit out of body**: Higher Self, astral travel, communion with Divine, authenticity and self-compassion

20. JUDGEMENT

RWS: **Laurel wreath**: completion, success, cycles, accomplishments, compensation
Four living creatures (corners): Four elements, fixed zodiac signs: *bull* (Taurus, earth), *eagle* (Scorpio, water), *lion* (Leo, fire) *angel/man* (Aquarius, air)
Two wands (similar to Magician's wand): dreams manifested, new chapters
LST: **4 corners platonic solids**: sacred geometry for 4 elements, 4 seasons, etc.
Ouroboros wreath: transformation, renewal, cycles of completion

21. THE WORLD

RWS: **Hand offering wand**: beginnings, creative insight, inspiration
Clouds: revelation, ideas out of nowhere, spiritual help, dreams and perception
Sprouting: budding creative energy, life force, new ideas sprouting, opportunity
Castle in distance: a journey towards success
LST: **Flame**: pineal gland lit up, inspired
Beads: Indra's net, Oneness, connection of all things, inspiration from the collective field, creativity in the ethers

ACE OF WANDS

2 OF WANDS

RWS: **Right wand (anchored down solidly)**: the option is to stay in place
Left wand: free to explore, travel
World: choices, evaluating current domain, possibilities, opportunities, dreaming, stay vs. leave
Rose and Lilly Cross (bottom left): competing energies, passion and innocence, beauty and hope, Spirit
LST: **Van and surfboard**: future dreams, desires to explore and travel
Windows: watching vs. experiencing

3 OF WANDS

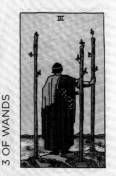

RWS: **Wands firmly planted**: stable foundations, reliability, strength, commitment, vantage point
Ships coming in: advancements in business or career, steady growth, waiting for the right moment
LST: **3 waves in distance**: opportunities on the way, skills, preparation
One purple wand (smaller, behind her): less interesting options in the past
Wands on fire: momentum, direction

4 OF WANDS

RWS: **4 wands with garland**: events, harmony, peace, festivities
Castle and people: community, coming together, gathering, support, home, stability
2 people with bouquet: marriage or milestone celebration, happiness
LST: **2 women dancing**: celebration, event, relaxation, success, community
Tent: peace flags, shelter, safety
Tambourine: traditions, self-expression

5 OF WANDS

RWS: **5 wands**: wrestling, competing, jousting, in-fighting, disagreements, tension
Colors of clothing: groups of people, different beliefs
LST: **Color of clothing**: competitive event
Stepping on one another: paying attention to competition instead of end goal (flame)
Reaching for flame: inspiration, goal, conquest, a win, working together

RWS: **Wreath:** victory, success, accomplishments, pride
Decorated white horse: homecoming, arrival, purity, strength
People in background: celebration, recognition, acclaim, notoriety
LST: **Hands below in front of stage:** fans, appreciation, being supportive, cheering
Lights: limelight, success, being seen
Wand with flame: momentum, spark of positive energy, triumph, celebration
White sweater: authenticity, strength

6 OF WANDS

RWS: **Holding wand:** defending position, holding back, valor, success
6 wands (attacking from below): insurrection, jealousy, disagreements
Cliff/Ridge: upper hand
LST: **Energy bubble:** magical/energetic protective mechanism
Algiz Rune: protection rune tattooed on arm and also above head as light
Prayer: meditative calm during attack

7 OF WANDS

RWS: **8 wands (flying through air as if thrown):** landing on target, swiftness, travel, destination, messenger.
No humans: shows focus on actions, times & events
Clear blue sky and small green hill: any challenges will not be overly significant

LST: **8 wands** flying through Universe, on fire because of speed and momentum
Tips together: pointed towards same direction/goal, focus

8 OF WANDS

RWS: **9 upright wands:** barrier or defense
Bandage: past injuries (on head suggests psychological or mental)
Green Hills: no hint of immediate danger, possibly multiple small challenges
Upright strong stature: strength, past success in battle, challenges overcome
LST: **Wand fence:** protection
Runes: *Hagalaz* (hail, past conflicts, challenge) *Thurisaz* (defense, Thor, strength), *Algiz* (protection), *Laguz reversed* (out of flow)

9 OF WANDS

10 OF WANDS

RWS: 10 wands: carrying burdens, responsibilities, can't see where he is headed, slow progress, persistence
Town: headed toward goals, continued perseverance needed

LST: Yak: accepting help with burdens
Wands on hill: dropped tasks, prioritization (some wands are still being carried), flames still lit for other opportunities in future
Wind at her back: help from Universe

PAGE OF WANDS

RWS: Young page: curious, sharing ideas, a strange message
Salamander print: fire elemental (eating its own tail signifies transformation), alchemizing negative to positive
Feather: a job well done, a "feather in his cap"
Pyramids: mystery, spirituality
5 leaves: sprouting potential
LST: Wand: creative sparks, enthusiasm
Landscape: blank canvas, anything is possible, limitless creativity

KNIGHT OF WANDS

RWS: Knight: departing, haste, being on a mission, salamander print (fire elemental, transformation, survivor)
Rearing horse: action, energy, speed
Pyramids/Desert: uncharted territories, mysteries, adventure, timeless wisdom, spiritual quest
Feathers: valor, Divinity, angels, self-expression
LST: Fire drum: passion, enthusiasm and adventure, free-spirited, expression
Rearing horse: on a mission, speed

QUEEN OF WANDS

RWS: Queen: confidence, authority
Sunflower: seeing bright side of life, joy, loyalty, beauty, vitality, radiance, growth in harsh conditions, enduring nature
Black cat: mysticism, intuition, rebirth, independence, curiosity, protection
Lions on throne: strength, courage

LST: Wand with fire element symbol: joy
Light in hand: ability to wield power
Cat: close connection to unseen realms
Candles: light, warmth, charisma

RWS: **Crown**: authority, mastery
Lion & salamander throne: courage, fire elementals, strength, transformation
Salamander: survivor (Aristotle believed salamanders could walk through fire and survive), adaptability, magical
LST: **Gecko/salamander shirt**: renewal, regenerative powers, fire elemental
Lion tattoos: Strength, royal crest, rebellious expression, bravery
Runes on wand: *Kenaz* (light, skills, knowledge), *Sowilo* (sun, leadership)

KING OF WANDS

RWS: **Chalice**: Divine offering, outpouring of love, emotional fulfilment
5 streams of water: five elements
Sea with lotus flowers: vastness of unconscious mind, spiritual awakening
Dove with communion wafer: Holy Spirit, peace, emotional renewal, love
Yods: Divine presence, potential, manifestation, blessings
LST: **Cup with heart**: new feelings being birthed, emotional intelligence, heart chakra, "filling one's cup"

ACE OF CUPS

RWS: **Winged lion** griffin (guardian of marriage) *or* Mithras (infinite time), *or* winged deity (protection, Divine authority) *or* St. Mark (courage, strength)
Caduceus of Hermes: (winged staff with snakes) exchange, healing

LST: **Rainbow and rainbow bracelet**: "love is love," the magic of love, alchemy
Ocean: emotional connection, intuition

2 OF CUPS

RWS: **3 cups**: a toast, joy, friendship, reunion, celebrating an achievement
Women: emotional bonds, communal support, dance party, happiness
Harvest: abundance, fertility, success after hard work, fulfillment
LST: **Celtic Triskelion**: *trios*: Earth, sea, sky, movement and life, death, rebirth
Lavender: devotion, serenity, ritual herb
Pleiades: star cluster "of the seven sisters," ancient bonds, soul family, starchildren

3 OF CUPS

4 OF CUPS

RWS: Young man: disenchantment, boredom, a "brat," taking things for granted, contemplation, meditation
Hand with cup: similar to Ace of Cups, new possibilities, awakening, growth, a missed opportunity
3 cups: disinterest, apathy, detachment
Tree: roots, protection, shade
Grass: abundance and fertility present
LST: Rainbow: opportunities that are not noticed even though they seem obvious
Hand: Universe lending a hand

5 OF CUPS

RWS: Cloaked figure: mourning, sorrow, focusing on what has been lost, inability to let go and move on
3 spilled cups: losses, disappointments
2 upright cups: hopes, potentials, positive aspects of life that remain
Bridge leading to castle: withdrawal
LST: Rainbow cup: healing and renewal, the energy to move forward
Foot pushing cup: Consciously allowing an energy drain, not seeing possibility
Path: The path of healing, the way home

6 OF CUPS

RWS: Children: innocence, gifting, nostalgia, simpler times, puppy love
Cups with flowers: purity, peace, reconciliation, memories, the past, remembrance of loved ones
Courtyard: protection, safety, guardians

LST: Rainbow cups: choosing timelines, inner child, future self, looking towards past
Dog: best friends, memories, change, impermanence

7 OF CUPS

RWS: 7 cups in cloud: choices, dreams opportunities:
Castle (material security, family),
Jewels (wealth), *Snake* (temptation),
Wreath (victory, success),
Dragon (fears, desires, magic),
Figure in cloth (unknown),
Tower (ambitions, dreams)
LST: Cups: as above but with chutes and ladders (ups and downs, the unknown)
River: intuition, illusions, the paths that seem easy but aren't

RWS: **8 cups stacked**: past relationships, stories or achievements that are no longer relevant, walking away
Moon: intuition, things not fully illuminated, the unknown path ahead
Looming mountain: challenges, obstacles ahead, spiritual pursuits

LST: **Bowl burning**: last ceremony to let go of memories or emotions (7 other bowls already under water)

8 OF CUPS

RWS: **9 of cups**: the arrival of emotional and material desires, the "wish card" (choose which cup you would like), dreams fulfilled
Sitting man: pride in accomplishments, success, contentment, smugness
Yellow background: happiness, joy
Blue tablecloth: calmness, truth, sincerity
LST: **Floating cups**: wishes granted, a happy heart, bright heart chakra
Treasure: choose the prize you desire

9 OF CUPS

RWS: **10 cups rainbow**: a state of enduring happiness and contentment
Family: partnerships, connection, joy, domestic bliss, supportive relationships
Home: security, stability, dreams realized
Clear blue sky: calmness, serenity, clarity

LST: **Bass clef hammock**: harmony, love, stability, unique frequency of each family, being able to relax and enjoy life
Couple: partnership, bliss, joy, stability

10 OF CUPS

RWS: **Fish in cup**: the unexpected, magical serendipity, creative inspiration, intuitive thought, spontaneous insight
Hat: creativity, unconventional ways
Water: comfortable at the edge of emotional and psychic realms
Floral tunic: blossoming ideas and emotional insights, potential
LST: **Legs above**: unexpected realizations, jumping timelines, a curious mindset
Hands with heart: romantic thinker, ability to quickly manifest his dreams

PAGE OF CUPS

KNIGHT OF CUPS

RWS: Armor: guarding heart, protection, readiness, bravery
Winged helmet: Hermes / Mercury, swiftness, adept communicator, Divine messenger, intuitive and emotional
Offering cup: proposals, messages
Water: feelings, intuition, the unconscious mind, fluid approach
LST: Envelope: proposals, messages
Winged sneakers: Hermes / Mercury
Roses: courtship, romance
Heart tattoo: romantic dreamer

QUEEN OF CUPS

RWS: Ornate cup with angel wings: connected to spiritual realm
Closed cup: deepest emotions, hidden emotions, intuition, sometimes keeping things to self
Flowing gown: connection to water/ intuition, emotional intelligence
Cherubs: innocence, love, connectedness
LST: Light streaming to hands: natural healer, working with emotions, Divine guidance, empath, love
Meditative state: peaceful, intuitive

KING OF CUPS

RWS: Throne in water: mastery of emotions, intuition, and depth
Fish necklace spirituality, the Divine
Decorated Robe and crown: authority, appreciating beauty
LST: Floating sound bowl: staying balanced, turning to spiritual practices in times of chaos or challenge
Ship: success, ability to navigate to calm seas, steering and direction, leadership
Water crown: intuition, emotional intelligence, connection to Spirit

ACE OF SWORDS

RWS: Hand with sword: conquest, force, power of intellect, mental clarity
Crown: success, authority, mastery
6 flame yods: Divine influence or inspiration, manna from heaven, potential, spiritual energy
Clouds: emerging from ambiguity, cutting through confusion
LST: Equation: thought, mental process
Nautilus shell: Divine ratio, Divine timing
Alchemy symbols: sulfur, mercury, salt, (3 prime substances), transcendence

RWS: **Crossed swords**: impasse, stalemate, weighing a decision, denial
Blindfold: need for impartiality, not knowing the way, can't see the way
Relatively calm sea: peace after navigating this rocky situation
Crescent moon: intuition, subconscious
LST: **2 crows/ravens**: Odin's familiars: *Huginn* (thought) *and Muninn* (memory)
Paths: crossroads, decisions, feeling lost
Divination with sand: grains blowing in both directions, no clear answer

2 OF SWORDS

RWS: **Swords in heart**: heartbreak, challenging times, loss or grief
Heart: psycho-emotional challenge
Clouds: turbulence, distress
Rain: purging emotions, catharsis
LST: **Tethered/stitched heart**: stuck, emotional difficulty, a broken heart that is healing, devastation, fragmented soul parts, feeling bound to emotions
Tree: no leaves, situation fruitless
Storm: turmoil, cloudy thoughts
Tattoo: from *RWS* 3 of swords

3 OF SWORDS

RWS: **Coffin/Tomb**: a time of withdrawal or deep rest, introspection and recovery, "sleep like the dead"
3 swords hanging above: unresolved matters, responsibilities
1 sword below: awareness, the issue being resolved, defensiveness, preparing
Hard exterior: protective mechanism
LST: **Nest**: time to cocoon and rest deeply
Tiny heart: healing fragments, healing through rest, protecting heart

4 OF SWORDS

RWS: **Victorious figure**: winning at all costs, hollow victories, ethical considerations, battles of ego
2 men in background: defeat, conflict
Swords on ground: giving up, arguments
Stormy sky: turmoil, unsettled emotions

LST: **Hand on head**: psychological impact of loss, ongoing issues because of defeat, sometimes literally a headache
Victor: sore winner, gloating, being strategic, not playing by the rules

5 OF SWORDS

6 OF SWORDS

RWS: Boat: transition, change, movement
Water: going from troubled waters to calmer shore
Man: assistance, guide, helpful strangers
Adult and child: being protected, seeking safety, a safe passage
Gray sky: troubled thoughts, worries
LST: Crows: pulling through, unexpected aid, help from strange places
Red scarf: emotional challenges, pain
Suitcase: transition, changing directions
Shore: new possibilities, groundedness

7 OF SWORDS

RWS: Stealthy figure: running away, deception, thief, caution, danger, "getting away with it"
2 swords left behind: taking only what is needed
Yellow sky: intellect, ego, joy (the community in the distance remains joyful as they are unaware of the missing swords)
LST: Crow: sounding the alarm
Moon: Universe witnesses true intentions
Small crows: taking only what you need

8 OF SWORDS

RWS: Bindings: feeling trapped
Blindfold: inability to see clearly
Castle: security and safety in view
Space between figure and swords: escape is possible, not seeing the way

LST: Mirror: seeing oneself as bound even though opportunities exist in real life, pessimism, fear, feeling stuck
4 Crows reflected in mirror: illusions, paranoia, negative thoughts

9 OF SWORDS

RWS: Figure: nightmare, anguish, anxiety
9 swords: internal difficulties more than external danger (swords not touching person), negative thoughts or burdens, rumination, troubled mind
Quilt: roses (beauty, emotion) and astrology signs (universal nature of fear)
LST: Crows: worries, troubles, illusions (one is a dove that goes unrecognized, potential for healing)
Bed: night terrors, bad dreams, awakened perspectives are possible

RWS: **10 swords**: backstabbing, psychological torment, betrayal, despair, an inevitable end
Hand gesture: same as Hierophant's (surrender, between man and Spirit)
Gloomy skies: conflict, challenges, lost in a negative mindset, depression
Dawn: new beginning, newfound hope
LST: **Woman**: getting up from the ground, walking into the dawn's sunrise, healing
10 birds: guidance, higher thinking, perspective

10 OF SWORDS

RWS: **Upright large sword**: thought, intellect, practice, mind as a tool, study
10 birds: broader perspectives, caution, messages, quest for spiritual truth
Clouds and Wind: being lost in thought, evolving/changing nature of thoughts
Ready position: prepared for new experiences and challenges
LST: **Lightbulbs**: display of intellect, ideas
Book: learning, studying, realm of mind
Birds: Frenetic energy, distractions, rumors ("a little birdie told me")

PAGE OF SWORDS

RWS: **Moving clouds**: speed, movement, action, urgency, turbulent energy
Charging Horse: action, heroism, not thinking about consequences
Raised sword: cutting through to truth of matter, clarity of thought,
Armor: protection, facing risks
Red feather courage, bravery, warrior
LST: **Crossbow and motorbike**: urgency
Binary Code on soles of shoes: being calculated, intelligence, quick results vs. thoughtful deliberation

KNIGHT OF SWORDS

RWS: **Upright Sword**: intellect, clarity
Above clouds: judgement is not clouded
Throne (adorned with cherubs and butterflies): transformation of the soul, authority, power, pure intention, adaptive nature of the mind
LST: **Flags**: peace, air element symbol in blue flag (she is "water of air" within the court cards. The air and fire flags are below, and all are grounded into earth.)
Locked Cup: using mind more than heart, having emotions under control

QUEEN OF SWORDS

KING OF SWORDS

RWS: **Throne butterflies**: transformation
Throne crescent moon: intuition, unconscious mind, communication
Upright sword: clarity, intellect, power
Clouds below: ability to think clearly, abstraction, rising above clouded thoughts
Sparse trees: top of mountain, realm of psychological thought and the mind
LST: **Wind and animals**: connected to element of air, flow of information, moving nature of thoughts, steadiness

ACE OF PENTACLES

RWS: **Hand with coin**: gift of abundance from material world, need to grasp opportunity, finances
Cloud: arriving out of nowhere, Divine
Archway: new paths, new investments, growth, transitions, steps to be taken
Mountain: future obstacles, adventures
Flowers: nature's reward, beauty, joy, life's pleasures, blossoming of ideas
LST: **Pentacle seed**: roots of success, planting ideas, working today for the future, flourishing ideas, material world

2 OF PENTACLES

RWS: **infinity loop**: continuous flow, balancing act, attention, juggling priorities, infinite possibility
Waves: ups and downs of life affecting balance, unpredictable external circumstances, making adjustments
Jester-like hat: performance, healing laughter, keeping up appearances, ability to say one thing & mean another
LST: **Moon and Purse pentacle**: balancing act (earth/heaven, thought/heart, spiritual/financial, wants/resources, etc.)

3 OF PENTACLES

RWS: **3 figures building church**: (architect, patron, and craftsman or mason) shared vision, teamwork, mentor, apprentice, group dynamics
Architectural plans: trades, experts, details, scope, plan, design, foresight
Workbench: practical application of skill
Clothing: different roles and social status
LST: **Weaving**: group work, common goal, community project, collaboration
Missing left hand: diverse abilities and unique skills, planning and visioning

RWS: Clutching Pentacle: fear of loss, possessiveness, wanting to control one's resources, greed
Pentacles under feet: grounded in material wealth, sense of security
Pentacle crown: thoughts and identity rooted in prosperity and the material
City at a distance: isolation, emotional distance
LST: Pentacle purse: worries, clutching belongings, financial fears, uncertainty
Othala rune earring: property, wealth

4 OF PENTACLES

RWS: Pentacle window of church: comfort, faith, community, feeling abandoned, cast out, lack of aid, barriers to support, "cold shoulder"
Crutches and clothing: health and financial difficulties, hardship
Snow: "frozen" in action or emotion
LST: Figure: feeling hopeless
Pentacle doorway: comfort and help available by opening new doors
Key: Invitation to new possibilities, assistance and belonging, help

5 OF PENTACLES

RWS: Figures: financial aid, generosity, power, dependency, charity, humanity
Scales of Justice: weighing resources and needs, good deeds, balance and equity
LST: Passing coins: giving and receiving (simultaneously), flow of money
Infinity: balance and harmony, merging of opposites, renewal and transformation, oneness and unity
Path: steps and movement, looking toward the future

6 OF PENTACLES

RWS: Farmer: contemplation, inspection of progress, a pause, the time it takes for plans to come to fruition
Crop pentacles: investments, time, a turning point, upcoming harvest
Hoe: hard work and effort needed to cultivate success, a short pause, a rest
LST: Pentacle roots: hidden growth, trust in the process, upcoming fruition
Energy from hand: positive mindset, energy healing, trusting yourself, having faith, taking time to notice details

7 OF PENTACLES

8 OF PENTACLES

RWS: **Craftsman**: mastery, dedication, hard work, practice, vocation, arts & crafts, attention to detail, perfectionism
Solitary figure: inner drive, initiative, self-criticism, flow-state, workaholism
Apron: protection, professionalism, being prepared, having the right tools
LST: **Pentacle moon**: cycles of time to perfect the work, repetition and change
Water and fire from desk: progress and act of creation, alchemy of skills, manifesting, day/night

9 OF PENTACLES

RWS: **Snail on ground**: enjoying the journey, patience, steady progress
Falcon: intellect, loyalty, discipline, training, keen sight, instinct, big picture
Enclosed garden: personal sanctuary, personal cultivation, being private
Robes: luxury, comfort, wealth
LST: **Hanging herbs**: fruition, success
Cauldron: creating prosperity, gains, manifesting goals, steady practice
Gold & silver sequins: sun/moon, god/goddess, power/intuition, reflection

10 OF PENTACLES

RWS: **Archway and castle**: generational wealth, achievements, legacy, prosperity, openness, sharing, family
Pentacles in tree of life formation: spiritual progression, presence of Divine
Dogs: home, loyalty, protection
Grapevines: fruition of effort, pleasure

LST: **5 Lamps**: 5 elements, wisdom passed to children, light, hospitality
Chandelier pearls: affluence, lived experience, relationships, familial bonds

PAGE OF PENTACLES

RWS: **Page**: youthfulness, enthusiasm, student of health and material wealth
Freshly plowed soil: fertility, potential, beginning stages of growth, new seeds
Garden: blossoming ideas, plans, attending to responsibilities, growth
Clear sky: optimism, clarity of purpose
LST: **Pentacle**: earthy abundance, roots reach to foot and root into earth
Mandala meditation: earth-based magic, creative mindfulness, practical action based manifestation, cultivating faith

RWS: **Knight**: presence, loyalty, steady pace, being methodical and consistent
Pentacle: being cared for, respected
Heavy armor: protection, slow to change
Still horse: grounded, fixed, stubborn
Plowed fields: hard work, future gains

LST: **Pentacle seeds**: consistent effort, long-term goals, future harvest
Shield: protection, stability, being prepared, having a plan
Decorated horse: luxuries, wealth

KNIGHT OF PENTACLES

RWS: **Throne with goats**: ambition, determination, Capricorn
Rabbit: fertility, abundance, cycles of growth, connection to earth and nature
Garden: lushness, nurturing energy, vitality, abundance, beauty
Crown: authority, material wealth
LST: **Pentacle**: material wealth, prosperity
Antlers: spiritual antenna, earth magic, ritual, protection, connection to nature
Leaf crown: royalty, Divine favor, enlightenment, sacredness

QUEEN OF PENTACLES

RWS: **Throne with bullhead and grapevines**: strength, determination, stability, abundance, willpower, Taurus
Scepter: leadership, power
Plants: cultivation, growth, harvest, bountifulness, connection to nature
Castle: security, achievement, material prosperity, legacy, generations
LST: **Library**: culmination of learning and work, enjoying fruits of labor, wealth
Wolf/Dog: animal familiar, loyalty, security, comfort, presence

KING OF PENTACLES

MAJOR ARCANA CORRESPONDENCES

MAJOR ARCANA	ASTROLOGY*	ELEMENT	
00 The Fool	Air / Uranus ♅	Air △ or Spirit / Ether ✶✿	
01 The Magician	Mercury ☿	Air △	
02 The High Priestess	Moon ☽	Water ▽	
03 The Empress	Venus ♀	Earth ▽	
04 The Emperor	Aries ♈	Fire △	
05 The Hierophant	Taurus ♉	Earth ▽	
06 The Lovers	Gemini ♊	Air △	
07 The Chariot	Cancer ♋	Water ▽	
08 Strength	Leo ♌	Fire △	
09 The Hermit	Virgo ♍	Earth ▽	
10 The Wheel	Jupiter ♃	Fire △	
11 Justice	Libra ♎	Air △	
12 The Hanged Man	Water / Neptune ♆	Water ▽	
13 Death	Scorpio ♏	Water ▽	
14 Temperance	Sagittarius ♐	Fire △	
15 The Devil	Capricorn ♑	Earth ▽	
16 The Tower	Mars ♂	Fire △	
17 The Star	Aquarius ♒	Air △	
18 The Moon	Pisces ♓	Water ▽	
19 The Sun	Sun ☉	Fire △	
20 Judgement	Fire / Pluto ♀	Fire △	
21 The World	Saturn ♄ /Earth ⊕	Earth ▽	

RUNES**	MUSIC***	BODY / HEALING****	
Raidho (ᚱ)	E	Respiratory Organs	00
Ansuz (ᚨ)	E	Cerebral & Nervous System	01
Perthro (ᛈ)	G#	Lymphatic System	02
Berkano (ᛒ), Feoh (ᚠ)	F#	Genital System	03
Tiwaz (ᛏ)	middle C	Head & Face	04
Othala (ᛟ)	C#	Shoulder & Arms	05
Gebo (ᚷ)	D	Lungs	06
Ehwaz (ᛖ)	D#	Stomach	07
Uruz (ᚢ), Thurisaz (ᚦ)	E	Heart	08
Isa (ᛁ)	F	The Back	09
Jera (ᛃ), Hagalaz (ᚺ), Perthro (ᛈ)	A#	Digestive System	10
Nauthiz (ᚾ), Tiwaz (ᛏ)	F#	Liver	11
Laguz (ᛚ), Mannaz (ᛗ)	G#	Organs of Nutrition	12
Eihwaz (ᛇ)	G	Intestines	13
Sowilo (ᛋ), Laguz (ᛚ)	G#	Hips & Thighs	14
Kenaz (ᚲ), Thurisaz (ᚦ)	A	Genital System	15
Hagalaz (ᚺ), Thurisaz (ᚦ)	middle C	Muscular System	16
Dagaz (ᛞ), Sowilo (ᛋ)	A	Kidneys, Bladder, etc.	17
Mannaz (ᛗ), Perthro (ᛈ)	B	Legs & Feet	18
Sowilo (ᛋ)	D	Circulatory System	19
Algiz (ᛉ)	middle C	Organs of Circulation	20
Ingwaz (ᛜ), Othala (ᛟ)	A	Excretory System	21

*Planetary Correspondences by The Golden Dawn except the newer planets (Pluto, Uranus and Neptune)

** By Chris-Anne ***By Paul Foster Case **** By Aleister Crowley

Runes Cheat Sheet

Rune	Symbol	Meaning
Fehu	ᚠ	Wealth, abundance, success, new beginnings, confidence.
Uruz	ᚢ	Strength, raw energy, good health, willpower, perseverance.
Thurisaz	ᚦ	Defense, reactive force, change, disruption, conflict, power.
Ansuz	ᚨ	Communication, wisdom, Divine messages, signs.
Raidho	ᚱ	Travel, journey, rhythm, progress, momentum.
Kenaz	ᚲ	Inner light, vision, knowledge, creativity, understanding, insight.
Gebo	ᚷ	Gift, partnership, exchange, sharing, generosity.
Wunjo	ᚹ	Joy, fulfillment, pleasure, celebration, victory.
Hagalaz	ᚺ	Disruption, change, chaos, uncontrollable event.
Nauthiz	ᚾ	Needs, desires, self-care, boundaries, friction, resistance.
Isa	ᛁ	Ice, stagnation, stillness, delays, inaction.
Jera	ᛃ	Harvest, reward, cycles, completion, closure.
Eihwaz	ᛇ	Stability, death and rebirth, transformation, eternity, initiation.
Perthro	ᛈ	Luck, mystery, fortune, fate, chance, change.
Algiz	ᛉ	Protection, defense, courage, guardian, awakening.
Sowilo	ᛋ	Success, inspiration, guidance, vitality, accomplishment.
Tiwaz	ᛏ	Victory, honor, justice, leadership, sacrifice, honor, determination.
Berkano	ᛒ	Growth, renewal, birth, fertility, healing.
Ehwaz	ᛖ	Movement, trust, faith, companionship, progress, harmony.
Mannaz	ᛗ	Humanity, support, self, community, social structures.
Laguz	ᛚ	Water, intuition, dreams, intuition, prophecy, flow.
Ingwaz	ᛝ/ᛜ	Potential, fertility, growth, pregnancy, beginnings, balance.
Dagaz	ᛞ	Dawn, clarity, illumination, positive outcomes, breakthroughs.
Othala	ᛟ	Heritage, inheritance, home, heirlooms, family customs, the past.

WANDS:
Element: FIRE
Elemental: Salamander
CUPS:
Element: WATER
Elemental: Undine
SWORDS:
Element: AIR
Elemental: Sylphs
PENTACLES:
Element: EARTH
Elemental: Gnomes

ELEMENTS and ELEMENTALS ←

TAROT LANDSCAPES

A quick reference for interpreting landscapes. (Based on RWS meanings.)

Castles: Security, ambition, achieving one's goals.

Cliffs: New beginnings, taking risks, vantage points

Cities/Towns: Ambitions, progress, movement

Clouds: Challenges

Crossroads: Decision making, life's pivotal moments

Deserts: Isolation, finding one's true self, new adventures

Fields/Wide-open spaces: Opportunities, vast possibility

Forests: Vitality, life, growth, abundance

Gardens: Fertility, abundance, new projects or relationships

Hills: Small challenges

Mountains: Obstacles, challenges, achievements

Nighttime: Shadow, the unknown, the unconscious mind

Oceans/Water: Intuition, emotions, mysteries, exploration

Paths: Journeys, lessons, fresh starts

Plowed Fields: Success, abundance, material wealth

Rivers: Flow, adapting to change, emotional cleansing

Rainbow: Joy, happiness

Stars: Hope, guidance, guidance, spiritual connection

Sunshine (and the color yellow): Happiness, joy, success

Waves: Ups and downs, instability, change, finding balance

AND

Into the grey we follow,
Like a thousand flickering stars,
And there in a sunlit hollow
We lose and find what is ours.

And into the SHADOW we wonder
What that glimmer of LIGHT has in store,
And then into the Light we Remember
That at some point we dreamt of much more.

May you find what is yours, sweet seer!

So into the grey we meander,
Holding hope as we anchor our hearts
Then we PRAY and we dance and surrender
Finding courage and TRUST in new starts.

And into the Light we face Bravely,
Like the faces of Love in the flesh
and we smile both wildly and gravely
and with SPIRIT and SOURCE we
                              enmesh.

SO...
  Into the grey we follow,
  Like a thousand flickering stars,
  And there in a sunlit hollow
  We lose and find what is ours.

We hope you enjoyed this Hay House book. If you'd like to receive
our online catalog featuring additional information on Hay House
books and products, or if you'd like to find out more about the
Hay Foundation, please contact:

Hay House LLC, P.O. Box 5100, Carlsbad, CA 92018-5100
(760) 431-7695 or (800) 654-5126
www.hayhouse.com® • www.hayfoundation.org

———

Published in Australia by:
Hay House Australia Publishing Pty Ltd
18/36 Ralph St., Alexandria NSW 2015
Phone: +61 (02) 9669 4299
www.hayhouse.com.au

Published in the United Kingdom by:
Hay House UK Ltd
The Sixth Floor, Watson House,
54 Baker Street, London W1U 7BU
Phone: +44 (0) 203 927 7290
www.hayhouse.co.uk

Published in India by:
Hay House Publishers (India) Pvt Ltd
Muskaan Complex, Plot No. 3,
B-2, Vasant Kunj, New Delhi 110 070
Phone: +91 11 41761620
www.hayhouse.co.in

———

Let Your Soul Grow

Experience life-changing transformation—one video
at a time—with guidance from the world's leading experts.

www.healyourlifeplus.com

♡

Join me for more
Tarot, magic and
wild creative musings
at
www.chris-anne.com

Giant magical THANK yous...

ACKNOWLEDGMENTS

- With giant gratitude to my husband, Alejandro. I love you, amor! Gracias for your support and for living inside of this tarot deck with me for so many years. (And for always making sure I eat when I lose myself inside of the creative cave.)

- Gracias a Valentina Abusabbah-Valladares, mi diseñadora, colega y amiga. I couldn't have done this without you! Eres lo maximo! Te quiero mucho. xo

- To my family, both in Canada and in Chile, I love you.

- Giant colossal love to the Kickstarter and Instagram communities for believing in the first edition of *The Light Seer's Tarot*, way back when it was just an idea.

- To the healers and all of the magical people in Collingwood and the Blue Mountains. I wouldn't trade this community and the friendships I've made here for the world. Your support through challenging times has been epic.

- And of course to Allison Janice at Hay House. Thank you for all of your support and stellar *editor-you-get-me* magic! Thank you for seeing me.

    xo I love you all!